ENTANGLING ALLIANCES

Also by John Maxwell Hamilton:

Main Street America and the Third World

Edgar Snow: A Biography

ENTANGLING ALLIANCES

How the Third World Shapes Our Lives

by

JOHN MAXWELL HAMILTON

with

Nancy Morrison

and contributions from

Erlinda Bolido
Yanina Rovinski
Lesley Anne Simmons
Wahome Mutahi

Seven Locks Press
Cabin John, MD/Washington, D.C.

Library of Congress Cataloging-in-Publication Data

Hamilton, John Maxwell.
   Entangling alliances: how the Third World shapes our lives
  John Maxwell Hamilton, with Nancy Morrison and
  contributions from Erlinda Bolido . . . [et. al.].
    p. cm.
  ISBN 0-932020-82-8: $24.95
  ISBN 0-932020-83-6 (pbk.): $12.95
    1. Developing countries—Foreign relations—United States.
  2. United States—Relations—Developing countries. I. Morrison,
  Nancy. II. Title.
  D888.U6H35   1990
  327.730172'4—dc20   89-48262
                                                CIP

Manufactured in the United States of America
Cover Design by Lynn Springer/Design Lines
Cover Illustration by Kathleen Carson
Typesetting by Bob Rand
Printed by McNaughton & Gunn, Saline, MI

Printed on acid-free paper.

For more information write or call:

   Seven Locks Press
   P.O. Box 27
   Cabin John, MD 20818
   (301) 320-2130

Table of Contents

Acknowledgments vii

Farewell to Independence 1

The Long-Distance Call 25

Cathedrals of the 21st Century 75

The Best of Strangers 123

If This Is to Be a Revolution 157

Notes 175

Index 191

Notes on Author and Contributors 203

For Maxwell

Acknowledgments

This book grows out of *Main Street America and the Third World*, an earlier volume that also looked at U.S.–Third World interdependence. That first book sought to trace the many ways that distant countries shape the lives of Americans every day, no matter where they live or what they do in work and play. In researching that book, I not only found an array of newsworthy connections but also began to see that those ties were more complex, subtle, and dynamic than I had imagined. Interdependence was not something that had happened; it was merely beginning to happen. And, it became more clear to me, those growing connections confront all citizens of this modern world with extraordinary challenges. Encouraged by the first book's surprisingly good reception—considering it was about a subject in which Americans are not supposed to be interested—and wanting to go a step further, I undertook this book, exploring the process of interdependence itself as it involves people in the United States and developing countries.

As did the earlier effort, this book has enjoyed the support of many individuals and institutions. And like the earlier project, it is part of a larger public education program, which will be carried out by the Panos Institute.

The help of some people will become obvious to anyone who reads the volume. Nancy Morrison, an American, contributed one chapter and ideas for other parts of the book. Erlinda Bolido in the Philippines, Yanina Rovinski in Costa Rica, and Wahome Mutahi in Kenya wrote shorter sections. Lesley Anne Simmons, an Englishwoman, worked on the whole book, helping research and think through the issues and write about them.

Rosemarie Philips, the first director of the Panos Institute's Washington office, helped conceive the idea for this book and masterminded the related education program. She has been an essential part of the writing process, giving the book shape and prodding me with editorial suggestions. Panos arranged for the written contributions by others. Ms. Philips and I both wish to thank the Ford Foundation for its grant support in the early stages of the project.

The World Bank, my employer, provided critical support. In line with its interests in promoting understanding about the development process among industrial countries, the bank gave me the time and logistical support to research and write the book. I want particularly to thank Judith Maguire, chief of the bank's public affairs division, who not only recognizes the value of projects like these but also shows that lawyers can be good journalists.

Others provided advice either in the beginning stages of the project or later in critiquing the manuscript. Those who contributed to the entire process include Regina N. Hamilton, Joan Joshi, Gabrielle Lecesne, William F. Schmick III, and John H. Sullivan.

Constructive suggestions for the Philippines chapter came from Hernando Abaya, Thomas Blinkhorn, Jane Bortnick, David Jarvis, Norman Hicks, Hugh Lantzke, Thomas Keehn, George Krimsky, Andy Rice, Carolyn Sachs, and Joel Swerdlow. The Organization for Tropical Studies provided invaluable help in Costa Rica: Ana Lorena Bolaños, along with Lucinda McDade, cheerfully organized a productive and ever-changing schedule; Ronald Suarez, assistant director of OTS's La Selva Biological Station, helped me in that part of Costa Rica; Luis Diego Gómez, director of OTS's Wilson Botanical Garden, proved an entertaining and valuable guide and host in the southern part of the country. Sheldon Annis, Janet Brown, Herman Daly, Robert Goodland, Gary Hartshorn, Jorge León, Donald Plucknett, and Charles Schnell offered ideas and editorial suggestions. For the chapter on Kenya, Wilfred Maciel and Lorna Hayes provided valuable guidance on the tourist industry; James Adams, Alan Donovan, Diana McMeekin, James Morrison, and Nathan Munyori gave helpful advice on the chapter itself.

David Anable, managing editor of the *Christian Science Monitor* until recently, showed his usual interest in projects that involve foreign reporting. The *Monitor* ran two articles adapted from the book. The *New York Times Magazine* adapted one chapter.

Jane Gold gave the book her typical, inimitable editing. I am also grateful to James McGrath Morris, president of Seven Locks Press, for his enthusiastic support for this book from the beginning.

It is de rigueur for acknowledgments to disabuse readers of the thought that those who offered advice, no matter how useful their contributions, actually made any difference. This book is no exception in perpetuating this formula: the ideas in the book do not necessarily reflect the views of the Panos Institute, the Ford Foundation, the World Bank, or any of those people who helped shape its outcome.

John Maxwell Hamilton
Washington, D.C.

INTRODUCTION

Farewell to Independence

On February 22, 1989, Sen. John Warner of Virginia stood in the U.S. Senate chamber on Capitol Hill and for the next 50-odd minutes read George Washington's 7,641-word farewell address. The first president's remarks, repeated each year on his birthday, extol U.S. self-sufficiency. They warn against "overgrown military establishments," "the accumulation of debt," and "the insidious wiles of foreign influence." Why, Washington asked, interweave "our destiny with that of any part of Europe, [and] entangle our peace and prosperity in the toils of European ambition, rivalship, interest, humor, or caprice? 'Tis our true policy to steer clear of permanent alliances with any portion of the foreign world."

Implored the president: "So far as we have already formed engagements, let them be fulfilled with perfect good faith: Here let us stop."[1]

For nearly two centuries Washington's farewell address was a beacon for U.S. policymakers. Today it illuminates the past far more than the future. Just as the staff of the British colonial office steadily increased after World War II while the number of colonies decreased, outmoded American reverence for independence and self-sufficiency has lingered beyond the realities that spawned it.[2]

However much Americans fancy themselves honoring Washington's dream, they have been inevitably drawn into alliances. In 1800, shortly after Washington's warnings, the United States had only 24 treaties and agreements with other nations. In 1980 it had 980 treaties—289 of them with more than one country—and 6,184 agreements.

What of "overgrown military establishments," which seemed to produce European strife? During his two terms, President Ronald Reagan emphasized the need to build up military power. According to the Defense Department, the United States spent 6.8 percent of its gross domestic product (GDP) on military power in 1986. By contrast, West Germany spent 3.1 percent and Japan 1 percent.[3] The United States has half a million servicemen and women overseas. Although Soviet military cuts have opened possibilities for American defense cuts, the United States is not about to give up all its overseas operations. Strategists will continue to worry that the United States does not have sufficient military advisers abroad to match the influence of the Soviet Union.[4]

And what of Washington's fear of indebtedness? In the mid-1980s, after 70 years of being a creditor nation, the United States became the world's largest debtor. "More than two hundred years after the Declaration of Independence," Felix Rohatyn observed of this indebtedness, "the United States has lost its position as an independent power."[5]

Interdependence has replaced independence. Dependence has replaced self-sufficiency. George Washington would not recognize today's world; nor would he be prepared to unravel the complex connections that inevitably bind the United States to the rest of the world.

The portraits in this volume of U.S. connections with the Philippines, Costa Rica, and Kenya illustrate both the transformation wrought by interdependence and the challenge this transformation presents today. But before these specific examples are considered, the next pages put interdependence into a *historical* context: Americans are facing not a brand new development but an old trend that is taking on new character.

The History of a New Phenomenon

Global interdependence is a modern term with old meaning. A time once existed when parts of the world had little intercourse with each other. That was a time, before Columbus, when India, China, the Fertile Crescent, and Central America and the Andean region of South America held great and distinct civilizations of their own. Individual regions then were as diverse from each other as they ever would be. For the trend since has been toward more and more contacts among nations and cultures. Correspondingly, people have become increasingly interactive, for good *and* ill, sharing each other's resources, catching each other's diseases, and craving each other's commodities.

Marco Polo and other adventurers trekked across Europe, the Middle East, and Asia to the Far East in the 13th century. Although Europeans marveled at Polo's tales, they initially saw little of practical use in his trips. Gradually, however, that changed. European courts imitated Chinese fashions and ideas, or at least fancied they did. In 1575 a Medici duke built a factory producing Chinese porcelain. In 1666, the British East India Company brought a mere 23 pounds of Chinese tea to Great Britain. But by the end of the century it imported 20,000 pounds a year. Tea was well on its way to becoming the national drink (though the British drank it their way— with sugar and milk).

As commerce grew, so did its by-products. Adventurous settlers brought viruses, bacteria, parasites—and the first rats—to the Americas. Disease proved a formidable weapon, cutting a devastating swath through native populations. Malaria and other scourges are often regarded as pantropical—a description sometimes taken as synonymous with the Third World. But often diseases that were started in one region spread, through the process of colonization, to others.

Features we commonly associate with our interwoven world today are actually old stories.[6] Dependencies of the kind that made the Organization of Petroleum-Exporting Countries (OPEC) cartel so powerful in the 1970s existed in 1201, when a salt cartel was formed by King Philip the Fair of France and King Charles II of Naples, who controlled salt mining. Salt in those days was essential in preserving food.

The specter of countries defaulting on their foreign debt, a fear today with Third World countries, has also roamed through many centuries. Shortly after he was crowned king of England in 1327, Edward III repudiated his country's foreign debts. British government securities were traded regularly in Amsterdam in the 17th and 18th centuries. And in the 19th century, the states of Pennsylvania, Maryland, Louisiana, and Mississippi defaulted on foreign loans; America, wrote an English lender, was "a nation with whom no contract can be made, because none will be kept."

Illicit drugs from abroad were a dominant issue in the 1988 presidential election, but concern with narcotics traffic is not new, either. During the last century, British merchants made a good business selling opium to the Chinese, 90 million of whom were considered addicted by 1900. Another hot political issue, migration of people into the United States, has old antecedents. Demographic statistics from Seville provide an early example of mass movements of people from one region to another: an average of one or two thousand Spaniards left that Spanish city for America each year in the 16th century. Political upheaval or economic deprivation of some kind prompted mass migration on a giant scale from 1820 to 1930. During that period more than 50 million Europeans—roughly one-fifth of the entire population of Europe at the beginning of the period—migrated to countries like Australia and the United States, which they essentially turned into Neo-Europes.

International cooperation to solve common problems is not a post–World War II innovation, though it is frequently seen as such. To improve weather prediction, the Florentine Academy of Science set up weather stations in 10 European cities in 1654. And concern that interdependence has gone too far is also an old idea. Said John Maynard Keynes in 1933, "There are serious questions whether the long-sought-after interdependence hasn't finally reached the point where its costs may be outweighing its benefits."[7]

The forces of global integration gained momentum in the 19th century. From 1837 to 1845, foreign trade excluding services equaled more than one-fifth of the total national products of Italy, Great Britain, Germany, Australia, Denmark, and Norway, among many other countries. In the 1920s, that trade equaled almost 40 percent of the total national product of Great Britain, more than 50 percent of France's national product, and more than 35 percent of Japan's.[8] Technological advances such as food canning, refrigeration, and railways in the 19th century reduced the importance of proximity for commerce or leisure travel. After 1874 the United States provided more than 50 percent of all British wheat, and shiploads of frozen New Zealand mutton first arrived on British shores in 1882, as British historian Geoffrey Barraclough observed in his brilliant study, *An Introduction to Contemporary History*. In 1870 Chile exported no nitrates; 30 years later it accounted for three quarters of total world nitrate production.[9]

Paul Scott Mowrer, a correspondent for the *Chicago Daily News* and the winner of the first Pulitzer Prize for foreign correspondence, discussed the implications of the trend for the United States. Using the word *interdependence* liberally in his 1924 book, *Our Foreign Affairs*, Mowrer explained how World War I had ended with the United States in a new position in the world:

> Through no conscious effort of our own, we became suddenly the world's greatest military and economic power. As at the waving of a wand, our status was changed from that of a debtor to a creditor nation. . . . We are acquiring Pacific and Atlantic submarine cables. . . . Our raw products are sent out to all manufacturing countries; our manufactures to all agricultural countries. We are exporting billions of dollars in the form of foreign investments. Our banks are everywhere establishing branches. Our vast organized charities are at work wherever there is suffering on a large scale, from the valley of the Hoang-Ho to Smyrna and Samara. Our energetic inquisitive, money-making citizens are to be found traveling or trading, for business, science, art, education, or pleasure, in every corner of the six continents and all the islands of the oceans. . . . I think the complacent, home-dwelling citizen would be astonished if he could be brought to realize the primary fact that there is probably to-day not a country, not a city in the world, in which the United States has not genuine interests of some description.[10]

Speed and Complexity of Interdependence

Mowrer was not alone in seeing ahead. A large number of thinkers, many of them in Europe, sensed global changes in the 19th century. In 1903, a German historian observed that the world "is, more than ever before, one great unit in which everything interacts and affects everything else, but in which also everything collides and clashes."[11] Indeed, so long have people seen the trend that we might wonder why we continue to talk about interdependence as though it were completely new.

Yet, it is. The speed and complexity of interdependence are growing beyond anything these forward-thinking people imagined. Although Mowrer shrewdly forecast American dependence on foreign petroleum, he could not anticipate the array of new problems that would confront nations. Indeed, the main thesis of this book is that the forces of interdependence are working at unprecedented speeds and levels of complexity for *all* countries, not just those in Europe. And no nations have identified the problems quickly enough, let alone found solutions to these entangling alliances.

The Third World: The Global Equation Revised

George Washington thought about Europe when he thought about foreign affairs, and so have most other Americans. The white colonists who settled and governed the country came from Europe. Europe gave them the social, political, and economic values upon which they built. When Americans began to travel, they typically went, like characters in Henry James's novels, to Europe. Not coincidentally, perhaps, Americans decided during World War II to fight all-out first in Europe and *then* in Japan, even though the Japanese had launched the first attack. That European orientation continued after the war, with the added American preoccupation with the Soviet Union, widely viewed in the United States as the guiding hand of worldwide communism. When President John F. Kennedy pledged the United States to creating a declaration of interdependence in 1962, he was speaking of "a concrete Atlantic partnership." The major exception may be Japan, whose dynamic economic growth first surprised Americans but now commands their attention.

But as logical as it may be from a historical point of view, Americans' tendency to view the world as simply running along an East-West axis ill serves modern, complex circumstances. The horizon over which the future lies also runs along North-South lines and involves what is often described as the Third World—the developing countries—whose number and power have changed the global equation.

When the United Nations was created at the end of World War II, 51 countries signed on as charter members. By 1989, 159 countries were members. A large part of the increase came as many former colonies gained political independence. The end of the British raj in India and the disintegration of informal Western control over China alone brought independence to nearly half the people of the world. In addition to all those newly sovereign African and Asian nations, Latin American countries became more determined to exercise the independence they had previously won.

The term *Third World* has a connotation of third-rate, last in order. Sensitive people often eschew the term not only for that reason but also because it puts under one roof countries as vastly different—and often as antagonistic—as poor Communist China and relatively prosperous Brazil. Many would dispute the inclusion of Hong Kong and Yugoslavia. While all broad terms are inherently flawed, however, groupings are essential first steps in making sense of the world. And the term *Third World*—once its origins are known—is rather more positive than negative.

Alfred Sauvy, a Frenchman, coined the term in the early 1950s. His idea was that freshly liberated developing countries, like the commoners that made up the Third Estate during the French Revolution, aspired to the same rights and opportunities possessed by other members of society. The concepts of First World (the industrialized countries) and Second World (the socialist countries) were afterthoughts. Today, with the remarkable political and economic strides many Third World countries have made since the term was first used, no leader of an industrialized country should dismiss these nations as inconsequential.

On the contrary, the emergence of the Third World over the last three decades has marked a fundamental shift in this century that has far outweighed the rise of communism, which has dominated thinking in the United States. The Soviet Union is far down our list of trading partners—number 32, behind Algeria and Spain and just ahead of Ireland. It has been singularly less successful at exporting its ideas to the United States than have developing countries, which have a tangible impact on how we dress, what we eat, and even how we think. The Soviet Union itself has recognized the need to think beyond superpower relations. In a speech to the United Nations in 1988, Soviet leader Mikhail Gorbachev spoke of "the interdependence of the contemporary world," with "the scientific and technological revolution" turning nations' problems into global problems.

Technology: The Engine of Interdependence

The growing influence of these developing countries is due to more than just their numbers. New technologies give them access and power they never had before. For centuries, advances in speed came only in small increments: "Napoleon moved no faster than Julius Caesar," Paul Valéry observed. In mid-18th century America, mail from Philadelphia was delivered to points south of the Potomac River only eight times a year.[12] But between 1944 and 1986, average airplane speeds for international flights increased from 150 miles per hour to 500 miles per hour. Between 1937 and 1973, the price of a flight from the West Coast of the United States to Japan dropped 85 percent in real terms; it fell by another 50 percent by 1985. Satellites and new communication materials such as fiber optic cables have meanwhile facilitated voice and data communications. The number of international telephone calls increased from 3.3 million in 1960 to 412 million in 1985, and in 1988 American Telephone & Telegraph handled more than 1 billion overseas calls. The total number of U.S. telephone conversations overseas was roughly equal to the number of letters to and from foreign addresses.[13] Thanks to these advances, no spot, however distant, is remote.

Peter Bell, formerly president of the Inter-American Foundation, recounted how surprised he was in the early 1980s to find people in a far-off Colombian mountain village tuning in their radios each morning to get London commodity prices. As an elderly leader of the local agricultural cooperative explained, world prices would affect prices for their crops. Many people understood the global stock market tumble in October 1987 as a demonstration of the global flow of money. But it also demonstrated the globalization of information flows. For the first time ever, average citizens in the United States and elsewhere followed stock market prices in other countries on a minute-by-minute basis and used that information to predict fluctuations in their own securities markets.

In this world of global communication networks, other countries complain that they are deluged with information from the United States that is often irrelevant and over which they have little control. But these complaints obscure the fact that the communication process is a two-way street: witness how other countries' tastes, talents, and technologies shape American entertainment. Foreign markets are so important to American television that one consideration in launching a new show is whether it will do well overseas.[14] The 1988 writers' strike against Hollywood producers revolved, in part, around royalty payments for reruns of shows sold overseas. When negotiations broke down, U.S. producers used foreign writers.

Developing countries are gradually becoming as important to this process as industrialized nations. Brazil has the fourth largest privately owned television network in the world, Globo, and the fourth largest television advertising budget in the world. Globo exports television programs and has clout with foreign producers who want to sell products in Brazil. India, for its part, produces almost twice as many feature films each year as Hollywood and, according to some reports, earns upwards of $100 million exporting movies each year.[15] The cultural give-and-take worries people in both developing and industrialized countries, as discussed in chapter three.

Easier travel and easier access to up-to-date information about prospects in other countries have facilitated the movement of people from one far-off land to another. At the beginning of the century, 85 percent of the immigrants to the United States came from Europe. Today, 85 percent come from Asia and Latin America. The current wave of legal immigrants into the United States, some have speculated, may exceed the previous high-water mark at the turn of the century, especially as newcomers bring their relatives. Immigrants made up 7 percent of the U.S. work force in 1985, Labor Department statistics show, but are expected to account for 22 percent of new entrants into the labor force between 1985 and 2000.

And not just the United States is so affected. All countries are subject to these migration trends. When Germany experienced its first postwar recession in 1967, one third of those who lost their jobs were foreign "guest workers." Today foreign workers comprise an estimated 30 percent of the Swiss labor force. They also build one-quarter of all automobiles and one out of every three kilometers of road in France, according to the French secretariat of state in charge of migrant affairs in 1983. Planeloads of Korean workers regularly land in Saudi Arabia and other Middle Eastern countries eager to spend oil profits on construction.[16]

Migrants often have visions of returning home, and with modern travel that has become an easy dream to realize. Often people slip into the United States or a northern European country to work; when they have earned enough money, they return to their homeland. The process, one observer notes, has contributed to the "progressive disappearance of national boundaries for labour and its transformation into a structural component of the international political economy."[17]

If anything, money moves across borders more quickly than people. With communications permitting global stock watching as well as investing, the amount of foreign investment not only in U.S. plants and equipment but also in stocks and corporate debt increased fivefold between 1980 and 1988. According to the Conference Board, nearly one-half of all new U.S. manufacturing projects in 1988 involved the acquisition of overseas facilities. Another third were joint ventures with foreign partners.[18]

In 1960, 8 U.S. banking institutions had 131 foreign branches; in 1982, 162 banks had 900 branches. The Third World debt crisis reveals how developing countries have become linked to depositors in industrialized countries. "The stock of recorded loans from banks in one country to nonbanking companies in other countries rose from $662 billion in 1981 to $1.06 trillion in the first six months of 1987, while cross-border deposits of nonbanks increased from $560 billion to $1.02 trillion in the same period," C. Michael Aho and Mark Levinson pointed out in a 1988 Council on Foreign Relations report.[19] On an average day in 1987, $300 billion was changed from one currency to another.

In trade, virtually every product and service seems to have global potential. Indians manufacture manhole covers for Phoenix, Ariz., and Newport News, Va., among other cities. Mexicans on the Yucatan Peninsula repair shoes flown in from Florida, Mexican social scientist Jorge Bustamante said in an interview. Writing about the shape of the 1990s, the *Kiplinger Washington Letter* told subscribers, "The biggest change will be 'globalization' of the marketplace."[20]

In 1988 world merchandise trade grew faster than production for the sixth consecutive year. "Between 1965 and 1978," economist Michael Steward observed, "the exports of developed market economies grew about 80 percent faster than [those markets'] industrial production, and nearly twice as fast as their GDPs."[21] And in 1989, the General Agreement on Tariffs and Trade (GATT) reported that "the volume of world merchandise trade is up nearly 40 percent, and world output up 25 percent, from their 1982 recession levels." This is a dominant post–World War II trend.

The United States is part of this process, ranking as the world's number one importer and tied with West Germany as its number one exporter. And so are developing countries part of the process.

Despite recent economic setbacks for many developing countries, many other Third World nations have shown great potential for growth, accounting for 39 of the 40 countries with the fastest-growing gross national products (GNPs) between 1973 and 1986 (see figure). While Third World countries accounted for less than 20 percent of total world manufacturing in 1985, their growth in production during the previous 20 years was nearly double that of so-called industrialized nations. The developing country share of world manufacturing exports increased by about 250 percent during the same period. The growth in exports of such sophisticated products as electrical machinery increased faster than that of textiles and apparel.

As a result of this shift, North American trade with Western Pacific nations grew more than 25 percent faster than transatlantic trade. In 1985, manufactured exports to the United States from just 4 newly industrializing countries of East Asia—Hong Kong, South Korea, Singapore, and Taiwan—amounted to three-fourths of exports to the United States from the then 10 members of the European Community. That same year the United States imported more manufactured products from all developing countries than it did from Japan and the European Community combined.

Technological developments and the proliferation of independent developing countries also put defense issues in a new context. In the past, countries worried most about those nations that were geographically closest. The United States, buffered by large oceans and able to declare its influence in Latin America through the Monroe Doctrine, had minimal defense worries. But today missiles carry their loads over long distances; nuclear bombs cut a much wider swath than their forerunners. Despite attempts to curb nuclear proliferation, developing countries are acquiring the capacity to make their own nuclear weapons. The number of developing countries that possess missiles increases each year. In 1988 Iraq and Saudi Arabia deployed missiles, and India and Pakistan engaged in missile testing. "In terms of strategic doctrine, being able to hit a target 1,500 miles away with precision has certain advantages," said an Indian government spokesman in 1989, underscoring the power that comes with owning medium-range ballistic missiles.[22]

"Those who persist in seeing India as a backward land of ox carts and spinning wheels will be startled to learn that it is today the world's fourth-ranking military power," observed Eric Margolis of

THE FORTY NATIONS WITH THE FASTEST GROWING GROSS NATIONAL PRODUCT
(ANNUAL AVERAGE, REAL GROWTH)

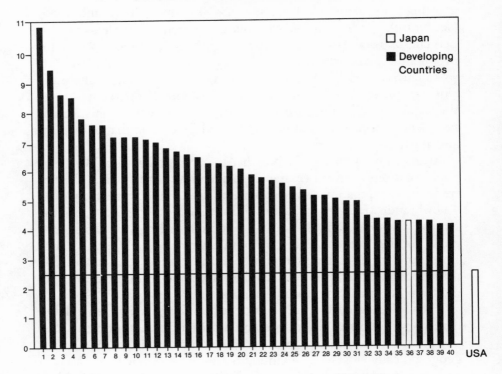

1. Botswana
2. Cameroon
3. Jordan
4. Hong Kong
5. Singapore
6. China
7. United Arab Emirates
8. Congo
9. Korea, Republic of
10. Malta
11. Solomon Islands
12. Oman
13. Egypt
14. Lesotho
15. Paraguay
16. Cape Verde
17. Malaysia
18. Pakistan
19. Yemen, Arab Republic
20. Indonesia
21. Thailand
22. Maldives
23. Burma
24. Algeria
25. Syria
26. Rwanda
27. Kuwait
28. Saudi Arabia
29. Tunisia
30. Saint Lucia
31. Sri Lanka
32. India
33. Bangladesh
34. Saint Vincent
35. Antigua and Barbuda
36. Japan
37. Kenya
38. Yemen, PDR
39. Comoros
40. Swaziland

Source: World Bank. Does not include data for some developing countries.

the International Institute of Strategic Studies. "The Bengal Lancers have been replaced by aircraft carriers, nuclear submarines and missiles. India is well on the way to becoming a superpower."[23] Brazil, North and South Korea, and Egypt have all built sizable arms industries.

No leader should doubt the ability of developing countries to dominate the crises on his or her foreign policy agenda. "Most postwar American presidents have been driven from office or disgraced by their policies in the Third World," wrote Charles William Maynes, editor of *Foreign Policy*, with only slight exaggeration.[24] Among the foreign policy issues that have bedeviled U.S. presidents are the Korean and Vietnam wars, including the secret, illegal bombing of Cambodia; the Bay of Pigs fiasco to oust Fidel Castro and subsequent efforts to assassinate him; the Iran hostage crisis; and Ronald Reagan's arms-for-hostages overture toward Iran.

Meanwhile, interdependence is shifting national security priorities away from military might. International competition now ranks much higher as a national security concern. One brand-new national security concept is the environment. The realization is gradually dawning that man's technological advances have put ever greater stress on the earth's resources. Previously, environmental concerns centered on local issues, such as the quality of one's water supply. Today people realize that untoward actions by other, distant countries can contaminate their local environment. The issues of ozone depletion and global warming generate international attention and action.

Interdependence: Out of Control

Interdependencies have grown faster than the tools to manage them. The traditional idea has been that governments should not meddle in other countries' domestic affairs, pointed out Harold Saunders, a long-term government official now at the Brookings Institution; today, it is impossible not to. "We live in a world in which whatever a leader says has an impact in somebody else's backyard." Just as a president can bypass journalists to get his message to the people directly—say, by speaking on television—leaders in one country can speak directly to people in another country, hoping to influence public opinion.

Whereas diplomatic relations between countries were once thought of as the province of national governments, the number of players has increased. Over 900 local governments passed their own nuclear freeze resolutions, according to Michael Shuman, founder and president of the Center for Innovative Diplomacy, which "helped pressure President Ronald Reagan to launch the Strategic Arms Reduction Talks in Geneva."[25] Similarly, the Davis, Calif., city council sent its own fact-finding mission to Nicaragua to evaluate U.S. policy. Business plays an ever larger role, one that is not always in sync with national goals. "The United States does not have an automatic call on our resources," a Colgate-Palmolive Company executive told a *New York Times* reporter. "There is no mindset that puts this country first." Colgate-Palmolive sells more products abroad than it does domestically. As a result, national leaders have more difficulty controlling and guiding their countries and working out accommodations with other nations.[26]

U.S.-Mexican relations illustrate how seemingly straightforward bilateral issues have become more complex. The proliferation of low-wage-rate, export-oriented *maquiladora* industries in northern Mexico has caused controversy. Some North Americans feel that these industries take away U.S. jobs; some Mexicans feel that American businesses take unfair advantage of Mexican desperation for work. But this problem cannot be understood only in the border context. Some "U.S. companies" taking advantage of *maquiladora* work are subsidiaries of Asian companies. And U.S. competitiveness worldwide may depend on its ability to use low-wage labor overseas. "The United States–Mexican relationship is itself becoming *more and more dependent on trends and forces through the world*," noted the Bilateral Commission on the Future of United States–Mexican Relations in a 1989 report. To cite one of its examples, "the positions that Argentina and Brazil take regarding their debt obligations will have major implications for Mexico's connection with its United States creditors."[27]

What has changed, above all, is that nobody can opt out of relations with the rest of the world. No country can think of advancing without acquiring products and ideas from other countries. If a government tries to cut off relations with another nation, it has little chance of complete success. The United States refused diplomatic recognition to Angola in the mid-1980s, but Americans continued to do business with that country—so much, in fact, that the United States was Angola's largest trading partner.[28] Banks can refuse to lend more money to indebted countries; but if those countries do not acquire the capital to develop, their citizens may emigrate to the United States. Nobody can afford to ignore international issues. Foreign affairs are now local affairs.

"The essential feature of the new age of interdependence that had solidified after World War II," Barraclough observed, "was that the world was integrated in a way it had never been before; and this meant that no people, however small and remote, could 'contract out.'"[29]

The United States' Response

No country may be able to "contract out," as George Washington urged the United States to do. But that does not necessarily stop a nation from trying. Even as the United States has been drawn into the world, Americans have fought the idea of greater involvement. When, after World War I, some people like Mowrer became internationalists, seeing U.S. involvement in a second world war as inevitable, most Americans hoped to keep their distance right up until the bombing of Pearl Harbor. The Great Depression had soured many American loans overseas. With both the war and the depression behind them, Americans "vowed that never again would they trust their fortunes abroad or respond to the requests of recreant foreign governments."[30]

There is more to this attitude than mere obstinacy. For decades the United States has had an enormous impact on other countries; its path-breaking technological advances, military strength, and economic reach have made other countries, to varying degrees, depend on it for capital, ideas, and protection. But until very recently, other countries have had relatively little impact on the United States. Thanks to its large internal market, its vast resources, and the special security provided by its dominance in this hemisphere, the United States has viewed itself as self-sufficient. It has had foreign interests, to be sure. But compared with the Europeans, for whom foreign affairs was a bread-and-butter issue, those interests have had little meaning for most Americans.

This can be shown in any number of areas, but one of the clearest examples is in trade. The United States has engaged in foreign trade throughout its history. After all, it started out as a colony. The New England colonists supplied England, France, Holland, and the

Danish West Indies with salt mackerel, horses, and timber, and they brought back molasses, sugar, and rum; some commercial ships traveled as far as the African coast and China. By 1900 the United States accounted for 23.6 percent of total world manufacturing output. But trade as a percent of the entire economy has hardly been decisive for most of U.S. history. While it equaled 30 percent or more of British, French, German, and Japanese GNPs in the 1920s, trade was only 10.8 percent of U.S. GNP from 1919 to 1928. "For all the *absolute* increases in America's exports and imports, their place in its national economy was not large, simply because the country was so self-sufficient," historian Paul Kennedy sagely observed.[31]

This situation continued after World War II. The United States accounted for one-half of the world's total production and about 20 percent of total world trade. Yet trade was then a smaller percentage of the U.S. GNP than it was in the 1920s. Between 1954 and 1963, trade, excluding services, averaged only 7.9 percent of GNP.

Little wonder that the United States has fancied it could free itself of foreign entanglements.

The United States cannot seriously entertain such notions today. With blinding speed it has been transformed into a nation that, like others, is dependent on the rest of the world. Foreign trade has become progressively more salient; U.S. strength has become progressively less overwhelming. In 1980 foreign trade amounted to 21 percent of GNP; in 1987 it was 26 percent—more than three times what it had been just after World War II. At the same time the U.S. share of the world economy dropped from 35 percent in 1960 to 28 percent in 1985.[32] "The United States," summed up economist C. Fred Bergsten, "has simultaneously become much more dependent on the world economy and much less able to dictate the course of international economic events."[33]

Signs of change appear throughout the economy. The United States has always enjoyed the advantage of agricultural exports, but that is slipping. Its share of world food exports to developing countries dropped from 59 percent to 41 percent between 1982–83 and 1985–86. All the while, developing countries have been selling more food to the United States. Foreign manufacturing competition inside the U.S. domestic market has also increased. In the early 1960s only 25 percent of American products faced foreign competition; more than 70 percent of American products had foreign competition in 1985.[34] Foreign companies have become the *only* suppliers of some products—for instance, compact disc players. Corporate America, not just consumers, relies on imports. Imports by businesses of capital goods increased 40 percent between 1985 and 1988, according to the *Wall Street Journal.*[35]

The United States rued its vulnerability to the OPEC cartel in the 1970s and took steps to make itself more independent. But today it is more dependent on foreign suppliers for its petroleum—particularly Middle Eastern oil—than it was in 1973.[36] Similarly, as of the early 1980s, the United States imported more than half its supply of 24 of the most important industrial raw materials it needed, many of them from Africa and other developing countries. Mineral imports, measured in dollar value *and* adjusted for inflation, doubled between 1950–54 and 1965–69 and increased by another 50 percent during the next five years. Although cobalt, manganese, and other minerals are purchased in modest quantities, they are essential to modern society—not only for defense but also for manufacturing production generally.[37]

U.S. dependence on foreign capital, which is needed to support the budget deficit, increases despite worries that such dependence is far too large already. "At the beginning of the 1980s, the balance of what foreigners owed Americans beyond what Americans owed foreigners amounted to some $2,500 per family. Today the balance *against* us amounts to more than $7,000 per family, and it is continuing to grow rapidly," said Benjamin M. Friedman in 1988.[38]

While the United States has fretted over this, Japan has become the world's number one foreign aid donor, and European countries have begun to play stronger leadership roles in solving world problems. As a reporter for the Montreal daily newspaper *La Presse* commented on National Public Radio in 1989, the time was when other countries waited to see what the United States would do before they acted. But George Bush did not have such authority when he took office and slowly began to plot foreign policy. "Mr. Bush promised that one of the first things he would do would be to call a global environmental conference," the reporter said. "Well, since the beginning of the year we have had three of those in Europe without Mr. Bush. So the world is not waiting for the American president anymore."

Even if the United States can cut its deficit and find alternatives to foreign oil, its links to the rest of the world will grow. Trade will remain important. With rapid travel, diseases will continue to spread. Ideas will continue to flow. People will continue to immigrate. And environmental problems in other countries—for instance, unsafe disposal of hazardous wastes—will continue to wash up on American shores.

The United States still has the largest economy in the world. It can remain powerful. But it will have to share world power and foreign problems more than it did in the past. Such change is inevitable. No country can aspire to being supreme in the world—yet apart from it—for long. That the United States did so at all is a historical accident, partly determined by its geographic good fortune and partly the result of the battering other countries experienced in World Wars I and II. The United States was the only great power whose economy advanced, rather than deteriorated, during both wars.[39]

All countries face enormous challenges in dealing with interdependence. The strains are seen in Japan, which is worrying about losing its competitive edge to Korea and Taiwan, and in Western Europe, whose nations are creating new systems for cooperation. Switzerland, once considered an idyllic oasis that avoided UN membership, is no longer free of foreign entanglements. It has foreign drugs, the highest per capita incidence of AIDS in Europe, and mounting fears that its economy will falter if it does not open its markets more.[40]

But because of its historic self-sufficiency and the swiftness with which change is coming, the United States has been extraordinarily unprepared among the great powers to cope with the labyrinths of interdependence. How it will ultimately adjust remains a big question. The American mindset is to pull back, to hope against hope that this is only a passing phase. Indicative of this sentiment is the remark of former Federal Reserve Bank of New York president Anthony Solomon: "The United States lost economic independence these last few years because our basic policies—as well as those of our leading trading partners—got out of balance."[41] All the United States need do to regain its old preeminence, Solomon implied, is change economic policies.

The instinct to pull inward is all the more likely when global changes are accompanied by decreases in living standards. Between 1983 and 1988, American workers, excluding those on farms, saw their average weekly pay decrease in real terms from $281 to $276.[42] Realizing that they are facing stiff global competition, Americans have shown greater interest in protectionism. A late 1988 survey showed that nearly 80 percent of Americans favor limiting foreign investment.[43]

Managing relations with other countries makes sense, of course. Trying to avoid relations does not. Many current signs point to a preference for the latter approach. Pollster William Schneider detected a shift in American attitudes away from internationalism in the 1970s.[44] In 1986 Thomas L. Hughes, president of the Carnegie Endowment for International Peace, observed that internationally minded organizations like his "are compelled to operate in an American milieu less favorable than at any other time in [the endowment's] history; even in the 1920s, there was confidence that internationalists were riding the wave of the future."[45]

The United States cannot extricate itself from the world's cultural, political, and economic machinery. But will it be ground up in the gears or mesh with them?

Coming to Terms with Interdependence

The term *global problems* did not appear in academic literature until sometime in the late 1960s, one Polish scholar observed recently. "Today representatives of almost all ideological trends and research orientations in social sciences are engaged in global issues."[46] Interdependence has itself become a major political issue, as the 1988 presidential election showed with its focus on competitiveness (and protectionism) and the inflow of illegal drugs. Both candidates ardently courted Spanish-speaking Americans.

The increased attention to interdependence in the United States is positive, yet much more must be done to think through the issues. Two impediments in particular have hindered the debate that should go on. The first is the narrowness of the investigation. The second is a tendency toward abstractness.

Narrowness. As a term, *interdependence* is fraught with problems.[47] People have used the term in ways that limit it when, in fact, interdependence is, by definition, a broad and complex concept.

The use of the word *interdependence* in political rhetoric has been unfortunately simplistic. In these realms the word has symbolized a world that is becoming smaller and more friendly. In reality, interdependence can actually increase conflict. At bottom, it is neither good nor bad. It is both.

In an effort to bring rigor to the discussion of the problems of interdependence, scholars and policymakers have concentrated on the costs of interdependent relationships. This is to say, some scholars argue that interdependence only exists in those cases in which countries have a great deal at stake in their relationship. Otherwise, there is simply "interconnectedness." While this provides a way of assessing interdependent relationships, however, it contributes to a tendency to see interdependence just in arenas where costs are easily measured.

Not surprisingly, given the emphasis on costs, the first serious discussions of interdependence were those dealing with economics.[48] Politics was the logical next target. With justifiable pride, Robert O. Keohane and Joseph S. Nye, Jr., two political scientists, noted that their work helped stimulate broader research: "It is now conventional to analyze interdependence as a political, as well as an economic, phenomenon."[49] Environmentalists have begun successfully to show that deterioration of the land, water, or air in one part of the world can hurt people elsewhere. But broader studies than this have been rare. Perhaps the most notable exception is Lester Brown's *World Without Borders*, published for a popular audience in 1972. Much of the book was farsighted and remains useful today.

Not only must investigations range over more issues, they must also explore connections using interdisciplinary approaches. A central feature of interdependence is that an economic connection can have consequences that go far beyond monetary matters. One classic example is the American manufacture for sale overseas of pesticides prohibited in the United States. Despite the restrictions on domestic sales, the pesticide comes back to Americans on the fruit they import. This play and byplay involves trade and health as well as politics. The exact costs of the transaction are not found on traditional balance sheets. Yet who would deny that the costs are high?

Another example of a multidisciplinary context for interdependence is the case of a Mississippi pulp paper company that stumbled on a reason for stepping up marketing efforts in Indonesia. On a trip through the Pacific Rim, the company's executives learned that Indonesia had just passed a literacy law, which meant the country would need more books—and, of course, more pulp to make books.

We must find ways to focus discussion of interdependence in ways that make the issues more manageable. But it is equally important to understand the breadth and depth of those relations and to look for ways to take our ties to other countries fully into account. For the time being, it is best to define interdependence as *a nation's increased sensitivity to external forces.*

Abstractness. Interdependence is often analyzed and described in terms that make it seem a remote, abstract concept. As a result, local implications are often overlooked and the public is not certain interdependence has anything to do with them.

The Treasury Department's statistics show that every $1 billion in exports is worth 25,000 American jobs. But people cannot relate to numbers this large. To their credit, Americans may sense that such statistics are only crude calculations at best. And, besides, people only pay attention to trends that tangibly touch their lives. If *you* have not lost your job or acquired a better one, interdependence can seem irrelevant.

The same pattern holds for other aspects of interdependence. Environmentalists, medical scientists, and other specialists who work on international subjects often assume that everyone shares their global understanding. But why should *we* care about tropical deforestation, I asked a world-class biologist. "If you live in Omaha and care about New York City, you should also care about Costa Rica," he replied impatiently. Colleagues might have understood his point, but most of us need to see connections explained in more detail.

Because specialists have not drawn these connections vividly for nonspecialists, most Americans have a hazy notion of interdependence. On the one hand, they talk about what a "small world we live in." They listen attentively as national political candidates talk about international issues that have come to have meaning in Americans' lives. Yet, at the same time, those who are elected to the House of Representatives are reluctant to apply for membership on the Foreign Affairs Committee: they know voters do not think the committee agenda has much of an impact on their lives.

Two readership surveys conducted in conjunction with a Society of Professional Journalists foreign news project illustrate how irrelevant the concept of interdependence seems to many people. In both surveys—one conducted in Hattiesburg, Miss., and the other in Richmond, Va.—readers were asked if they agreed or disagreed that, with growing interdependence, "what happens in one country influences another country." In both cases more than 80 percent of respondents agreed. Given their response to this first question, it would be illogical for respondents to answer "no" to the second: whether political and social upheavals or economic growth in poorer countries affects people in their state. Yet positive responses were more than 25 to 50 percentage points lower.[50]

Irrelevancy is one by-product of the abstract discussion of interdependence. The other is loss of complexity. Foreign connections manifest themselves locally in ways that are sometimes hard to predict based on the reading of national news stories. This became especially clear in writing an earlier book, *Main Street America and the Third World*, a precursor to this volume. In traveling around the United States in search of local connections, I discovered angles that had been missed by concentrating on the big news.

As one example, considerable concern had arisen over the Third World debt crisis. Large money center banks had cut off the flow of new credit to indebted nations, a decision that seemed sensible to many people across the land. Yet a bank in Lincoln, Neb., provided a new wrinkle on the story. The bank did not make foreign loans and never planned to do so, but it wanted the large banks to keep up their level of loans abroad. Without new capital, the Nebraska bank understood, developing countries would not grow and therefore could not import U.S. products. The bank had traced the escalating number of its local farm loan defaults to the inability of countries to import Nebraska-grown food.

The tendency of specialists to look at interdependence on a grand scale is not surprising. The subject is, in the first place, international; the specialists have been drawn to the issues surrounding interdependence because of their interests in the world. Local implications, in contrast, seem provincial. But the tendency can create international parochialists, people who care only about the "little man" in some far-off country and ignore the involvement and aspirations of the "little man" at home. If interdependence is to be understood, the local aspects of it must been seen as well.

This Book

This book does not pretend to provide a complete picture of interdependence between the United States and the Third World. It *does* intend to look broadly at the process of interdependence as it reverberates between the United States and three developing countries. It looks at a computerized data entry facility in the Philippines that is part of the global flow of information revolutionizing business and touching the lives of common people everywhere. It looks at Costa Rica's tropical forests, richly endowed with plants and animals of great value to citizens in the United States. And it looks at Kenya, a tourist mecca that is also an example of how cultures clash and create new tensions.

This is not a book designed to make readers feel all is well. The three profiles show that global interdependence has created a tangle of connections. These connections liberate some people but bind others. They raise difficulties never before confronted. Observations offered by journalists in developing countries (see boxes) are meant to give additional perspectives on the complexity of interdependence. Throughout readers are not told what to think. The intention is to suggest ideas people might start thinking about. In that spirit, the concluding chapter does not solve the problems raised in the book. It talks about problem solving.

George Washington's observations may not be as fitting today as they once were. But one aspect of his farewell address does remain valid: that "it is essential that public opinion should be enlightened." This book hopes to make a modest contribution to that end.

CHAPTER ■ 1

The Long-Distance Call

Whether in Manila or Dayton, most people go about their lives as they always have. But if routines are the same, the forces underlying them are not. Hard-to-see global communication grids link not only the Philippines and the United States but countries everywhere. The resulting global work forces, making brand-new information products sold worldwide, are rewriting the theories of Adam Smith and Karl Marx. "These are the days of miracles and wonder," sings Paul Simon of the astonishing implications of modern technology. "This is the long-distance call."

very workday morning at 7:30 Marian Tabjan (pronounced *tab-han'*), a fresh-faced woman in her late 20s, begins her long, familiar journey to a job the world has only begun to understand.

Outside her parents' simple plywood-walled home, which like others in the government housing project in the northern Manila municipality of Malabon has electricity but no telephone, she hails one of the many motorized tricycles that cruise the neighborhood. It taxis her five minutes to within a short uphill walk of a jeepney pickup point. Jeepneys, a distinctive Philippine cultural institution, come in gaudy combinations of bright colors, are decorated with streamers and silver horses mounted on the hood, and have names like "Holy Mary," "Milwaukee," and "Mobile Lounge." Though viewed by foreign visitors as chaos-on-wheels, these vehicles with jeep fronts and two rows of benches facing each other in the back are efficient small buses that ply routes throughout the city. The 5- to 10-minute jeepney ride Marian takes drops her within walking distance of a train station. The LRT (Light Rail Transport), as it is called, whisks her through the old part of Manila to the Makati commercial center on the south side of the city. She exits at Sen. Gil J. Puyat Avenue and squeezes on a double-decker bus that lumbers up the street. After 10 minutes she climbs off the bus and darts through the heavy traffic to the other side of the broad thoroughfare. Entering one of the simple steel and glass buildings that have become the dominant modern architectural style throughout the world, Marian walks to the back of the lobby, ascends a flight of dingy stairs to the second floor, and goes through the doors of Saztec Philippines. She freshens up, chats with her colleagues for a few minutes, and is at her desk by 9 a.m., poised to communicate instantly with the world.

Saztec Philippines, one member of the Saztec family of information facilities spread around the world, does data entry. In the lingo of modern communications, that means its data entry operators sit at electronic terminals, converting information printed on paper into computer files. On a given day Filipinos employed by Saztec can be found "keying" American patient records for hospitals in Pomona, Calif., or Greensboro, N.C.; consumer credit reports on British citizens; names and addresses of Stride Rite shoe clients in the United States; switching networks for the Mountain Bell and Pacific Bell telephone systems; articles in *Playboy* and the *Christian Science*

Monitor; U.S. presidential speeches; French novels; European patent records; and the Helsinki, Finland, National Library book catalogue.

Saztec is one component of a technological revolution that is reshaping our lives as profoundly as the industrial revolution in the 19th century reshaped the lives of our forebears. Weighing little and operating at speeds that have no meaningful relationship to old-fashioned mail delivery, computers and other modern technology create global interdependencies unimagined only a generation ago when the experts thought that each country would never need more than one computer.

Global industries spawned by this technology create brand-new services that have become indispensable virtually overnight. As the provider of one of the first services to go abroad, data entry companies like Saztec have helped rewrite the theories of Adam Smith and Karl Marx, who thought that only manufactured goods were economically important and that services must remain as local as a haircut and shoeshine.

Communication networks using high-speed facsimile machines, computer terminals, and satellites and transoceanic fiber optic cables knit together far-flung operations. It is now possible, indeed imperative, for traditional manufacturing companies to function as if borders did not exist at all. Rather than worry about how far corporate headquarters are from manufacturing facilities, executives search for countries that have workers who will toil for low wages or that possess a promising market for sales.

This revolution has also created noneconomic global interdependencies, such as the one that shocked Swedes when it came to light: the Malmö, Sweden, fire department reached its database of street routes by contacting a General Electric computer in Cleveland, Ohio.

The manufacture of computer hardware, software, telecommunications gear, and other information technologies is the largest industry in the United States and "will be the largest industry worldwide by the mid-1990s," says Michael Tyler, a telecommunications consultant with Booz-Allen and Hamilton.[1] But the meaning, if not the magnitude, of this revolution is less clear. As with any sweeping change, new concerns have surfaced. Some are as fundamental as fashioning standards for telephone plugs and dial tones so they will work in all countries. Some are as profound as whether information technology will let developing countries surge ahead or will push them further behind—and what it will mean for the United States and other industrialized countries.

So quickly is change coming that the most basic implication of this revolution—global interdependence—is hard to see.

"What are you doing here?" a worker in Saztec's London office asked when I visited.

"Researching interdependence."

"What," she said with dead seriousness, "does that have to do with us?"

New Enterprises, New Entrepreneurs

Alan Fraser, a New Zealander, founded Saztec without the kind of business plan that Harvard Business School teaches its students is essential. What he did have was the self-confidence to act quickly and creatively on an untested global business opportunity.

Fraser's self-confidence is partly natural and partly, no doubt, derived from his military service. New Zealand does not have its own West Point. Instead, it sends a small group of young men each year to Australia's Royal Military College, Duntroon. Fraser, a farm boy who won an appointment to the military academy, graduated as an infantry officer in 1958 and served in Malaysia during the Communist-led insurgency. According to Conrad Lealand, who graduated with him and is now an executive with Saztec, Fraser became something of a legend when an insurgent leader said he would surrender only to Fraser. Fraser, Lealand says, was mentioned in dispatches and seemed on his way to a star-studded career.

But after serving first with a small contingent of New Zealanders stationed in Vietnam and then in what he perceived as the wasteful military bureaucracy in New Zealand, Fraser became disillusioned. In 1968, when he was 30, he bought his way out of the military, paying the equivalent of half a year's salary to the government, and took some business courses. Although IBM prefers to hire young salesmen, whom they can mold, Fraser convinced the New Zealand office to give him a job. Dressed in what he calls his IBM uniform—a blue pinstriped suit and white shirt—and armed with his IBM-style briefcase, Fraser went to work in 1969.

Fraser seems physically larger than he really is. Six feet or so in height, he is lean and muscled. His sandy hair is cut close, military style, accentuating his jug ears, angular features, and large toothy smile. In keeping with the common impression of New Zealanders, he is outgoing and frank. It is not hard to imagine prospective clients succumbing to his sales pitches or to understand why someone with his command presence preferred to start his own company in 1972 rather than work in someone else's.

"While shaving one morning," he recalls of his first business venture, "I thought what is the simplest thing to sell, and I saw the cap." The cap belonged to his aerosol shaving cream can. He figured he could redesign it with distinct new selling points. It would be a quarter of an inch higher, making the product stand taller on the store shelf; it would have serrated edges, making it easier to take off; it would have the customer's logo imprinted on the top; and it would have a pinhole in the middle so that "unsightly" moisture on the can nozzle would evaporate. Enthused by the idea, he wasted little time looking for a company name. He opened a magazine at random and, finding a story about Aztec Indians, called the company Aztec. Today he admits that the selling points for Aztec caps, especially the pinhole, might not have made much difference to consumers. But the pitch worked well enough with a shaving cream manufacturer, who placed large orders with him. In a year Fraser had enough capital to go into a business with a real future—data entry.

Data entry appealed to Fraser both because it built on his IBM experience without requiring extraordinary technical expertise and because he saw a market. Data entry was changing from the primitive method of punching holes in paper cards to electronic computerization. Businesses were learning the value of managing information, and they wanted help. Although some giant companies like General Motors might have had enough work to keep in-house data entry operators busy every day, many smaller companies then, as now, did not; and those that did have a steady volume of work often preferred not to be distracted by maintaining an operation whose task was peripheral to their central job. IBM stopped selling data entry services for just that reason: it wanted to concentrate on selling equipment.

From the very first, Fraser planned an international operation that would provide high-quality work at a low cost. He targeted the Australian market and set up a small office in Sydney. He planned to subcontract the data entry work in Singapore, where wage levels were about one-half those in Australia. With the help of a silent partner, who continued to work at IBM, Fraser registered the company in Singapore, although not as Aztec. Because another Singapore company had already taken that name, he put an "S" for Singapore on the front of Aztec, making it Saztec.

Fraser's approach to building Saztec was to make bold promises and then find ways of delivering. He got his first contract by challenging a Sydney customer, Computer Accounting Services, to give him a small job as a trial. If he couldn't deliver a high-quality product at the low price he quoted, and do it in four days, he would forgo payment. The problem was that Fraser had not yet tested any data entry facilities in Singapore himself.

Fraser jumped on an airplane and, shortly after landing in Singapore, located a local car dealer with a computer to do the work. But when the data were entered, Fraser discovered many errors, and although the car dealer was willing to do the job again, he did not have time until the next week. Fraser, who was staying in a cheap Singapore hotel room to conserve his dwindling resources, desperately looked for another company that could do data entry. Recalling that *Reader's Digest* had such work done in the Philippines, he found Pacific Data in Manila and called the general manager, a Chinese Filipino named Emmanuel B. Cu. The gist of Fraser's call was: This is Saztec; we're doing a test to see how fast you can turn around a data entry job; meet me at the Manila airport tomorrow and I'll give you the data; you must send it to Sydney within 24 hours by plane. (Fraser could not afford to stay overnight in Manila.) Cu agreed to do the job and met Fraser at the airport. Pacific Data delivered on the day promised. "That," Fraser says, "was the start of Saztec."

Within three years, Fraser's daring strategy had created a client base of one-half million Australian dollars annually (about U.S. $600,000 at the time). Saztec gave most of its data conversion jobs to Pacific Data, though some were sent to Singapore to spread what was becoming a large work load.

Fraser experimented with other aspects of the computer business, always with the same bravura. When he wanted to sell Hitachi's upscale hand calculator in Australia, the Japanese company balked. They had never heard of Saztec. Fraser convinced them to test Saztec by giving him 2,000 computers. In just a couple of days he was back in Japan to announce that he had sold the whole lot, a feat he accomplished by offering the calculators at cost to a discount house.

Hitachi gave Saztec more calculators and other equipment to market in Australia.

Fraser eventually split the company with his partner, who by now had left IBM to work full time at Saztec. The partner took the equipment side of the business, which did not interest Fraser as much. Fraser kept the data entry activities and aggressively expanded sales into the U.S. market. In 1980 he opened his own data entry facility in Manila on Sen. Gil J. Puyat Avenue.

Fraser's decision to open the Manila facility changed his life, which seemed to him to have fallen into an empty routine. Since the mid-1970s he had lived a few months each year in Australia, Singapore, the Philippines, and the United States. He was divorced from his wife and was, by his own reckoning, "a wild, hard-drinking man." The Manila facility forced him to put down at least temporary roots. One reason he chose Manila was that he liked the Filipinos. Eventually he fell in love with one of his Filipino employees. Shortly before marrying Dinah, Fraser happened to attend church with her. Inside, in a shattering moment, he says, he actually heard God chiding him for his selfish ways. Within a few months he became a Catholic. He gave up drinking and shifted his horizons.

"People became my first priority," he says. He called Thomas L. Reed, whom he had taken on as a partner to manage the American marketing arm of Saztec. "I am out," Fraser recalls saying. "You can buy the company." Specifically, Fraser wanted to keep the Manila data entry operation, which he owned with Emmanuel Cu of Pacific Data and another Filipino businessman, who had minority shares. Reed could have the U.S. operation, for which he was to pay Fraser about $200,000 whenever he could. Saztec Philippines would continue to do data entry jobs sold by Reed's Saztec operation. Fraser would use his personal profits and some of those from the company for charitable works in the Philippines. Reed was free to expand the company.

Saztec's progress since then has not been uniformly up. Data entry, Fraser says, "is a barometer of the global economy." Companies experiencing financial difficulties do not commission big jobs converting data on paper into computerized databases, which can be expensive. When the world economy slumped in the early 1980s, Fraser "thought God might be sending him a message to go teach

Bible classes in the islands." Business was so slow he had to let 300 Filipino employees go, reducing the Saztec Philippines staff to six. But within a month of the layoffs, he was hiring again, and within half a year, he was at full capacity. In mid-1989 the facility had 1,000 employees. Each year since 1982, when business rebounded, Fraser has seen at least 100 percent return on equity, he says. In 1989 Saztec Philippines grossed $3.1 million.

The Saztec U.S. operation has become Saztec International, under chief executive officer (CEO) Tom Reed. In 1985 it opened a European sales office in London and, two years later, a data entry facility on the western coast of Scotland. It also set up a small sales office in Toronto, Canada. It acquired Presstext News Service, a Washington, D.C., database, which it later sold. Additionally, it has absorbed two companies with which it had worked closely: a data processing and software development company called LMI in Dayton, Ohio, and a data entry facility, Information Control Inc., in an industrial park outside Kansas City, Mo. The latter has a division that sells used computer hardware.

In 1986 Saztec International made a public stock offering on the over-the-counter market. The stock had a large run-up in value in the first months, something that often happens with new issues. The high expectations, however, quickly collapsed. The company experienced a $1 million loss the first year after going public, which Reed attributes to investments needed for long-term growth. When the stock market tumbled in October 1987, the stock dropped from $7 a share to $1. But in 1989 Saztec International posted a profit of $1 million, sales were double those of the previous year, and the stock was on the rebound.

Noting how changes in the data entry business influenced his previous seat-of-the-pants business style, Fraser says, "You can't do it the way I did before with a suitcase and a telex machine." Norman Bodek, president of the Connecticut-based Data Entry Management Association, says that competition and the natural process of maturation have forced some companies out of business and encouraged others to expand and take on more sophisticated work, as Saztec has done. DEMA, which claims a membership of 1,500 firms involved with data entry, does not try to keep an accurate count of the number of data entry facilities in operation, but the industry is healthy and expanding.

The fastest-growing category of jobs in the United States is computer programmers and systems analysts. Businesses that once paid little attention to information management have found they cannot afford to neglect the subject today. "We are keying stuff no one ever dreamed of keying a few years ago: newspaper articles and *Playboy*, or how to grow roses in California," Fraser says. "The reason this has happened is that the cost of storing data is so low and access is so fast. The time will come in the near future when every book is stored on a computer . . . and we will read books on computers. We have the technology. It is possible."

Saztec specializes in library catalogues, hospital patient records, legal documents, and telephone line records. "The most technically interesting job," Fraser says, "is the line record for telephone companies so they can track errors in the system. We get information on lines down to a point that a computer can identify a break at a house on the corner of such-and-such a street and [warn] that the repair man should watch out for the dog. This is one of the most sophisticated examples of a database."

The number of commercial databases for sale has expanded as the use of computers has become more widespread. The 1979–80 edition of the *Directory of Online Databases* listed 400 databases and 59 online services worldwide. The 1987 *Directory* identified 3,487 databases and 547 online services. Subjects include Physician Data Query, which contains cancer treatment measures, and *Zeitschriftenkatalog der Bayerischen Staatsbibliothek Muenchen*, which "contains citations to the periodical holdings of the Bavarian State Library." Presstext, which Saztec owned for a time, puts official White House and State Department statements into a computer database. The White House is a subscriber.

Thanks to the database boom, membership in the Information Industry Association more than tripled between 1983 and 1989 to 800. The Washington, D.C.-based organization represents companies that create information products, as Saztec does, and sell them, as many of Saztec's clients do. "We get two or three new members a week," said David Y. Peyton, IIA's director of government relations in 1988. "It is all we can do to remember the new names. Most of them are small companies."

If industrial growth is not diminishing, neither is one other aspect of the information revolution—the global flexibility it engenders. In the days since Fraser jumped on a plane for Singapore—and then

Manila—with his first data entry job, businesses of all kinds have become more adept at using information to knit together workers from vastly different locations and cultures.

Flexibility, Speed, And the Global Work Force

Todd Stein is a programmer in Saztec's most sophisticated and free-wheeling facility, located in an industrial park of one-story brick buildings about 10 miles outside Dayton, Ohio. Like many Americans of his generation, Stein has found computers a liberating obsession. He gave up full-time college study to become one of the first three employees hired by LMI, which was formed in 1981 by two Dayton-area men, Dan Leggett and Kent Meyer, and merged with Saztec in 1987. An amiable football player-sized man in his mid-20s, Stein works on computers during the day and then stays to play games on them in the evening.

In keeping with Leggett and Meyer's relaxed management style and the rapid growth of the company, the offices are spread haphazardly in four bays. A brick props open one door; tables are not in rows; and space is so scarce that private offices also serve as hallways between rooms. Stein and the 20-odd other employees work in blue jeans and sport shirts and take breaks to play a quick game of basketball in the court behind the building. Stein attends college in the evenings, except in the summer, when he enjoys being outdoors. During those months, he often works through his lunch hour and goes home early.

The work environment is not as casual at other Saztec work sites. In the Philippines and Scotland, where large staffs do basic coding jobs, regular work hours are essential to ensure efficient use of equipment and to monitor output. Rather than dress in sports attire, as Stein does, Filipinos wear blue uniforms. This reduces the amount of money they must spend on clothes for work. Chris Dowd, an Australian who is managing director of the Scotland facility, smiles as he tells of the Scotswoman who was uncomfortable with breaks from tradition, such as calling him by his first name. She preferred he wore a suit to work.

Even so, the Saztec watchword is flexibility, not rigidity. When Saztec CEO Tom Reed complains about "having flexibility but it is not as great as we would like," he is really talking about how much freedom he has come to expect. As the integration of vastly different work forces in Scotland, the Philippines, and the United States shows, Saztec believes in a world liberated from traditional constraints of time and space.

With a telephone call to Madras, India, almost as easy as a call next door, distance is becoming a meaningless concept. Whereas people were once satisfied to send memoranda through interoffice mail, they have begun to use facsimile transmission—fax—over telephone lines, even if the recipient is only one floor away. The need for fast turnaround and low transport costs traditionally dictated putting production facilities close to the customer. But information products do not travel like steel bars or bags of grain. Magnetic computer tapes holding information copied from tons of paper can be slipped into an envelope and tossed on a jet plane.

Distance and time are also of decreasing importance in constructing data entry facilities. A steel company has to think carefully about setting up a mill in another country. It takes three to six years to build a plant and to train its work force; then, once the mill is constructed, the decision to move is costly. But silicon chips and other computer components used in data entry are lightweight, small, and relatively cheap. Between 1972 and 1981, the number of transistors and other components that could be put on a silicon chip doubled annually.[2] Thus, data entry facilities can be started quickly—as Saztec proved shortly after opening its London office in 1985, when it heard that the British Library had decided to computerize its General Catalogue.

The General Catalogue consists of a series of bound volumes listing a large share of the library's holdings, about one-half of which are in languages other than English. Although a major innovative convenience when it was first printed in 1900, the catalogue had become a bulky, unwieldy operation by the 1980s. It took so long to prepare an updated version that the most recent 360-volume edition published in 1987 did not include books published after 1975. Entries were listed almost solely by author, rather than cross-referenced by book title and subject matter.

When Saztec first heard of the plan to computerize the catalogue, the British Library had already decided to award the lucrative contract to a U.S. company that planned to do the work in New York City. To get the contract open to competitive bidding, Saztec launched a major lobbying campaign. Among the main lobbying points was that Saztec hoped to open a facility in Ardrossan, on the west coast of Scotland, which would give jobs to British subjects, not foreigners. Ardrossan was chosen because a defunct U.S.-owned facility in the vicinity had earlier computerized the Library of Congress card catalogue. Saztec expected to find a potential pool of trained workers in an area that suffered from high unemployment.

With the help of people like David Lambie, a member of Parliament who represented the Cunningham South electorate that includes Ardrossan, the contract was eventually opened to competitive bidding. While bids were being considered in late 1986, Saztec started a small test center with 15 people—the sort of facility, says Conrad Lealand, who took the lead in competing for the British Library job, that meant they could have "pulled up and gone home if we didn't get the contract." In January 1987, Saztec won the 4-year, £1.8 million job and acquired the rights to market the resulting computerized index worldwide for 10 years. Saztec's use of British labor also made the company eligible for British government cash grants.

A month after winning the contract, Saztec Scotland began work in earnest in a two-story red brick building that stands only 75 yards from the grey Irish Sea. It proved difficult to recruit people who had worked in the earlier facility, as many had taken other jobs. Nevertheless, Saztec hired and trained about 100 people in six months. By early 1988 the facility was profitable. Despite the enormous task of devising methods of keying languages as difficult as Greek and Cyrillic on English-language keyboards, the Scottish work force turned out computerized data ahead of the British Library schedule. Yet even this was considered frustratingly slow by Saztec, which in late 1987 briefly considered doing the work elsewhere.[3]

Technological advances have not made proximity entirely irrelevant. The Dayton facility has five full-time data entry operators who do small jobs. Almost daily a local "fulfillment company" sends a cab driver named Rocky to Saztec with coupons received from sales promotions promising calendars and other gifts. Saztec operators key master mailing lists from the coupons. The jobs are not big enough to justify sending them to Manila.

Some complex keying tasks require close contact with the client to check specifications or questionable data; others require turnaround in one day. Work of this nature is important enough for Saztec to have a facility with 180 full-time data entry operators in Kansas City, Mo. Other data entry companies have a much bigger U.S. presence. In 1988, Appalachian Computer Services had more than 1,400 data entry operators in six plants in rural Kentucky, Illinois, and California.

Nevertheless, the trend is increasingly to go offshore, where wage rates are lower than in the United States. In an interview, Norman Bodek of DEMA ticked off data entry operations in the Dominican Republic, Mexico, Haiti, Grenada, Barbados, Martinique, St. Kitts, Jamaica, India, Sri Lanka, China, Taiwan, South Korea, and the Philippines. He had not heard of the Saztec operation in Ardrossan. In 1985, after 20 years of operating strictly in the United States, Appalachian Computer Services bought a small facility in Jamaica. Perhaps the only data entry operations that will never send work offshore are those run by prisons in Connecticut, Michigan, Kentucky, California, and Texas.

"There are [offshore information] capabilities out there people just don't realize," says W. Patrick Griffith, who was president of AMR Caribbean Data Services in 1988, before he became vice president of AMR Information Services. "That's why I am so enthusiastic." CDS was established in 1983 when AMR, its parent company and also owner of American Airlines, decided to move its data entry facility for airline tickets from Tulsa, Okla., to Bridgetown, Barbados. In addition to processing an estimated 70 million tickets each year, CDS began to sell its services to other companies. In 1987 it opened a second facility in the Dominican Republic, which had 650 operators in mid-1989 and is expected to grow to 900 in the near future. CDS executives talk about opening a third facility at another site in the Caribbean.

The incentive, Griffith says, is that all kinds of work can be done offshore as a result of improved communications. In one of its biggest jobs, acquired in 1988, CDS keys medical claims for a large Manhattan insurance carrier. The documents arrive by plane; after the information is encoded, it is transmitted back to New York via satellite and leased communication lines, thus shortening the turnaround time. The client can also beam information, such as computer formats, directly to the Dominican Republic facility.

In 1988, Griffith expected that his work force would soon do medical transcription using this two-way electronic communications capability. U.S. physicians would dictate remarks about patients into a microphone; the comments would then be transmitted to Barbados, where they would be typed and beamed back to the United States. The whole process, Griffith said, could be done in four to six hours.

Although by 1989 that job was still on the shelf, as one executive put it, the idea of receiving documents electronically, rather than on paper, was very much alive. The company was vying for a new insurance contract in which claims information would be transmitted to the Caribbean over satellites. "Pure data entry has changed drastically in the last three years because of changes in technology, and it will change just as dramatically in the next three years," says Gary Barras, CDS's vice president for finance, who already regards the sending of information on paper as passé. "A couple of years from now we will be able to offer a product we haven't even conceived now."

Griffith's emphasis on doing more than just keying data offshore is typical of the trend in information industries. Conrad Lealand of Saztec describes his own company as the Rolls Royce of data entry companies. He means that Saztec provides high quality and can, in addition to data entry, do programming and other services needed to actually use the data. Equidata, a Manila-based operation owned by an American, recently started data entry operations with plans to provide data processing services as well. Equidata owner and president James Conway can use processing technology to analyze the Malaysian Yellow Pages, for which he already does data entry, and identify which parts of Kuala Lumpur show the greatest potential for the sale of Yellow Pages ads later.[4] And Augusto C. Lagman, a Filipino entrepreneur, has a financial interest in about 20 computer-related companies in the Philippines, including one that does data entry and another called Systems Resources Inc., which produces customized software. One of SRI's biggest jobs, Lagman says, was a $2 million contract to produce an air base inventory management system for Boeing Services International and to train Americans in its use.

The path a job can travel to take advantage of special skills and technology in one place and cheap labor in another is as complex as the circuit diagram of a computer. Take, for example, the various stops required for the job of cataloguing part of the Helsinki Library: The library card catalogue was microfilmed in Helsinki. Reading from the microfilm, data entry operators in Manila keyed an abbreviated database that listed all book headings. This computerized list went by plane to Sydney, Australia, where a specialized company put it into a computer format compatible with a database in Toronto, Canada. Once this was done, the Toronto database supplied full citations for many standard book titles and thus reduced the amount of information that had to be keyed by hand. Saztec's Dayton processing facility converted the Toronto entries into the proper Finland catalogue classification system and sent them on to Saztec's London office for checking. Filipino workers keyed full citations for the books not in the Toronto database. Saztec's Ardrossan facility did the final editing and quality control on the Manila entries. The Helsinki Library integrated the two sets of entries.

At times it seems as if Saztec is perversely testing the limits of information to unite its work force. In 1988 Saztec moved its headquarters from Los Angeles to Kansas City, Mo., where its large U.S. data entry operation is located. But many executives did not uproot themselves. Kent Meyer, who handles sales and for a time was in charge of all operations, including the Saztec Scotland facility, resisted moving from his home in Dayton. His wife liked Dayton, where she grew up. "We can be anywhere in the United States as long as we have telephone service and Federal Express," Meyer says of the irrelevance of location. Two employees who provide technical support for projects and work on company research and development live in Eugene, Ore. In addition to its full-time data entry operators in Kansas City, Saztec employs about 80 Kansas Citians who work part time on personal computers in their homes.

The ability to use information to manage a company applies not only to information industry companies like Saztec. The quick, cheap transmission of information has made traditional heavy industry light on its feet.

For all the "buy America" talk in the car industry, for instance, truly American-made automobiles are fast becoming as much a myth as the American family farmer. By 1981, Ford Motor Company produced more than one-half of its cars outside the United States and Canada. The Ford Escort assembled in England and Germany may use wheel nuts from the United States, defroster grills from Italy, starters from Japan, exhaust flanges from Norway, and tires from Austria.[5] Ford manages its parts procurement system with one of the largest private communication networks in the world.

"With modern transport and communications," a 1987 World Bank report noted, "it probably is no more difficult for today's merchants to organize a putting-out [cottage industry-type] system between New York and Hongkong, or between Tokyo and Seoul, than it was for the early English merchants to organize their putting-out system between London and the surrounding villages."[6] According to Booz-Allen and Hamilton, Inc., the number of leased international telephone lines, the backbone of private communication networks, is expected to grow from 17,000 in 1988 to 34,000 in 1995.

Dallas-based Texas Instruments is a prime example of a company that has created its own dedicated communications system. One-half of its 50 facilities are in Attleboro, Mass.; Johnson City, Tenn.; and other U.S. cities. The other half are located in such spots as Nice, France; Miho, Japan; Buenos Aires, Argentina; Elizabeth, Australia; and Baguio, a city high in the Philippine mountains, where workers cut microchips and configure them for use in computers. The facilities can beam messages to each other via channels leased on eight satellites. As of April 1988, Texas Instruments had 43,500 computer terminals for its 77,000 employees. Dallas can send messages giving Baguio microchip design specifications; Baguio can order raw materials for production.

With this network, many design and engineering jobs can be done far from the home office. In 1986, Texas Instruments opened a facility in Bangalore, India, where Indian specialists create software used in designing semiconductors. One hundred percent of the designs are exported via satellite. Access to cheap labor was not the chief reason for opening the plant, says Bob Bledsoe, market communications manager for Texas Instruments' data processing group. India has become a leading world software production center, thanks largely to its sizable, well-educated work force. The plant enabled the company to establish a presence in a potentially good, long-term market without raising Indian concerns about being overwhelmed by foreigners.

IBM, which has long had a sales operation in Manila, started buying computer chips in the Philippines in 1985. Worldwide computer networks permit staff to locate needed parts or to send a message to a colleague in any of 55 countries, telling of travel plans and proposing they have lunch when he arrives. When a Filipino salesperson makes a sale, he can connect his computer terminal to a system in Toronto that will "display" model sales contracts; IBM's 80-person repair staff in Manila can diagnose computer problems by connecting their computers to IBM computers in Tokyo, Japan; Tampa, Fla.; or Boulder, Colo.

Global banking, one of the chief economic integrators in the world, also relies on such information networks. The *Economist* estimates that telecommunications accounts for as much as 10 percent of commercial banks' operating costs. Although only a tiny percentage of the 50 million people who live in the Philippines use the automatic bank tellers in Manila and carry Diners Club credit cards, the country's banking system is hooked into the Society of Worldwide Interbank Financial Telecommunications, a global network for transferring money that began operation in 1977. In the mid-1980s, SWIFT handled about one million messages daily between member banks in more than 50 countries.[7]

Improved communications has helped companies create and maintain joint ventures and partnerships such as Fraser's with Saztec International. The SGV Group, a Filipino multinational that calls itself "the largest professional services firm in Asia," formed a joint venture with the large U.S.-based firm of Arthur Anderson in the mid-1980s. Working on 55 IBM computers in blue cubicles, SGV employees write sophisticated software programs. These programs are transmitted to an Arthur Anderson terminal in Chicago, which relays them via telephone lines to clients. In one of its first jobs, SGV converted an Atlanta, Ga., hospital management system—which included everything from billing to patient records—so that it could be used on a more powerful computer system.

Saztec, Texas Instruments, IBM, SGV, and companies like them are breaking down virtually the last bastion of "domestic" economic activity: services. The United States has bowed to the inevitable consequences of global financial markets and agreed that local banks can offer foreign currency accounts. A Danish company has office cleaning operations in 15 countries; its U.S. subsidiary employs 16,000 people.[8] Telemarketing—for instance, selling magazine subscriptions by telephone—is cheaper than the door-to-door selling techniques made famous by the Fuller Brush Company. With declining costs of telecommunication, the day is not far off when English-speaking work forces in tropical Caribbean climes will sell storm windows to Bostonians.

Increased global manufacturing and trade in goods and services mean countries are linked in ways they never were before. Interdependence, however, is not a precise equation, both sides equal in every way. Todd Stein in Dayton and Marian Tabjan in Manila, both valued employees, worry about keeping their jobs in the changing world economy. But Stein's opportunities outside Saztec far exceed Tabjan's, who is reminded daily of the vulnerabilities workers in developing countries face.

Staying Competitive

Marian Tabjan's personal history is marked, above all, by hard work, a family trait. The eldest of six children, she was born in 1959 in Tondo, one of the poorer sections of Manila. Her parents moved to the Malabon government housing project, situated on reclaimed land, in 1985. Two married brothers were given the Tondo home for their families. For 32 years Mr. Tabjan worked as a mechanic on government tugboats dredging Manila Bay. After retiring, he did what many Filipinos do these days: he took his services overseas to work for a German company dredging the Tigris River in Baghdad, Iraq. He returned after about a year and a half when the Iran-Iraq war broke out. The family jokes that he is now the janitor and principal of the small preschool run by Marian's mother. Named affectionately after Marian, the 40-desk Marian Learning Center fills what otherwise would be the Tabjans' living room. Tuition is 40 pesos, or about $2 a month. After teaching two hours in the school each morning, Mrs. Tabjan commutes to Tondo, where she teaches at a government-run kindergarten from 11 to 1 and then teaches grade six for adults from 6 to 9 in the evening.

After high school, Marian worked while attending college. Her first job was with the Coconut Planters Bank, where she typed information about the replanting program onto primitive data punch cards. After five months she went to the Philippine Coconut Authority. To her disappointment, she was not trained as a programmer as promised; not having a college degree, she was instead assigned clerical work. When a keypunch operator left to have a baby, however, Marian filled in for her. She worked hard to improve her typing skills and kept the job. The next year, 1980, she went to Saztec as a data entry encoder on the night shift. At Saztec she completed her college degree in industrial engineering, rose to become a line supervisor over seven other men and women, and later moved to the statistical department. By 1988 Fraser spotted her as someone to be groomed for more responsibility. He moved her to the quality control department to broaden her experience and then to a supervisory role in the department that sets specifications for work before it is coded and keyed.

"No one knows how many data entry companies there are in Manila," says Eduardo Bagtas, who manages the Saztec finance department. "They are like mushrooms." Most people in the industry guess there are 35 or 40 companies, some with just a few computer terminals. Emmanuel Cu, one of Fraser's partners and now head of the Philippine Association of Data Entry Corporations, formed in 1987, estimates that the number has doubled in the last two years. He has also seen many data entry companies fail during the 20 years he has been in the business.

Saztec's offices are unadorned but clean and air-conditioned. On both the first and second floors of the building, data entry operators sit at 11 rows of tables, eight operators to a row. The humming and beeping of their computer terminals collectively give out the sound of an orchestra tuning up. Statisticians, accountants, engineers, and coders, who prepare documents for the typists, are located in smaller rooms.

Base wages for data entry operators are about one-third those of keyers in the Kansas City facility (who earn $5.00 to $6.50 an hour) and about one-half those paid to Androssan workers. But these wages are attractive for a country with an annual per capita GNP of less than $600. Data entry operators with four years' experience average $2,650, not counting overtime. (The basic workweek is 35 hours, Monday through Friday.) Marian, who has advanced steadily, earns over $4,000 a year.

Comparisons between Saztec and other data entry companies in the Philippines are difficult. Companies do not like to give out salary data for fear of losing a competitive edge, and in any case, actual wages depend on complex systems of bonuses for high-speed, accurate work. Workers at Saztec talk about some firms providing unpleasant employment and paying less than the minimum wage. The data entry facilities that let me visit provided comfortable working conditions and paid the legal minimums at the least. But their wages and benefits were substantially lower than Saztec's.

Saztec provides free medical and dental care in a building behind the office, and it gives employees hospitalization coverage for a small fee. It also gives employees material and money to have their uniforms made, and it has set up a commissary where workers can buy food at cost. Thirty staff members are deaf. Fraser provides slightly over $2 a day to employees who are sent home when work slows down temporarily. After three and a half years on the job, employees receive $25 worth of company stock and the right to buy as much more as they want. As an added bonus, 2.5 percent of the company's before-tax profit goes to a Christmas party and summer outing for staff, the former usually at one of Manila's five-star hotels. "If we don't have a benefit," says Fraser, "it's because we haven't thought of it."

The concept at Saztec, says Erlinda Lorenzo, the administration manager, is that "seniority doesn't count for much. Performance counts." Two-thirds of the staff are women, and women have come to dominate senior positions. Lorenzo started as a clerk. The production manager is Theresa U. Joson, who earns over $12,500 a year.

Fraser, the only non-Filipino working in the facility, thinks of himself as making a contribution to the Philippines. "We are in pioneering days. That is why I love it here." He is scrupulous about running an honest company. In 1986 Saztec was listed as the 1,473d largest company in the country in gross revenue but 38th in return on equity, a factor that reflects the tendency of some companies to understate earnings to avoid taxes. Ed Bagtas, head of Saztec's finance department, says Fraser once wrote a letter to the government asking why he hadn't been taxed more.

To some people Fraser comes across as too confident, too self-righteous. He is capable of defending a decision with utter conviction one day and changing his mind the next—again with total assurance. Not surprisingly, employees are often intimidated by him. But if his level of conviction is extraordinary, he is not alone in his enthusiasm for pioneering in the Philippines. Others, such as James Conway of Equidata, which is just down the street from Saztec, also talk about making a contribution to the country.

Even so, Saztec and its competitors are businesses and, as such, are out to make a profit. Keying is a tedious and carefully monitored job. Using computers, Saztec management can precisely measure a worker's number of keystrokes and accuracy of performance, information that is used to weed out inefficient employees as well as to reward good ones. Fraser sets other tough standards and swiftly fires people who violate rules. New employees cannot become full-fledged staff members with all the benefits unless they have worked one year without being tardy more than one hour. When I first spoke to him in early 1988, the staff numbered well under 500, only about 60 percent of whom were "regular" employees. Each month Saztec workers are rated on a one-to-five scale, a technique Fraser says he drew from his military experience.

Even those companies that do not treat their employees well can make good profits in the Philippines, for the Filipinos offer handsome returns. Part of the reason for this lies in their history.

The country is sometimes thought of as the most Oriental of Western nations and the most Western of Oriental nations. The 7,100 islands that make up the Philippines are peopled by Malay, Chinese, and other Asian groups, who were ruled by the Spanish for 300 years. Then, at the turn of the last century, they were "liberated" by the United States, which stayed, creating schools and building American-style institutions.

English is so widely spoken that Americans sometimes fail to notice that the concept of "face" and other Asian values run deep in the culture. English-speaking abilities are not essential to data entry; Chinese and Latins can key data with high accuracy rates. But English is the language of the computer and of most databases, which gives Filipinos an edge.

So does widespread education. Although Philippine universities are not generally on a par with those in industrialized countries, few countries anywhere approach the Philippines in the percentage of people who attend college. Saztec does not have precise figures on college education, but Marian Tabjan is far from the exception. Of the employees at Equidata, 85 percent are college graduates. (By contrast, the personnel director at the Scotland facility reports that "only one or two people have a university degree.") Saztec bookshelves hold English-language translation dictionaries in Italian, German, French, Latin, Finnish, Swedish, Hungarian, Danish, Norwegian, and Spanish—all languages with which the staff has worked. Accuracy and speed are slightly higher in the Philippines than in Scotland or Kansas City even though wage rates are lower.

The pay differential can produce considerable profits. "One of the requirements in this business is high quality," James Conway of

Equidata says. "And that means you have to put a lot of labor into it." Saztec often keys data twice. This produces two sets of data, which can then be compared to ensure near-perfect accuracy. The use of low-wage labor means that the cost of such accuracy is much lower than it is in the United States.

Despite the extraordinary benefits Saztec offers, employees feel frustrated. To some degree this is natural in any company. The options for Philippine workers, however, are far narrower than those for their U.S. counterparts. As Saztec CEO Tom Reed notes, turnover among data entry operators in the United States is very high; they can find other, more interesting jobs. That is not the case in the Philippines. Interesting work is scarce.

Many data entry jobs are monotonous, requiring dexterity but not imagination. With the exception of those who repair computers, few employees at Saztec work in a field for which they were educated. They were trained as dentists, teachers, architects, accountants, mathematicians, nurses, and engineers—people for whom there are no jobs, or at least no jobs that pay close to wages at Saztec. One data entry operator, who has a degree in business administration, told me she would take a cut in pay to get experience in her field, if she could. She can't, however, because she must take care of her family. Others have had small businesses that failed. Two-thirds of the Saztec staff are under 30, eager to start ambitious careers. But as Marian Tabjan puts it in her straightforward way, "It's hard to find a job based on your degree."

The contrast with Todd Stein in Dayton is poignant. He could have moved to a better-paying job with a bigger computer-related company long ago, his supervisor told me. Instead, Stein stays at his $34,000-a-year Saztec job because of the opportunities it affords him to take on more responsibility. In 1988, for instance, he supervised sophisticated final mainframe computer programs performed on data that were keyed in the Philippines.

Joblessness is hard to measure in developing countries, but about 40 percent of the work force is generally thought to be under- and unemployed in the Philippines. When Eduardo Bagtas advertises for an accountant to work in the Saztec finance office, he gets 100 applications. The biggest reason data entry operators leave Saztec is to marry or to emigrate to another country where wage levels are higher. In 1988 Fraser estimated his turnover to be about 1 to 2 percent a year. For data entry companies in which pay is not so good, the rate is higher.

The frustration is made all the more intense by workers' fear that instead of moving ahead, they may lose the jobs they have. In the data entry business, as Emmanuel Cu describes the uneven flow of contracts, "it is typhoon or drought." When Saztec hit a dry spell in November and December of 1987, workers were sent home for a few days. Some have thought about unionizing as a way of protecting themselves, but most seem to recognize they have little to gain in benefits and much to lose. A militant left-wing union made life difficult for the Mattel toy company's manufacturing operations, which employed 3,400 Filipinos. Says one Saztec employee ruefully, "The owners left with their money."

Labor unrest is not the only turmoil that can drive business away. Violent political contests are a way of life in the Philippines. The ongoing rivalry between the forces of the late Ferdinand Marcos and Corazon C. Aquino are only part of this; there is also the threat of Communist insurgents. Fraser insists this is not a problem for Saztec. "We keyed all through the revolution," Fraser says of the period in which the Marcos regime fell. "If the Communists take over the country, do you think we are going to stop keying?" Saztec International's CEO, Tom Reed, reckons the risk roughly this way: "Fraser is 100 percent certain the Philippines will not collapse into political chaos; I am 99 percent certain."

Workers express greater concern. As they know, foreign clients want stability, and even the appearance of unrest can drive these clients away. During the unsuccessful coup attempt against President Aquino on August 28, 1987, one prospective Saztec client became worried and sent its business elsewhere. Reed and his colleagues have considered alternative sites they can use in case of emergency. From time to time, Saztec has sent work to facilities in Mexico, China, India, South Korea, Barbados, Puerto Rico, and Singapore. It has also scouted firms with facilities in Brazil, Haiti, Bolivia, and El Salvador, and it has considered acquiring a company in the Caribbean, where many countries offer investors financial incentives. "I wouldn't want to make a commitment to any one place," says Kenneth Noble, an information industry analyst with the Paine Webber brokerage firm in New York City. "I would rather have something I could shift out of."

Lack of strife alone is not enough to keep the country competitive in data entry. With the imposition of martial law in 1972, President Marcos achieved a high level of stability, and yet the Philippines information industry lost ground. "We were known as *the* training center in the region" for computers in the early 1970s, says Dr. William T. Torres, managing director of the National Computer Center. But the martial law government clamped down on information, and a military officer directed the computer center Torres now heads. "Some people believed that telecommunications was suppressed because the less people knew, the better," Torres says.

Escalating economic problems have also made it difficult for computerization to thrive, says Roberto Romulo, president and general manager of IBM Philippines when I interviewed him in 1988 and now the Philippines' ambassador to the European Community and Belgium. Long-term foreign debt, just under $3 billion in 1975, soared to more than $24 billion by 1982. In the early 1980s, real growth slowed to a crawl and within several years began to slip into the negative column. In per capita terms, GNP fell from $790 a year in 1981 to $570 in 1986. The Aquino government, which inherited the economic mess created by Marcos, has concentrated on immediate pressing problems of rural development. To conserve foreign exchange needed to service the debt, it completely banned computer imports from the end of 1983 to the end of 1985.

"Starting in 1986 we released ourselves from this bondage," says Torres, who represents the change from the old military rule days. One of the central purposes of his center is to train government workers. An aggressive apostle for computers, Torres has even arranged for his driver to take computer courses. He believes the private sector can build on the low pay scales the country has to offer foreign investors. "Our niche in the global information industry is to make software, not to compete in hardware."

Augusto Lagman, the Filipino entrepreneur who did the $2 million job for Boeing, estimates that Philippine exports of computer software total about $10 million a year. Within five years, he guesses, they will soar to $100 million. Although only "a rounding error" when measured against total software exports worldwide, he says, labor-intense software production will make a big difference to the Philippines.

Being released from bondage and moving quickly ahead, as Torres and Lagman hope will happen, are different matters. The costs of computers have gone down. In one decade, the price of a silicon chip went from $10 to one-fifth of a cent.[9] South Korea and other advanced Third World countries have learned to manufacture computers that are compatible with IBM equipment but sell at a fraction of the IBM price. But basic costs are high by Philippine standards. While sales of computers in the Philippines are back up to 1977 levels, the government remains concerned about using foreign exchange to import such technology. Thus, while financially healthy Singapore has made communications a central component of its development strategy and allowed computers to be imported tax free, the Philippines places high duties and taxes on them. As a result, at the beginning of 1988, a computer in the Philippines cost 50 percent more than a computer in the United States.

Only a handful of Philippine companies can afford IBM's most sophisticated equipment. One Filipino executive with IBM says that computers at his university are roughly as sophisticated as when he attended 20 years ago. When a computer programmer is trained on outdated equipment, observes Dr. Alfred Tong, associate director of Ateneo University's graduate computer program, "his worth in the commercial market is three times less."

Technical expertise does not always match technological capacity. "I can give away computers," says Romulo, who donated equipment to schools as part of IBM's charitable efforts, "but schools can't afford to maintain them." In 1986 the government-run Technobank in Manila, an information resource center, subscribed to DIALOG, a U.S.-based database service that includes newspaper articles, trade statistics, and profiles of individual businesses. Two years after first subscribing, Technobank still was not connected electronically to the system. Its modem—the device that links a computer to telephone lines—was broken, and Technobank had been unable to fix it. The best Technobank could do was request written copies of DIALOG information through the mail. Even when modems do work, database companies charge fees that can amount to several dollars a minute. That is over and above the basic membership cost and long-distance charges—and often beyond Third World financial means.

The Philippines is hooked into the international communications system.[10] It has access to two satellites through earth stations outside Manila and has oceanic cable connections. The problem, as is often the case in developing countries, comes in the "last mile"—the distance from the international jumping-off point into the Philippine domestic system.

The Philippines has fewer than 2 telephones per 100 people, compared with 80 telephones in the United States. Thirteen of the country's 72 provinces have no telephone service at all. "Around 300 municipalities and towns do not even have the basic telegraph service," says Filipino legislator Vicente C. Rivera, Jr., chairman of a committee on communications. Providing at least one telephone for each of the more than 1,560 Philippine municipalities is still a long-term aim. Telephone density in metro Manila—much higher than the national average—is not close to meeting demand. It can take five years to get a telephone installed in some sections of the city, and it sometimes seems to take just as long to squeeze a local call through the overburdened system. The seven "record carrier" companies that handle data and telex transmissions—as distinct from voice communications—must use telephone lines. The poor quality of these voice lines causes garbled and slow transmission of written information.

Investments to upgrade telecommunications equipment pay off as fast as telephones are installed. But as noted by a special International Telecommunications Union commission, the initial costs are high, and about 60 percent of the investment must be made in imports, which requires spending foreign exchange.[11] The growth in telephone services has slowed since economic problems began to bite in 1981.

In addition, heavy surcharges on international calls make it much more expensive to call the United States from Manila than the other way around. The pricing arrangement has the advantage of helping the Philippines husband foreign exchange resources and the disadvantage of discouraging foreign businesses from locating in the country.

Yet another impediment to better service is the fragmented nature of the national system. Nearly all of the 50-plus telephone companies are private—an unusual situation in developing countries, which generally prefer public ownership. By far the most powerful company is the Philippine Long Distance Telephone Company, which has over 90 percent of all subscribers and controls the switching point for international calls. The smaller companies that fill in the gaps left by PLDT generally operate in different geographic areas without rivals. The large number of tiny telecommunications companies makes regulation difficult and does not create competition, as officials such as Mercedes F. Garcia, chief of telecommunications planning in the Department of Transportation and Communications, are quick to point out.

Nevertheless, the Philippines is far better off than many other developing countries. More than half the world's population live in countries with less than one telephone per 100 people. For Saztec, the situation has so far been tolerable. The company typically has sent raw data to Manila on either paper or microfilm via airplane; the final product has been sent back on magnetic tape or computer disk. The biggest problem has fallen on the shoulders of Rene Purificacion, who shepherds Saztec's incoming shipments through the airport. Shipments generally range between 10 and 1,500 pounds; the largest ever was more than two tons. Getting shipments through customs requires as many as 42 separate signatures. (Under Marcos, only 25 were needed; worried about corruption, however, the Aquino government instituted more controls.) To send a shipment out of the country requires 10 signatures. With the help of expediters who greet shipments arriving in California, Saztec can promise seven-day turnaround to its clients.

How long the Philippines will stay competitive with current technology is unclear, though. James Conway of Equidata thinks that Manila should be the data entry capital of the world, just as Dublin, Ireland, was when he originally got into the business. But other countries are vying for the title. And, as Conway admits, "businesses gravitate to places where they can get a better bottom line."

In a joint venture with American Telephone & Telegraph and the British-owned Cable & Wireless, a Jamaican telecommunications company is building an $8.5 million teleport that will provide a direct online link between the United States and the proliferating information facilities in Montego Bay. It will also ease communications for other service industries, such as local hotels that need worldwide communications to book rooms. The government is equipping a small section of the business district in Kingston with modern fiber optic cable, which permits a greater volume of high-quality communications traffic.

When I first talked with him in the spring of 1988, Alan Fraser dismissed in his self-confident way the threat of competitors like

Caribbean Data Services electronically beaming data from the Dominican Republic and Barbados back to the United States. "Either you provide 24-hour service or you don't," he said. One-day service is not possible when documents must be first shipped into the overseas facility. The one threat, Fraser acknowledged, was creation of ultra high speed, low-cost facsimile transmitters and other devices that could send many pages of raw documents per minute. When that technology was ready, Saztec would consider receiving raw documents electronically—rather than shipping them in by airplane—and sending the computer data back to the customer electronically as well.

Within a few months, that threat seemed real to Fraser, who now said 24-hour service was what "the business was all about." Saztec started practicing electronic transmission via satellite and decided to make two-way electronic transmission part of its routine operations by the end of 1989. About that time the Philippines would be hooked to the United States via newly laid fiber optic transmission cable. Saztec was not about to abandon the old routines of getting raw data via airplane, but the use of this communications technology, Fraser and others hoped, would give them access to time-sensitive work they had not enjoyed before. "Because of the time difference with the Philippines," Tom Reed said, "we can do the work while Americans are home at night."

In 1989 Saztec paid $15,000 to lease special transmission lines, with which it bypassed the unreliable telephone system inside the country. For other companies, such fees can seem too steep. In early 1988, Conway of Equidata said he thought about using satellite transmission but ruled it out as too expensive. Conway also decided against putting his facility in the mountain city of Baguio because just getting a telephone there was problematic. If Fraser is correct that 24-hour service is now what the business is all about—and if the Philippines want to attract offshore investors in data entry— improved telecommunication facilities inside the country have become more urgent.

The creation of adequate, cheap communications infrastructure to support entrepreneurs like Fraser may help bring in foreign companies. It does not ensure, though, that developing countries will come abreast of industrialized countries in know-how.

Data entry operators, who comprise the largest part of the Saztec staff, acquire few skills beyond basic familiarity with computer terminals. Saztec coders, who write format instructions on documents before they are sent to data entry operators, have received special training in oil well terminology, in calculating corporate financial statements, and in telephone switching networks and other Saztec specialties. For some coding jobs they are more skilled than coders in Kansas City.

Engineers and programmers do better. When Fraser started the Manila facility, a consultant brought from the United States trained engineers for two weeks. With this minimal instruction the Filipino staff persevered and learned to maintain the "equipment from the chip level up," as Fraser puts it. Since then, the engineers have trained a steady procession of newcomers hired out of college. A retired marine sergeant was brought in to teach staff how to write software programs needed for different data entry jobs. Filipinos, who dislike confrontation, suffered through his ill-tempered outbursts, which left dents in computer keyboards. Yet while engineers and programmers have acquired the most marketable skills, they complain privately that they should receive more new training.

An executive with A. C. Nielsen, which uses countries like Mexico and Haiti to count "cents-off" coupons used in American grocery stores, describes the situation this way: "Technology is on one side of the company and labor is on the other." Saztec finds it easier to develop and use sophisticated technology in the United States, where it has more equipment and a pool of better-trained workers. Tom Reed and other Saztec executives talk about perfecting new programming techniques in the Dayton facility and later assigning the work to the Kansas City data entry operation, where wages are lower. The next step is to send the work to Manila.

SGV's joint venture with Arthur Anderson brings American computer software technology and training to the Philippines, says Frank Holz, the only American among the 80 partners at the Philippine company. In addition to learning to work according to recognized international standards, SGV gets access to the U.S. market and eventually, he hopes, to Europe. But such plans do not always work. SGV has broken partnerships with American firms that did not transfer technology as expected.

Developing countries with large domestic markets have leverage in dealing with American companies. In exchange for letting a foreign company sell in the country, the government can insist that the firm produce all or part of the product there. In the process, the developing country acquires new technical expertise. In the same way, countries with relatively strong economies can develop technologies themselves while protecting their young information industries from foreign competition.[12] The Brazilian government has done this and boosted national mastery of computer technology.

These protectionist policies can have a negative side. Because the government is trying to keep out competing computer technology, other Brazilian businesses often cannot acquire new, sophisticated equipment developed overseas. This limits their ability to be competitive internationally. Thus, what Brazil gains in competitiveness one way, it loses in another. But Brazil is far better off than sub-Saharan African countries, which together have fewer telephones than Tokyo. They have neither the critical technological mass to become self-sufficient nor large enough markets to make stiff demands on foreign investors.

When Fraser hears people talk about the $5 trillion investment needed to get advanced developing countries up to the same telecommunications level as the United States, he grows impatient. He believes computers to be as essential for any business as small calculators, but he is troubled that developing technological capabilities too quickly may put people out of work. "Frequently," he says, "the computer salesman will draw charts to show how many people you can wipe out of your organization. In the Philippines, and in many other countries where jobs are at a premium, this is morally indefensible."

Fraser's point that foreign technology is not always best suited to developing countries is widely shared. For all the trouble Technobank has using DIALOG, the staff recalls getting only one request for the service. Its job is to help Filipinos acquire information to run and manage toothpick factories, pig farming, and other small businesses that have little need for databases set up to service First World clients.

Yet the Filipinos can hardly turn away from telecommunications and computers. How can they run their airline without access to the computer tapes that contain international airline timetables, which are published in Oak Brook, Ill., by a subsidiary of Dun & Bradstreet?

If properly adapted, better communications can help with development. In Sri Lanka, installation of telephones helped small farmers find out the prices of coconut, fruit, and other produce in Colombo, the capital. The farmers were able to sell to middlemen at 80 to 90 percent of market price rather than at 50 to 60 percent. On the other hand, Rodolfo Romero, president of Business Development Services and a consultant to the Philippine Central Bank, tells of a client who lost money when good data could not be found. The client, who was on Negros Island, wanted to produce milk and needed information on the size of the local market. Romero's staff went to six agencies without success. "The project stalled," he recalls.

Technobank is taking steps to apply computers to local problems. In a small, windowless room, on the day I visited, two people sat at computer terminals typing titles from the library onto a database. The information will initially be used by people who want to find documents quickly in the library. Many of those who use the system are so poor they cannot afford to photocopy material once it is located. Instead they must copy the information by hand. But such efforts could be a first step toward sending information electronically to other parts of the country.

A 1987 International Telecommunications Union study in the Philippines calculated that the benefits of telecommunication investments outweighed costs by more than 30 to 1 in the health sector, and by more than 40 to 1 in the agricultural sector.[13] A Philippine computer study noted that computers would be useful in voter registration and tax collection. (According to one Filipino businessman who imports computers, the Philippine internal revenue service had trouble calculating taxes on imports because it could not afford to import computers.) A telecommunications project for Luzon and islands in the southwestern Visayans, under way with Japanese funding, will help Filipinos predict foul weather. Computers and satellites can also help monitor the use of Philippine resources, especially its dwindling tropical hardwood forests.

Always, in the background, is the realization that the Philippines cannot afford to pull back from the world's information industries, that it must be a competitor. "A new pecking order among nations is being created by the computer," a National Computer Center study concluded in 1987. "This awareness explains the mad scramble for supremacy between Europe, Japan, and the United States. While the Philippines cannot hope to become a major league player, it can at least avoid becoming a victim by being able to chart out a course to where it can capture some of the economic spoils."[14]

That competitiveness is constantly being expressed by Filipinos. Manila data entry companies that cooperate one day may try to steal each other's business the next. Filipino entrepreneur Augusto Lagman worries about competition from India, which has lower wage levels for programmers than the Philippines and is also English speaking. Torres and others worry that, in the rush to get business, Manila firms will not produce a high-quality product, which will give the Philippines a bad reputation. Singapore, which recently created four centers graduating 600–700 computer professionals a year, already has vastly outdistanced the Philippines in computer sophistication.

The Overseas Development Council has pointed to the resulting frustration for Third World countries generally: "The emerging structure of the world economy makes development difficult *without* integration and competition, yet the price of integration is greater dependence on the industrial world and less flexibility in domestic policies."[15] But not just developing countries feel hemmed in. At the economic level, industrialized countries have also lost flexibility and independence. To even compete in their own home markets (where foreign investors become more of a threat every day), large companies must take advantage of opportunities globally. Major U.S. companies worry about losing ground to competitors in other industrialized countries—not least of all Japan, which has outdistanced Americans in more than one area of high technology. Workers in Britain and the United States worry about losing data entry jobs to low-paid overseas workers, a trend union and political leaders describe as taking away "the last large group of jobs that the economy is supposedly going to have available."[16]

Ultimately this interdependence between the Todd Steins and the Marian Tabjans is more than just a matter of economics. Even if the Americans and the British could keep jobs at home, they would not sever links with developing countries. The interdependencies created by the information revolution reach far beyond jobs to culture, politics, and virtually every other aspect of modern life. Compounding this feeling of vulnerability is the awareness that the surge in information technology has outstripped people's ability to manage it.

Keeping Up with Information

When John Berry went to work for a consumer credit agency called the United Association for the Protection of Trade in 1965, privacy was about as complex an issue as over-the-fence neighborhood gossip. But at the same time that UAPT has been transformed into an energetic company with global aspirations, advances in communications have taken it—as well as entire nations—into uncharted thickets of information policy.

UAPT was started in 1842 by tailors on London's swank Saville Row, who gathered in local coffeehouses to discuss which clients paid and which did not. Deciding they needed a slightly more reliable information system, they formed an association to collect the reports in one place. The clothiers' association was like many that emerged during that period except that it survived, attracting a wider array of businesses. The handwritten minutes of the December 9, 1909, board meeting list 116 new members—not only tailors, dressmakers, and hatters, but also manufacturers of umbrellas, scientific equipment, and motorcycles; pork butchers and fishmongers; coal and seed merchants; the *Times of Ceylon*; and the Rosie Film Company. By the 1960s, the association operated some 20 more or less autonomous consumer credit report bureaus in cities and towns throughout Britain.

"It was a sleepy company; I can imagine it being treated like a gentlemen's club," Berry said in an interview in his trim new offices. "In the early days, when I first joined the company, the way we used to keep the records was in these enormous handwritten ledgers. They were vast books, and when you ran out of space you had to turn [the ledger] on its side and write in the margin. To try to find Joe Bloggs in these books was a nightmare." Berry's first assignments were in bureaus in Southampton, Plymouth, and Exeter. Mr. Minear, an elderly gentleman who ran the Plymouth office when Berry arrived, was hard-of-hearing. And Myrtle Hillman, the secretary, went home each day after lunch, leaving no one to answer telephone credit inquiries.

When Berry went to work, the telephone was ringing more and more. With the country fully recovered from the war, consumers were ready and eager to buy automobiles and washing machines. Finance companies emerged to give them the credit they needed. Credit card companies and soon mail order companies proliferated.

UAPT faced a choice of clinging to the past and surely fading away, or providing centralized nationwide credit reports quickly and reliably. Expanding rapidly, it created 60 bureaus by the early 1970s. In 1973 it used primitive computers to create microfiche files to replace the old handwritten system, and in 1978 it started a national online computerized register of names. By 1981, UAPT had a fully computerized system and needed only four regional offices in addition to its headquarters in Croydon, South London.

Berry, a competitive redheaded Englishman born four days after D-Day in 1944, advanced with his company and was named a director in 1978, when he was 33. Between 1982 and 1984, when he was in charge of marketing, the percentage of clients connected to the computer system increased from 0.4 to 66. Today, more than 90 percent of the clients dial directly for consumer credit reports. Berry calculates that INFOLINK, as the company has been called since 1987, handles 23 million information requests a year and has roughly half the British consumer credit information market.

The idea behind choosing the corporate title INFOLINK, Berry said, was that it is "a go-ahead name." And in going ahead, INFOLINK has reached beyond British borders. It hired an Indian company to design its sophisticated computer software program, and it has recently begun to look for clients overseas. That job has fallen to Berry, who said, "We're anxious to expand our marketplace because the marketplace in the U.K. is not limitless."

By far INFOLINK's largest international activity has involved Saztec. The United Kingdom is divided into 412 voting districts, each of which keeps its own voter rolls. Wanting to have a reliable way of verifying where credit applicants live, INFOLINK decided in 1983 to put the rolls into a single database in its computer. It sent the job, which required 1.5 billion strokes on computer keyboards, to Singapore. When Singapore's prices increased, Berry began sending the annual job of updating the names and addresses of British subjects to Saztec's Manila facility. Since then, Saztec has also calculated and then keyed corporate financial credit reports for INFOLINK.

INFOLINK's go-ahead, limitless approach to business creates efficiencies unimagined in the days when Mr. Minear dozed through his afternoons. Clients expect the INFOLINK computer to respond to credit inquiries in five seconds. But the age of the computer, with dreams of information uniting peoples, has also brought nightmarishly intractable inefficiencies, management problems, and misunderstandings that require new methods of thinking and organization.

The information industry, which prides itself on organizing data, cannot keep track of itself. Computers, integral to international communication networks, work so fast that a new system for calibrating their speed is only just being developed. Computers have introduced new services, such as automatic tellers, without creating ways to measure the increased productivity that results. And as refashioned companies like INFOLINK have gone abroad for data entry services and in search of new markets, the old measurement systems for trade have fallen apart.

Services, once considered insignificant by economists, have become major components of most national economies. By 1987 services accounted for almost 70 percent of the U.S. GNP, and they are calculated at about 40 percent of the Philippines' GNP. With reason, some economists suspect such domestic figures may be too conservative. With even greater reason, they worry about calculating *international trade* in services, which the International Monetary Fund estimates to have increased 1,000 percent from 1970 to 1987.[17] Even a haircut is tradable, as one wag has put it, thanks to easy global travel, which is itself a service. But how can statisticians capture such realities in their numbers?

"There are a lot of grey areas. Everybody has his own definition of what an exported service is," observes Sidney Marcus, who conducts a U.S. Census Bureau economic survey that includes data entry services. "Say a foreigner comes in and buys a computer program at Radio Shack. Is that an exported service?" Even if agreed-upon export definitions cover such a case, "how does the company even know that it was a foreigner who made the purchase?"

In the case of some exports, hardware and services are lumped together. "The sale of a new computer by a U.S. company inevitably will involve design, consulting, installation, and software services," J. Steven Landefeld of the U.S. Commerce Department says, "but the entire transaction will probably be recorded as merchandise trade rather than services trade."[18]

Equally confusing, statistical classifications sometimes combine services that are only loosely related. In the mid-1980s, the federal government expanded the Standard Industrial Classification system list of domestic services. In the new system, the SIC number for data entry, 7374, also includes the rental of computer time. Similarly, the Philippine tariff system classifies computer tapes and magnetic disks in the same category as gramophones.

The British traditionally call services "invisibles," and they have largely remained so. Unlike a keg of nails, a barrel of oil, or a box of sweaters, information easily bypasses customhouses, which also serve as statistical mills. The best the Commerce Department can do is conduct periodic surveys of American businesses in hopes of developing a rough statistical picture. The lag between the time a service begins to be traded internationally and the time the first survey is done, however, can span more than a decade.

The Commerce Department did not even look at data entry trade until 1987, when it did a special benchmark survey. Data entry is now measured in annual trade surveys, but it is lumped with custom software design and computer maintenance. Obei G. Whichard, who worked on the initial survey, describes one of the biggest problems as identifying companies to be surveyed. It is not uncommon for a traditional heavy industry to send data entry work abroad, something that is not always obvious to government statisticians.

"No one knows how to measure these transactions, let alone value them," says Arthur A. Bushkin, a telecommunications consultant. Corporate information transmitted by one branch in one country to an office in another country has no established monetary value, Bushkin says, although "a change in an international telephone rate goes as quickly to the bottom line as a change in interest rates." Saztec puts data on disks and magnetic tapes, which for tariff purposes are generally considered "returned U.S. goods" and thus are not subject to duties. When duties *are* levied—say, for a database on a magnetic tape—the charge is based on the dimensions of the tape rather than on the value of the information on it.[19] "The disk is worth only a couple of dollars," says one American labor union official who objects to jobs going offshore. "What's on it may represent many thousands of dollars." Levying tariffs on information that is beamed from overseas is more difficult yet.

According to a 1987 U.S. Office of Technology Assessment (OTA) report, conservative calculations show that statistics underestimate exports of services by 36 percent and imports by 28 percent.[20] *National Journal* financial correspondent Bruce Stokes has pointed out one of the repercussions of bad recordkeeping: the U.S. government was not able to anticipate the dip in services trade that came in the early 1980s. Since then critics have worried that faulty measurements may have led to overestimates of the drop.[21]

The fuzzy trade picture makes it difficult for policymakers to devise trade and trade negotiating strategies. "The data on services trade are poorest for precisely those industries—the knowledge-based services—where the United States should have the greatest dynamic comparative advantage, and where the greater strategic benefits for other American industries lie," the OTA report concluded. "Better data will do little good unless the government finds better ways to use it. But improving the database is the first step."[22]

Similar statistical problems impair the Philippines' ability to plan domestic development. In an interview, Dr. Filologo Pante, deputy director general of the National Economic and Development Authority, expressed surprise that companies the size of Saztec operated in Manila. "Our statistical system is not geared to get this kind of [services] information," he said. In 1983 the UN Conference on Trade and Development surveyed developing countries about their service industries. Most were unable to provide useful data.

Difficulty monitoring trade accentuates the feeling that information and other services are whizzing around the world, out of control. It is not that anyone suspects Saztec or the Philippines of doing something untoward with the British voter rolls; rather, it is the thought that a private company like INFOLINK each year sends five tons of paper with British names and addresses outside the country, beyond the bounds of British sovereignty.

Countries go about protecting their interests in vastly different ways. Worried about computerization, Europeans have created omnibus laws and regulations protecting the privacy of electronically stored information. Rather than concentrate on information in computers, Americans think *all* information should be protected. But arguing that the U.S. Constitution already provides basic privacy protection, the U.S. Congress has not passed an overarching privacy law, preferring instead to rely on piecemeal national and state legislation to protect consumer credit reports, school transcripts, medical records, and other data computerized by Saztec.

Europeans have not always been comfortable with the resulting U.S. guarantees of privacy, but they are themselves not always of the same mind on how privacy should work. Sweden created a Vulnerability Board in 1973 as a result of such revelations as the one that the Malmö fire department depended on a General Electric database in Cleveland. Now Swedes do not allow *any* "name-linked" data out of the country without approval. The British Data Protection Act, on the other hand, requires INFOLINK to give notification only if it exports computerized information; the company does not need approval to send the raw British voter rolls to Manila to be computerized.

One problem with addressing wrongdoing is the absence of commonly agreed-upon definitions of what constitutes a communications crime. Two U.S. states have passed laws against "junk fax," unwanted advertisements sent over facsimile machines. Other states have yet to catch up with the technology. Easy access to information in one country can put a researcher in jail in another. For a report on North Atlantic Treaty Organization installations, a Norwegian researcher drew on computer databases in the United States. Although he didn't know it, the data were restricted in Norway. Following publication of his research, the Norwegian was found guilty of espionage.[23]

Computer viruses—disabling messages or codes introduced into software programs and able to spread rapidly across borders when an "infected" computer communicates with others—have created new ways to perpetrate old crimes. Viruses that wipe out entire computer files can be used for extortion. The University of Delaware discovered a virus and an accompanying message that said an "immunizing" program could be purchased by sending $2,000 to a Pakistani address. Sales of equipment and software to prevent undesired access to computers may exceed $2 billion in the United States in 1989, according to an estimate of International Resource Development Inc., a Connecticut research group.[24]

Modern technologies that permit wide dissemination of information electronically have undermined copyright protections. It is easy to spot the illegal use of copyrighted material when it is published in a book or article. But it is not so easy to pick up violations that take place between two people using computers. "With these technologies, the situation is no longer simply one of an individual trading or giving away a book to someone else; rather, it is one in which individuals can inexpensively and privately share the contents of an entire library," a U.S. government study concluded.[25] Without effective traditional copyright protections, some experts say, an entirely new system will be needed in place of the royalty system for authors and the standard book-selling approach for publishers.

The North-South information debate often portrays issues in stark them-and-us terms that miss complicated grey areas. Disagreements over patents, copyrights, and protection of other intellectual property are often seen as disagreements between the industrialized countries (who try to protect their ownership with tight restrictions) and developing countries (who want access to information needed to advance and therefore do not want restrictions).[26] To some extent this is the case. But it is also true that some fears about information technology span both sides, often depending on whether a developing country has a competitive advantage over other Third World countries.

In 1989 American diplomats said that one of the biggest problems in relations with China and Thailand was piracy of foreign software; neither Chinese nor Thai governments honor copyright protection on software. American movie producers have complained about Filipinos pirating U.S. movies. But a National Computer Center study in the Philippines has argued for protecting local software entrepreneurs, lest they be discouraged from making investments to develop the Philippines into a software production center. India and South Korea include software products under their copyright laws.

As for the United States, it may have pioneered the concept of putting software under copyright protection, but it was far less enthusiastic about promoting such guarantees not so long ago. The first American copyright laws protected only American works; foreign works were explicitly excluded. The United States argued that it was entitled to foreign works to further its development—not so different from Thailand's point that it cannot afford to pay higher U.S. prices for the software it needs for development. The United States did not join the Berne Convention for the Protection of Literary and Artistic Works until 1988, 102 years after it was drafted.

Like Sweden, developing countries worry that foreigners will get access to vital information. The Philippine Congress has openly questioned the propriety of SGV, the Filipino-owned multinational working with Arthur Anderson, exporting financial data on Philippine companies. Another worry for Third World countries like the Philippines is that an American-owned satellite can collect valuable agricultural information and sell it to the Filipinos at prices they cannot afford to pay. And both developed and developing countries have worried about computer technology becoming a subversive tool.

With good reason, Ferdinand Marcos saw that free-flowing information could undermine his control in the country. And when the leaders of the Communist National People's Army were apprehended in Manila in early 1988, Philippine authorities found radios, personal computers, and 95 computer disks in the insurgents' safehouse.

For all of their talk about having an open society, U.S. policymakers have fiercely debated the wisdom of permitting the flow of information. For national security reasons, a National Academy of Sciences report worried that direct, easy person-to-person communications via global networks "may be outside the reach of current control mechanisms." Meanwhile, the Association of American Universities decried the Reagan administration's attempts to block scientists from delivering papers on government-funded research. Such steps, the AAU said, retard research and development. Rumors floated around Washington, D.C., of the government wanting to license database users, a concept that would run straight into constitutional guarantees *against* such information restrictions.[27]

Just as Brazil loses something by limiting imports of technology, so do nations lose something by controlling information. For the Philippines, successfully combating Communist insurgents may depend on the ability of the government to reach the countryside with positive messages. David Peyton of the Information Industry Association characterizes foreign reactions to the rumors of licensing databases as going through three stages: "First they said 'you guys are crazy'; then they said, 'ye gods, we will be cut off from information'; finally they said, 'go ahead, we'll create the databases ourselves.'"

Concerns are not limited to the perceived dangers of information seeping out of a country. Being on the receiving end of global information is also considered dangerous. The United States has refused to let leftist foreign journalists enter the country to speak and, as is discussed in chapter 3, has worried about foreign culture destroying American values. In Brazil, the executive secretary of a group set up to study informatics, as information technology is sometimes called, declared that "the information process threatens the cultural identity of people. Informatics is not neutral. It bears within itself the culture that produced it."[28]

The difference between the views of people in industrialized countries and those in the developing world is often one of degree— degree based on each country's ability to control information. The United States and other industrialized countries possess the largest share of global communications. Developing countries see themselves as suffering the consequences.

Foreign influences have had an enormous impact on the Filipinos and their national sense of self. The people the Spaniards conquered thought of themselves as members of tribes. Under the Spanish, the sound range of the local bell defined the size of the community; the bigger the bell, the bigger the community.[29] The term *Filipino* was first applied to Spaniards born in the islands. Although the term now covers the roughly 60 million people spread throughout the islands, local and regional loyalties remain very strong.

As a result of U.S. influence during this century, unifying elements in the country are often American ones. Anyone making a telephone call to a number that is out of order hears a recorded message that says, in perfect American English, "The number you have dialed is not yet in service." The LRT train Marian Tabjan rides to work plays the same song every day, performed by a Barbra Streisand sing-alike named Kuh Ledesma. The domestic television system broadcasts American boxing matches and soap operas. More than 40 percent of all the movies imported into the country come from the United States. Best-seller book lists in Manila have been dominated by American histories of the country and by such volumes as *His Way*, the biography of Frank Sinatra, and Bill Cosby's *Fatherhood*. One of the world's last Playboy Clubs overlooks Roxas Boulevard, along the Manila waterfront. And advertisements for American goods are everywhere. "We crave PX goods," one Saztec employee commented one day, referring to the desire of Filipinos to have the products U.S. armed forces personnel can buy on the military installations in the islands.

But even as Filipinos "buy American," they fret about the destruction of their culture. The Apo Hiking Society, a celebrated local music group, has a famous song, "American Junk." "Leave me alone with my Third World devices, I don't need your technology," the lyrics say in a typical Third World lament. But the song is sung in English, not the national language, Tagalog.

Every conversation between an American and a Filipino seems to turn to the local "colonial mentality." Often bitterness creeps in. One night at a hotel bar, a young Filipino sat next to me. "Here to make fun of the country?" he asked with uncharacteristic Philippine harshness. "There is a joke," says Rico Raymundo, the Saztec engineering manager, "that people don't have to go to Saudi Arabia to be expatriates. They can stay in the Philippines and work for a foreign firm." The saddest part of the common Filipino refrain that "we don't have a culture of our own" is that they do. The feeling of weakness, though, makes it difficult for them to honor fully their music, history, or social customs.

To some extent, misunderstandings are a natural consequence of different cultures and different languages facing each other in new ways. As the Apo Hiking Society song shows, technological advances that make it easier to telephone long distance do not ensure that people will communicate better.

Some miscommunication can be humorous. Relying on translators in foreign countries who know little about computers, Western businesses have ended up with computer manuals that used the Indonesian term for *underwear* to mean *software* and the Arabic term for *false pregnancy* to mean the specialized term *dummy load*.[30]

Fundamental misunderstandings can also exist among industrialized countries, which are often presumed to share more standards and procedures. Saztec was not quite sure why the Scotland facility was not showing better financial performance until Kent Meyer traveled to Ardrossan, scrutinized the accounting system, and found it worked differently from the U.S. method. To avoid just such problems with the Philippines, Saztec International brought a Filipino accountant to the United States to help with bookkeeping; his accountant wife now works for the company, too.

Implicit in many such anecdotes is another story—one of inequality. The language of modern business is English, which automatically puts non-English-speaking countries at a disadvantage. And although Filipinos may speak English, they often feel victimized when their native tongue is involved. Dr. Tong at Ateneo University explains why. In addition to his teaching chores he is general manager of a computer import company. In a typical instance, a word processing software program he imported did not have the Spanish ñ used in Tagalog. He contacted the American manufacturers to ask if they would work with him to modify the software. The American company said no. The Philippine market was too small to justify the expense.

"There can be no doubt that in the next 10 years there will be serious new concerns about electronic neo-colonialism," says Joseph Pelton. Pelton is on the strategic planning staff at Intelsat, a Washington, D.C.-based telecommunications consortium owned by 114 countries, including the Philippines, and providing services to 172.[31]

Such instances of inequality show up in international negotiations, not least of all the General Agreement on Tariffs and Trade. The GATT was created in 1947 to promote and regulate open trade. In effect, it has covered manufactured products, some agriculture, and no services except motion pictures. The United States, which did not even mention services in trade legislation until 1974, only began to quarrel with the hole in GATT regulations in the 1980s.[32] Brazil and India, meanwhile, have led the way in mounting resistance to new, broader GATT rules on privacy, copyright, and other services issues. Bringing services into the GATT and setting up international disciplines for them, Third World critics argue, would prevent developing countries from erecting protective trade barriers to nurture their fragile services industries and would enable the United States to maintain its enormous advantage in services trade.

The Philippines, which joined the GATT in 1980, reluctantly agreed that services should be included in discussions but did not commit itself to any timetable. "It took 40 years to deal with trade in goods," says Victor Gosiengfiao, director of the government's Bureau of International Trade Relations. "We cannot solve services in one sitting."

As might be expected, the Philippines has sought ways to accentuate its advantages in services—which is people, not technology. [See story by Erlinda Bolido.] About 500,000 Filipinos left the country between 1975 and 1986. Many work as domestics; some are nurses, opera singers, and computer experts; others are skilled construction workers, like Marian Tabjan's father, who went to Iraq. As one American expatriate puts it, "What the Filipinos have to sell is high education, but they have to leave the country to use it."

Gosiengfiao thinks that the GATT should permit Filipinos with marketable specialties to ply their trade freely in international markets. The idea is neither new nor without precedent. The recently negotiated U.S.-Canadian trade agreement allows people to go from one country to the other to perform service-type work.

Indian Prime Minister Rajiv Gandhi has suggested a similar understanding with the United States: India will let U.S. banks and insurance companies do business in his country if Americans let Indian carpenters and mechanics work in theirs. The thought of waves of people from developing countries, however, scares industrialized nations. Not surprisingly, early GATT discussions have stalled on such basic questions as what should and should not be considered a service. "When you get into it," Gosiengfiao says of the GATT talks, "you begin to see there are consequences."[33]

All countries face a double bind. None can consider disengaging from tough global bargaining and withdraw inside its borders. But winning on a trade issue may only mean that a country pays the consequences in some other way.

Some Americans might consider the following scenario a major victory: that high technology continues to bring major improvements in automation, thereby making low wage scales in the developing world less attractive to U.S. business. But such a scenario could have other troublesome implications for the United States— as well as for the Philippines—as trends in the computer industry show.

One new piece of technology in data entry is the optical character reader. OCRs scan paper electronically, entering data into a computer without the help of a typist. Although Fraser and Reed insist that OCRs will not totally replace human beings, who can perform qualitative functions that machines cannot, Saztec has begun to use OCRs in Dayton and Kansas City. Jane Bortnick, an authority on the information industry with the Congressional Research Service, foresees OCRs steadily improving. American Express, which already uses them to handle bills that are printed on machines, is developing technology that will convert signatures on credit charge slips to electronic codes and looks ahead to the day when OCRs can read handwritten receipts.[34]

The impact on the Philippines and other developing countries could be disastrous. A 1985 report of the OTA predicted that, as a result of OCRs, "off-shore keying may have an effective life span of only 15 to 20 years."[35] If this comes to pass, hardworking people like Marian Tabjan could realize their worst fears: no jobs. Lack of personal opportunity and stalled national economic growth would damage the Philippine education system, central to the country's advancement; it would lead to lower levels of health and raise mortality rates.

A developing country that has made large investments to attract foreign data entry operations might be in even worse trouble: it would also be left with large bills that need to be paid. "For the developing countries," economist Peter Drucker has said, "the trend [toward less reliance on low-wage labor] threatens to close the broadest avenue toward rapid economic development: exporting development based on low-wage but productive labor."[36]

If Filipinos cannot catch up to the technology train or, once aboard, find that it is going nowhere in their country, the United

---

Service Industries:
Filipinas Go Global

by Erlinda Bolido

Four days a week, the sidewalk in front of the Japanese embassy becomes a campsite. Philippine women, some of whom have arrived at midnight, sit or lie on grass mats and old newspapers. They cook food and talk to each other, awaiting their turn to apply for a visa.

The crowds in front of the American embassy can be as large. Less numerous, but no less determined, are Filipinos in the lines that form at the Australian, Canadian, Italian, and Middle Eastern embassies.

Saztec imports service jobs into the Philippines. A visa from a foreign embassy is a way for individual Filipinos to export their own services. Filipinos work abroad as nurses, seamstresses, and domestic helpers. Some are bureaucrats in the U.S. government. One Filipina is a concert violinist in Germany; another is a lead dancer in an American ballet company.

One thing these positions have in common with Saztec's jobs is that they are mostly performed by women. In 1987, 129,000 Filipinos left to work in foreign countries as service workers, according to the Philippine Overseas Employment Administration (POEA). Fewer than one-sixth of these were men.

Filipinos also travel abroad to take nonservice jobs such as in construction and agriculture, traditional jobs that remain male dominated. Altogether 380,000 Filipinos took foreign jobs in 1987, according to POEA statistics. Of these, 202,000 were men.

Of the women going overseas to work in service jobs, 52,000 went to neighboring Asian countries, 48,000 to the Middle East, 4,200 to Europe, 1,700 to the Americas, and 19 to Africa. About four out of five worked as domestic helpers.

States will feel the repercussions. An experience of SGV's Institute of Advanced Computer Technology reveals one reason why. Enrollments, never lagging at IACT, took a sharp upswing in 1983. The number of "walk-ins"—people who pay for their own training rather than attend at the expense of their company—tripled over the 1980 level. The reason for the sharp increase could be found by reading what the students wrote on their admission forms, says Fides Alviar, IACT education manager. Concerned that the assassination of Marcos opposition leader Benigno Aquino would spawn a period of political and economic unrest, the students wanted skills that would help them emigrate to the United States and elsewhere.

The percentage of women going overseas will increase as skill requirements abroad change, according to Carolina Rogge, president of Northwest Placement, Inc., which has recruited Filipinas for service jobs abroad. Women are often viewed as being better suited to computer-related jobs than men. Women are more persistent, more patient, and more dedicated to their jobs, good qualities that a lot of bosses admire, says Erlinda Lorenzo, who handles personnel matters for Saztec.

Nevertheless, says Cora Doloroso, president of the Cora Doloroso Career Center, more men are enrolling in secretarial and computer courses offered by her company. These men, often with college degrees, typically have had trouble finding work. Secretarial skills are a way to get a foot on the corporate ladder.

Service industries give women hope of breaking out of traditional dead-end work into positions that earn money for the family and develop new skills. The rise of women into managerial positions, as has occurred at Saztec, is not unusual in service industries.

Often, however, an overseas service job ends in sadness, sometimes tragedy. Women have ventured overseas in hopes of finding worked and failed. Stranded, they turn to prostitution. Women who leave for a prearranged job cannot be certain what awaits them. One typical story is that of a woman who worked 19 hours a day as a dressmaker in Saudi Arabia and then was not paid. Other horror stories tell of rape and murder. In a strange land, women workers often have little recourse to legal remedies.

Overseas workers are a valuable source of foreign exchange to the debt-strapped Filipino government. The Department of Labor and Employment reported that remittances from all Filipino overseas contract workers in 1987 amounted to $725 million. A regular check from a daughter in Tokyo or San Francisco can vastly improve life for a Filipino family back home.

And there is always the prospect, however remote, that something better will result from a foreign visa. Just as Filipinos know the sad stories, they also know about the maid who married her millionaire employer.

Even before the assassination, this exodus was at work. Although statistics are sketchy, studies show that the number of illegal *tago-ng-tago* (always hiding) Philippine immigrants to the United States increased by more than 300 percent between the late 1960s and the early 1980s. Of those Filipinos who enter the country as tourists and students—and therefore cannot stay—as many as 87 percent may never return home.[37] Americans would be wrong to think they can simply deny visas to people wanting to escape troubles in the Philippines. One product of modern information machinery is forged documents, which are easily acquired.

Illegal immigration is only one repercussion of Philippine poverty that is felt in the United States—and data entry is only part of the work picture. According to some calculations, developing nations need 1 billion *new* jobs in the next 30 to 40 years to accommodate the young people who will come into the work force. Failure to get work could mean that more Filipinos will have to live off their land and, in the process, put more pressure on their natural resources, including one of the world's finest stands of tropical hardwood timber. Those forests, which are of global importance, are already in grave danger (see chap. 2). Failure to give people a chance to achieve their aspirations also means economic and political instability in a country considered of major strategic importance in the Pacific to the United States.

Of course, automation may not put Filipinos out of work. Large companies realize that access to developing countries' markets requires putting jobs there as well. And there is the argument that as old data entry jobs disappear, new low-wage jobs will surface. "True, INFOLINK may not use those people," says Daniel Siegel, an associate professor of finance at Northwestern University, "but some other industry will." People, he says, too often take a static view of world business. They look only at what Saztec is doing today, when they should see that other tasks or other companies will develop no matter what happens to Saztec. Too often, he says, political leaders, economists, and businesspeople look "for a point at which there is no need to worry and we can relax."

"Data entry is dying. Sure it's dying—but with every death there is a rebirth!" Norman Bodek has proclaimed in a DEMA membership newsletter. "Technology is changing so fast today that we in data entry can't expect to stay the same or to do the same work. If you think you can, you're foolish and not very practical."[38]

The Future

Each character in the Saztec story steers through an uncertain future, marked by stiff competition and rapidly changing technology. Tom Reed is aggressively looking at new technologies and lines of business. At the Dayton facility, Todd Stein and other technicians experiment with CD-ROM (compact disk-read-only memory) technology. The disks, the same size as those used for music, hold the equivalent of 550,000 pages of information. When the disk is inserted into the computer, an image of the actual pages is flashed on the terminal screen.[39] Dayton is also creating software for a computerized cash register invented locally.

Alan Fraser must balance his personal charity work, which includes leading Bible study at the local mental hospital, with business concerns. Although he had hoped to drop out of daily management of the Manila facility, he has had to remain actively engaged in the operations. In 1989 he began construction of a $2.5 million office building near the airport that would accommodate 2,000 workers. If he doesn't keep up, Saztec International could be forced to send business elsewhere. Although he finds Fraser a charismatic figure, INFOLINK's John Berry makes clear that he would use a different company—or perhaps set up his own data entry facility—if it made better economic sense to do so.

Saztec executives talk of losing freedom as a result of selling stock publicly. They now must hew to the restrictions imposed on companies that sell stock to the public. Reed's loyalty to Fraser, who sold him the company, is today balanced by pressures of satisfying stockholders. "One of the challenges for the future," says Chris Dowd at the Scotland facility, "is to make the transition from a small family kind of trusting business to a larger, well-run business operation."

The continued existence of the Ardrossan facility depends on getting new contracts after the British Library job is completed. "Feeding the monster" in Scotland, as one Saztec executive calls it, is a problem. Although Ardrossan can take additional work now, Saztec finds it easier to attract clients based on Philippine wage rates.

Marian Tabjan has good prospects of moving up in the company if it and the Philippines can remain technologically competitive. And like workers everywhere, she has other goals. She has thought about becoming a missionary and getting married one day. As is customary for Filipino women, Marian says she would defer to her husband.

She has plenty of time for such thoughts on her ride home. Rather than retrace her steps by tricycle, jeepney, rail, and bus, she rides in four jeepneys. That way is slower. But at the end of the day, Marian says, she is tired. By taking only jeepneys, she is certain of having a seat.

Yet while each person has his or her own agenda, how all of these people fare may ultimately depend on what global understandings can be reached.

CHAPTER ■ 2

Cathedrals of the 21st Century

Costa Rica is an out-of-the-way nation with little-appreciated wealth: the microscopic genes that belong to the plants and animals that reside in its dark tropical forests. Or so it has been until recently. Powerful industrialized countries are coming to realize that they will depend on these genetic resources more and more, even as the forests shrink and shrink. In the words of one Costa Rican, the disappearing forests "will become the cathedrals of the 21st century."

Tropical forests confront strangers with a world seemingly divorced from the organized life most of us in the United States lead among paved roads and carefully arranged flower beds. At the La Selva Biological Station in northeastern Costa Rica, army ants march by in long columns; leaf-cutter ants build subterranean condominiums 10 yards across. Dragonflies, propelled by two pair of improbably iridescent blue wings, flutter in and out like some optical illusion. Brightly colored birds with unimaginable beaks appear among the dense tangle of vines, and a caramel-colored snake, no bigger around than an index finger, imitates a tree branch. Three-foot-long iguanas climb out on limbs that hang over the river; below, fat trout-shaped machaca fish wait for giant figs to drop into the water while bright green lizards, called Jesucristos, run on the water's surface. Trees stretch 50 yards into the air, their branches blocking sunlight and holding in the 157 inches of rain that fall each year. At the base of their trunks they have developed supports that look like fins on a missile. From time to time, a giant tree can be heard crashing to the ground somewhere in the forest, clearing an open space that permits regeneration. Everything is dark, wet, close, unfamiliar.

Costa Rica is not a country North Americans think about often. Called the Switzerland of Latin America because of its long succession of democratically elected, peaceful governments, the West Virginia–sized nation offers no specter of political instability. The biggest news Costa Rica made recently was when its president, Oscar Arias Sanchez, won the Nobel Peace Prize for mediating someone else's problems—the violent disputes engulfing its northern neighbor, Nicaragua. A tourism article in the *Indianapolis Star* reported that "Costa Ricans have found the fountain of happiness. Store clerks don't hassle, pretty ladies smile without flirting and little girls skip happily along holding their arms out so they won't wrinkle their dresses."[1] To visitors, Costa Rica's tropical forests and long, sandy beaches on both the Pacific and Caribbean coasts are a peaceful relief from the normal routine of 9-to-5 jobs, air-conditioning and central heating, and taking out the garbage.

Yet this small Third World nation and its plants and animals are a matter of urgent concern for all of mankind. Weird, seemingly chaotic worlds like La Selva are biological cornucopias. In addition to the vital role tropical ecosystems play in maintaining the quality of air everyone breathes, the assemblage of wild creatures and plants holds vital new medicines, new foods, new industrial products, and new ways to manage agricultural pests without chemicals. Harnessing these riches depends on the survival of fragile tropical habitats—not only the forests but also the savanna around them and long stretches of coastline. And that survival is in grave doubt.

The mere cataloguing of tropical species has not kept pace with their destruction. Tropical forests and woodlands throughout the world, located almost exclusively in developing countries, are disappearing at the rate of 42,000 square miles a year, an area that amounts to more than twice the size of Costa Rica. Although statistics are little better than educated guesses, a 1980 U.S. government report estimated that 100,000 to 333,000 species of plants and animals would become extinct in Latin America alone by the end of the century.[2] Worldwide, from 15 to 20 percent of all species would disappear.

Costa Rica, often said to have more biological diversity per square foot than any other place on earth, has one of the best conservation programs in the world. But it also has a long tradition of exploiting resources as a path to development. With one of the world's highest per capita foreign debts and a burgeoning population, pressure on the environment has not abated even as the country realizes that its natural resources are oversubscribed. At current rates, Costa Rica will run out of forests in less than 10 years, except for land in parks and other protected reserves. And even those protected lands cannot be considered secure.

"I am convinced that our tropical forests will become the cathedrals of the 21st century—you know, what the cathedrals of the Middle Ages are to us now," says Alvaro Umaña, Costa Rica's minister of energy and natural resources. "In the 21st century, the tropical forests will be like cathedrals because there will be so few of them left."

What should be done to reverse destructive environmental trends? This is not a question just for Costa Ricans. Environmental interdependence is taking industrialized and developing countries into a realm as mysterious and uncharted as the forests themselves. Understanding our dependence on these tropical cathedrals and devising global systems for maintaining them may be two of the most important tests of whether the United States can cope with interdependence.

The Importance of Diversity

"This very small country is biologically like a superpower," says Minister Umaña, sitting in his office overlooking a largely residential section of Costa Rica's modest capital, San José. But to most citizens of the world, Umaña's statement means little.

People around the world are familiar with the color photograph of the earth on Umaña's wall. The blue, partly cloud-covered planet, photographed from Apollo 17 as the spacecraft returned from the moon in 1972, is a symbol of the great modern feat of human beings propelling themselves off the ground into outer space. But while space launches capture worldwide attention, scientific research with microscopic genes found in tropical flora and fauna goes largely unheeded and receives scant support. A single space shuttle launch by the National Aeronautics and Space Administration costs about $200 million. Yet only about $50 million—half of it from the United States—is spent worldwide each year on tropical biology research, excluding applied forestry and agricultural work, according to W. Franklin Harris of the National Science Foundation.[3]

Nevertheless, Costa Rica and other tropical countries *are* biological superpowers. With continual exposure to sunlight and large amounts of water—essential ingredients for life—they are better equipped to nurture plants and animals than are regions with long, cold winter nights and uneven precipitation. The tropics hold well over three-fourths of all plant and animal species although they occupy only 42 percent of the earth's land area. In fact, just the tropical forests alone, which cover only 6 percent of the earth, may hold three-fourths of the world's species.

In absolute terms, Costa Rica has fewer different species than larger countries like Indonesia, Brazil, and Texas-sized Madagascar. Its superpower status comes from the high diversity of different species, a blessing conferred by geography. Costa Rica sits at a biological crossroads. It borders on both the Atlantic and Pacific Ocean systems and lies on the thin thread of land that joins North and South America. It is also one of the world's rainiest countries and has both low coastal land and high mountains. (The highest point on the Pan-American Highway is in Costa Rica.) Holland, which is flat, has a single "life zone" as defined by one common classification of ecosystems, Umaña notes. Costa Rica has 12, the same as all of the United States east of the Mississippi River.

Costa Ricans enjoy rattling off the extraordinary diversity of plant and animal life their country supports. Nobody does so with more authority than Rodrigo Gámez, an affable, internationally famous plant biologist in his early 50s. Gámez, who has a doctorate from the University of Illinois, is the personal environmental adviser to President Arias. He is working on a plan for saving Costa Rica's biodiversity. "Even in absolute numbers, you find that Costa Rica has more species of birds than North America, including northern Mexico, the United States, Canada, and Alaska," he notes. "That's incredible. You find that Costa Rica has more species of butterflies and moths than Africa. The La Selva Biological Station has almost two times the number of plants and animals of the state of California. And we're just talking about 1,300 hectares [3,200 acres]."

The list can go on. Costa Rica has more plant varieties than are found in the United States between the Mississippi River and the East Coast, more kinds of ferns than in all North America north of Mexico.[4] When coupled with similar statements for other tropical countries, the comparisons make industrialized countries appear distinctly underprivileged. A 25-acre forest in Borneo has in excess of 700 tree species, more than are found in all of North America. Madagascar is estimated to have five times as many species of trees as temperate North America; one forested volcano in the Philippines has more woody species of plants than the United States. Panama, just south of Costa Rica, has as many different kinds of plants as all of Europe. A Brazilian river has more varieties of fish than all the rivers of the United States combined. Harvard biologist Edward O. Wilson talks of finding 43 ant species on a single Peruvian tree—roughly the same number as in all of the British Isles. "Every time I visit Central and South America on field trips," Wilson commented at a Washington, D.C., meeting in September 1989, "I turn up new species within hours of walking into the forest."

The Spanish arrived in Central America at the beginning of the 1500s with far less enthusiasm than Gámez for the dense forests, which seemed forbidding more than anything else. They called the land Costa Rica—rich coast—because the presents given by Indians suggested the prospect of vast stores of gold. Just as the Spanish thought oil in Venezuela's Lake Maracaibo was valueless "excrement of the devil" and eventually sold the country to German bankers, they paid relatively little attention to Costa Rica when they found instant wealth was not available. The Spanish did not establish a permanent settlement in Costa Rica until 1560, and that country remained the poorest, as well as the smallest, of Spain's Central American holdings.

In the slow process of taming new lands, the Spanish were more interested in introducing plants and animals with which they were familiar than in finding novel ones. The Spanish crown required all ships sailing to the Americas to take seeds from Europe. The process fit into a general historical pattern that has been called biological imperialism and is exemplified by the conquest of the eastern Atlantic island of Madeira and its neighbor, Porto Santo. The Portuguese brought rabbits to Porto Santo when they arrived in the 1420s. The rabbits, which had no natural predators, proliferated, overrunning native plants and animals and disrupting the ecosystem to the point that the settlers left for a period. "The Porto Santo of 1400 is as lost to us as the world before the Noahian flood," Alfred W. Crosby wrote in his fascinating account of this pattern.[5] In the meantime, the name of the island of Madeira, the Portuguese word for wood, quickly became a misnomer. The settlers were in such a hurry to clear land for sugar plantations that they burned large stretches of the island, rather than cutting the trees for timber. The process again destroyed native species, though no one can say how many.

The European colonists sometimes put plants and animals from the tropics to work. Sugar, a tropical crop, came originally from Asia. Coffee, oil palm, and even pasture grasses, which are essential to Costa Rican agriculture today, came originally from Africa, via Europeans. The British took rubber from Brazil and planted it in Southeast Asia and, during World War II, in Central America. The Portuguese transplanted South American cassava in Africa. Generally, however, the tropics have been a place to plunder. Only recently have scientists become interested in conserving and employing the biological wealth that exists there. One reason for the change is that modern technology has created capabilities and needs that did not exist before.

A good place to start looking for the biological importance of developing countries to the United States is in advances in modern farming.

Genes, microscopic molecules, bear an inherited code that determines whether cells develop into plants or animals and that imparts specialized characteristics—for instance, drought resistance. Beginning early in this century, U.S. scientists and businesspeople created hybrids of corn and other food crops by systematically crossing varieties with different genetic properties. Such hybrids have borne more fruit and resisted insects and diseases. Between 1930 and 1980, per acre yields increased 100 percent for soybeans, 109 percent for rice, 136 percent for wheat, 157 percent for cotton, and 333 percent for corn.[6] According to more than one estimate, breeding contributed to about one-half of those increases. The U.S. Department of Agriculture (USDA) calculates that such improved germplasm, as genetic material is called, contributes $1 billion a year in increased U.S. crop productivity.

With progress has come dependency. Farmers now rely on hybrids to boost yields and stay competitive. But while new varieties produce more food for people, they also provide pests with "banquet tables," as one agricultural scientist puts it. To keep ahead of thriving pest populations, farmers must constantly change to different hybrids with new resistances, sometimes switching as often as every four or five years.

In the search for germplasm, scientists look to the places where such food crops originated or have been used the longest, for it is at these centers that the greatest genetic diversity exists. To an overwhelming extent, these centers are in Third World countries, which lie largely in nurturing tropical climes and, though seen as developing today, were yesteryear's great civilizations.

Sunflowers may have originated in North America, but about 98 percent of all food production in the United States is based on crops native to other parts of the world. Rice comes from Africa and Asia, citrus from Southeast Asia, wheat from countries around the Mediterranean, soybeans from China, and sorghum from southern Africa. Gámez's list of foods from Costa Rica and other Central American countries includes corn, beans, tomatoes, cassava, avocado, squash, and cacao.

Of course, as wheat spread through Europe and corn into North America, they acquired new genetic characteristics as a result of genetic mutation and natural selection. But in this process, too, the tropics have special advantages. They have been hospitable to the newcomers they have received, which have also evolved into distinctly new varieties with unique genetic properties. Ethiopia is now a center of genetic diversity for wheat although the crop probably did not originate there, and Central America has produced coffee varieties different from those in the crop's African homeland.

The Irish potato famine is a grim lesson in the horrors of not having wide access to foreign germplasm. Potatoes originated in the Andes, not Ireland, and those varieties introduced in Ireland came from just two South American samples, both of which were highly susceptible to the blight that struck in 1846. Use of a wider range of species could have limited the damage, which resulted in 2.5 million deaths and the immigration of 2 million Irish to the United States.

A smaller but similar tragedy struck in 1970 when a fungus mutation, which may have originated in the Philippines, attacked corn with a genetic characteristic common to 80 percent of the U.S. crop. National yields fell 15 percent. Then, true to the form of modern day interdependence, the disease traveled overseas.

Also true to the form of interdependence, the genes to breed resistance to such maladies come almost exclusively from the tropics, says James Brewbaker, a horticulturist at the University of Hawaii. "The corn based in the Midwest has a very narrow genetic base. We are terribly worried about that."

Techniques for using genes have become progressively more sophisticated. The term *gene* did not even exist until 1909; today, scientists have developed techniques for combining genetic properties from entirely different species. The process is roughly akin to breeding a cat with a dog, except that scientists move only one of the hundreds of thousands of genes a plant might possess. Scientists at Washington University in St. Louis have put a gene from a virus into a tobacco plant, a sort of "inoculation" giving the plant resistance to the virus. Antipest properties produced by genes in cowpea, a tropical plant, have also been imparted to tobacco. The ability to control genes has become so elegant that scientists can modify when a gene will express itself, limit its expression to only a part of the plant, and even control the degree of expression.

These scientific advances have created a voracious appetite for genes that is only beginning to be met. Rather than taming the environment by introducing familiar species of plants and animals, scientists look for genes with diverse characteristics that have not yet found their way into use. Prime candidates are plants that grow anonymously in the wild, where they have developed special genetic properties for survival without the help of man. Gene banks—

collections of genetic material used in breeding—have an estimated 75 percent of the rice varieties already used agriculturally but a mere 10 percent of the wild species. Although 125,000 distinct samples of wheat are stored in gene banks, only 60 percent of the wild species may have been collected. Collections hold an estimated 30 percent of wild soybeans, 15 percent of wild corn, 5 percent of wild yams and cassava, and 1 percent of wild sweet potatoes.[7]

"What we need now are the genes themselves," says Karel R. Schubert, a plant biologist at Washington University's Center for Plant Science and Biotechnology who works with *pejibaye*, a tropical palm found in Costa Rica. "And that's where we realize that in terms of the future we need to think about the diversity of genes we don't know anything about. That's why we are concerned about the conservation of genetic resources. These [resources] come from things that would have no known commercial value."

Scientists look for new genes the way explorers once searched for the headwaters of the Nile. Armed with camping gear, they roam fields and mountains. Their quests have produced tales of perseverance and of serendipity such as befell a botanist who discovered a new variety of citrus in Malaysia when he happened to pick up a fruit that had fallen in his path. Over lunch in San José, Jorge León, a veteran of many such expeditions, excitedly told me of the discovery just the week before on the Osa Peninsula, on the southwest coast, of a tree that was thought only to exist in the Amazon.

On an expedition to Panama, León himself once discovered a plantain in an old woman's backyard. She would not let him take sprouts for replanting, but he quietly returned in the night to get some. At the time León worked for the Centro Agronómico Tropical de Investigación y Enseñanza, a Costa Rican–based research and education center funded by countries in the Caribbean region. The plantain showed so much promise at CATIE that León told a watchman to keep it under close guard. Instead, however, the watchman accepted a bribe and gave seeds to a businessman, who used them commercially. It is now the most widely used variety of plantain in Costa Rica.

León also talked of the famous tomato discovery associated with Hugh Iltis of the University of Wisconsin. During an expedition to the frigid altiplano region of Peru in 1962, Iltis and a colleague spotted "a tangled, yellow-flowered, sticky-leafed, ratty-looking wild tomato." They mailed the seeds to Charles Rick, a tomato geneticist at the University of California, Davis. In 1980, after years of breeding experiments with the seeds, Rick created a new tomato strain that, among other attributes, has an unusually high sugar content. Iltis figured the value of those genes to the commercial tomato industry at about $8 million a year.

Iltis was also involved in the discovery of a species of perennial wild teosinte, an ancestor of corn that could be bred with modern varieties. A young Mexican student named Rafael Guzmán found the teosinte in a 10,000-foot-high mountain range in southwestern Mexico in 1978 and sent the find to Iltis. It may take years to develop, but commercially productive perennial corn could have important labor-saving and soil conservation advantages for farmers. Perhaps more important, Iltis claims, the wild species resists five of the nine major viruses affecting corn and has the only known resistance to three of those.[8]

These are not isolated examples. Altogether wild genes have given modern tomatoes resistance to 15 major diseases. A gene from Ethiopian barley has been used to breed resistance to yellow dwarf virus. One wild rice variety is the only source for genetic resistance to grassy stunt virus disease. Genes from African cattle help create disease resistance in U.S. herds. And new finds may help ward off another potato famine; resistance to a potato virus was discovered recently in a variety used by the Chilote Indians on an island off Chile. With the number of species of pests developing resistance to chemical pesticides between 1970 and 1980 doubling, modern farming faces an obvious choice: use more chemical pesticides, which threaten the health of people, or explore ways of tapping Mother Nature's capacity for creating safe pesticides.

And disease resistance isn't the only advantage of these new finds. A species of tomato found on the Galapagos Islands has a jointless stalk that assists mechanized harvesting, making it worth millions of dollars a year. Several species of wild coffee have been found to have no caffeine. A leaf used by Indians in Paraguay is 300 times as sweet as sugar and has no calories; a West African plant is an even sweeter sugar substitute.

Surviving Indian cultures that use traditional subsistence agricultural techniques are ideal places to look for new genetic characteristics—even for new foods. Not producing for a mass market, these farmers do not seek a high level of standardization in the appearance and taste of foods. "There is a very interesting connection between the economic condition of people and number of plant species used," Gámez says. "The more economically developed an area is, the fewer number of species you find. The more uneconomically developed, the lower the standard of living of people, the larger the number of plant species they use."

Gámez calculates that Costa Rican Indians use at least 300 different species of plants for food, medicine, building material, and ornamentation. The industrialized world attaches little value to many of these species. Latin American colonists viewed crabgrass and amaranth, formerly eaten by Indians, as weeds. "The amaranth was extensively and intensively used in Costa Rica" as a food, Gámez says. "It's a small grain that was prohibited by the Spanish because it was associated with ritual ceremonies and things of that nature. Part of the disruption of the [Indian] culture was due to the prohibition of the use of this."

Changes in eating tastes do not come quickly to a world that relies on about 30 plants for most of its calories. Nearly a century passed before American farmers and consumers took to soybeans. But many Indian crops could translate into brand-new products for the rest of the world. Rye and oats, once considered weeds, are important food crops today. Because amaranth has a higher protein content than wheat or meat, it is making a comeback. According to the Rodale Research Center, a nonprofit research organization that has experimented with amaranth, U.S. farmers planted 3,000 acres of the crop in 1988, double the area of the previous year. USDA taste tests in 1980 showed that people liked amaranth greens as well as they did spinach.

Victor M. Villalobos, a Mexican scientist, heads a program to improve tropical crops at CATIE, where germplasm explorer Jorge León once worked. CATIE, located in a pleasant valley in eastern Costa Rica, has the world's largest collections of chili pepper and squash. Villalobos talks about it as a center for biological diversity. In the search for new foods, CATIE has started collecting amaranth and annatto, which is used in food coloring. CATIE also collects violets on the verge of extinction. Villalobos planned to explore from Mexico to Peru in 1989 for different species of a sweet-tasting tuber called jícama that is just becoming popular in North America. Denmark is financing the exploration. Referring to the international value of CATIE's collection, Villalobos says, "Every week we have a request for seeds now."

The hunt for tropical plants and animals yields medical as well as agricultural benefits. "Half of all prescriptions dispensed have their origins in wild organisms," according to estimates cited by the World Commission on Environment and Development chaired by Gro Harlem Brundtland, Norway's prime minister. "The commercial value of these medicines and drugs in the United States now amounts to some $14 billion a year. World-wide, and including non-prescription materials plus pharmaceuticals," the Brundtland Commission noted, "the estimated commercial value exceeds $40 billion a year."[9]

Before coming to CATIE, Villalobos looked for wild yam species that had diosgenin. Diosgenin, a compound used by Central American Indians to avoid pregnancy, is used in today's birth control pills. Due to the recent demand for diosgenin, the two species with the highest concentrations of the compound are disappearing.

Brazilian pit viper venom was used to develop a drug for high blood pressure. Purple foxglove, from western Europe and Morocco, is used in making the heart stimulant, digitalis. Surgical suture derived from the shells of crustaceans and insects dissolves in wounds and promotes healing. Doctors use the seeds of the levant berry, found in Southeast Asia, to treat schizophrenic convulsions. And the rosy periwinkle, first identified in Madagascar and perhaps originating in the West Indies, was used as a substitute for insulin during World War II; later, it was used in vincristine, a drug that gives a 95 percent cure rate for childhood leukemia.

The National Cancer Institute has a five-year, $8 million program to collect and test native plants in Africa and Latin America in hopes of finding cures for cancer and AIDS. A botanist has screened 1,500 tree species in Costa Rica and concluded that 15 percent might be useful in treating cancers. Daniel Janzen, a University of Pennsylvania biologist who works in Costa Rica, has said that three tropical plants offer potential cures for AIDS; these plants come from Australia, Panama, and Costa Rica.

Nevertheless, only a small number of plants have been investigated for their medicinal properties. "Between 25,000 and 75,000 species of plants—about 10 percent of known flowering plant species—are used by traditional healers," Dorothy Bray, a pharmacologist at the London School of Hygiene and Tropical Medicine, told a *New African* reporter. "Only 2 percent have been chemically examined, and it is these, directly or indirectly, which have yielded virtually all the drugs we have on the market today. We need to look at the other 98 percent."[10] Norman Myers, one of the most enthusiastic proponents of the medical discoveries that await tropical explorers, has calculated that "we shall find one drug-yielding plant out of every 122 species subject to pharmacological evaluation."[11]

Tropical plants and animals also offer new industrial products such as dyes or fibers. One rain forest vine potentially outdistances palm in oil production. USDA researchers have created a potentially valuable source of the acid used in making plastics, nylons, and high-temperature lubricants.

Simply maintaining tropical ecosystems, without using them at all, has value. Tropical rain forests have an extraordinary capacity for storing water, which is then recycled into the atmosphere. Green plants, so abundant in tropical forests, consume carbon dioxide and release oxygen as a waste product. In contrast, slash-and-burn techniques to clear tropical forests add carbon dioxide to the atmosphere. This contributes to the so-called greenhouse effect, trapping the sun's infrared radiation around the earth. Scientists speculate that the earth may be headed for the greatest temperature rise in human history. With such temperature change, sea levels will rise, and certain species, including some that carry disease, might be more widely dispersed while clams in the Chesapeake Bay might become extinct. The major contributors to global warming, by far, are industrialized countries, which burn fossil fuels at a furious rate. But burning and other destructive practices in tropical forests may account for 20 to 25 percent of carbon dioxide buildup.[12]

Biodiversity losses give new meaning to concepts of national security and diplomacy.[13] Neglecting destruction of the atmosphere is as dangerous as neglecting missile defense systems; access to genetic resources is more crucial than keeping sea-lanes open. Despite the creation of synthetics, for instance, natural rubber is still essential for sophisticated industrial and defense products. And rubber tree breeding still depends on access to wild rubber tree germplasm in the Amazon basin.

Lack of genetic diversity in the Cuban tobacco crop may have contributed to one of the major international political incidents of 1980, the Mariel boatlift to the United States. That year, blue mold destroyed 90 percent of the Cuban tobacco crop, which shut down cigar factories and possibly contributed to the Cuban government's decision to let people leave by boat.

In a less well known incident shortly after, scientists wanted to visit China, a point of origin for citrus. They hoped to find trees resistant to citrus canker, which was afflicting the Florida industry. As a result of Sino-American trade disputes, the Chinese canceled the trip.

Political leaders everywhere confront difficult trade-offs. While they begin to develop new ways of thinking about the value of genetic resources, the old colonial impulse to wring food and wealth out of the land continues. Growing populations like Costa Rica's must put increasing demands on their land to meet basic food needs. International economics and other expressions of interdependence encourage overuse of resources while simultaneously undervaluing them.

Overused, Underexploited

Fidel Mendez is what development is all about: enterprise and toil. He also exemplifies the way traditional development patterns destroy tropical forests at a frightening pace.

Don Fidel was born in Puntarenas, a town in the Gulf of Nicoya on Costa Rica's Pacific coast. He worked for many years as a fisherman, plying his small boat through the tropical waters. Then the fishing industry hit a resource crunch: the number of fishermen was increasing and the number of fish decreasing. Unable to support his wife and five children, even supplementing his income by working as a chauffeur, he reached for the time-honored Costa Rican dream—a piece of land of his own. On March 5, 1985, he and 147 other Costa Rican families with similar aspirations invaded La Flaminia, a 4,600-acre cattle ranch near the La Selva Biological Station.

Whether invaders stay on the land or are evicted depends on the political influence of the landowner—and his willingness to sell. If squatters stay, owners have a right to compensation. Owners are especially interested in selling if the Instituto de Desarrollo Agrario, the government agency set up to help squatters, will intervene. While invaders are usually too poor to pay for land, IDA can pay a high price in cash. Don Fidel's group actually visited the owner of La Flaminia before the invasion. Although the owner went through a pro forma complaint procedure, he secretly gave them food while they waited for IDA to make a settlement. Realizing they depended on the owner's good will, the invaders were careful not to disturb his 1,000 head of cattle during the early stages of the invasion.

Even with this help, Don Fidel and his colleagues found it difficult to endure the eight-month wait for IDA to make a decision. They sold their bicycles and clothes for food. Police put some of the squatters in jail. Finally, out of frustration, they marched on IDA headquarters in San José. Twenty-eight days later, on October 26, IDA decided in the squatters' favor.

Don Fidel acquired a 30-acre parcel that had been cattle pasture; his daughter and son-in-law got a plot in a densely forested part of La Flaminia. Don Fidel talks about both pieces of land as if they were under one owner and fits them together in his planning. One of his crops is cassava, sold through a farmers' association for export. Cassava is a good cash crop, he says, because he can harvest it in the rain. The parcel settled by his daughter's family is a study in tentativeness. In one small section, between the trees, are a few ornamental plants they hope to sell for cash; nearby is a pit in which they have tried to make charcoal. On another uneven piece of land are some withered stalks of rice, which died of disease.

Nothing about Don Fidel suggests easy living. His face is gaunt, his eyes deep set and intense, his sun-baked skin the color of gingerbread. His plastic brown hat, cracked where the broad brim meets the crown, is held together with nylon string. His two-story wooden house is one of only six in the settlement with a wood floor; all the rest have dirt floors. He has no indoor plumbing, and he has no electricity. His one convenience, a television, is also an inconvenience: it is run off a car battery. Each week, he straps the battery to a horse and lugs it to town to be recharged.

Still, Don Fidel prefers farming to fishing. Walking through the ankle-deep mud along the ugly road cut through the forest near his daughter's home, he talks with pride of protecting the trees rather than cutting them all down. They are an investment, he says, to be harvested as needed by the family. He can name different varieties and is experimenting with growing 10 types that he thinks might have commercial applications. The experimental plot is located in a small banana grove near his house.

But immediate needs press down on such farmers. Don Fidel admits that only one other squatter is raising trees on his land. Whatever his future plans, Don Fidel must sweat to eke out his basic food supply. How much the poor tropical soil at La Flaminia can yield is a big question. For all their lushness, tropical forests do not possess rich soil. When the forest is cut and burned, the ash and decomposing vegetation release a rush of nutrients adequate to support new growth for only a couple of years. The hot, wet climate, which promotes fast decomposition of dead material, ensures that the nutrients that do exist are rapidly recycled. Squatters throughout the country typically say that each crop is smaller than the last, even if they have been on the land only three or four years. "By subsisting today, I know I can destroy the future of the forest and the people," Don Fidel acknowledges. "But I have to eat today."

Environmental statistics of natural resource use make a grim tally. Before the Spanish colonists arrived, trees covered 99.8 percent of the country. By 1950, 75 percent of the land was still in natural forest. Since then, deterioration has been rapid. By 1977 about one-third of Costa Rica was in forest. Deforestation is currently running at 60,000–70,000 hectares a year, or about 231–270 square miles, according to a study by the San José Tropical Science Center, a 25-year-old environmental think tank. Reforestation may be 4,000 hectares annually. At this rate, Costa Rica will have no forest outside its parks by the middle of the next decade and, the U.S. Agency for International Development (AID) estimates, could be importing $50–200 million in wood by the year 2000.

Meanwhile, the environment is not improving on the Pacific Coast, where Don Fidel fished. One-half the mangroves there have disappeared. Costa Ricans have used bark in mangroves for tanning and have used water for salt production; pollution and the cutting of trees for fuel have contributed to destruction. Nor can Don Fidel expect to find things better on Costa Rica's Caribbean coast. There reefs are dying, smothered by sediments and contaminated by pesticides that have run off the land.[14]

The pattern of environmental destruction is repeated worldwide. At one time forests covered virtually all of Central America; today they cover only 40 percent of the region. About 90 percent of the genetically rich, wet tropical forest on Brazil's coast is gone. Côte d'Ivoire, India, Nigeria, and Sri Lanka are also on their way to losing their forests entirely within a generation or so. At current rates of destruction, all tropical forests may disappear in 50 to 75 years. Already 1.5 billion people in 63 countries experience fuelwood shortages. Costa Rica's rate of deforestation to reforestation is 10 to 1, about average in the tropics; in Africa the ratio is 29 to 1. With the best of care, the most severely damaged regions would take a millennium to rejuvenate—and even then the process can never be complete.[15] Restoration will not bring back species that have been completely destroyed.

With extinction only a recently perceived problem, quantification of species loss is still crude guesswork. Widespread agreement does exist, though, that extinction rates are at least on a scale of major prehistoric climatic cataclysms and the worst in probably 65 million years.

Not much has to go wrong before potentially valuable plants and animals are lost. The rare perennial corn teosinte was found in three patches totaling only 11 acres, an area that could be bulldozed in a matter of hours. The construction of a new airport in Indonesia obliterated stands of wild rice. So did a 1983 forest fire in Borneo. Major disasters, like the recent African drought, kill off large numbers of unique species. The greatest losses occur in the dark tropical forests, which have the largest resources to begin with.[16]

The Brundtland Commission offered specific examples in 1987. A quarter of a century of forest clearing in western Ecuador took place at a cost of perhaps 50,000 species. Madagascar, the home of the cancer-curing rosy periwinkle, has lost over 90 percent of forest cover; with that, half or more of the vast array of the species on the island have also been lost since 1950 or are on the verge of extinction. That situation is made all the worse because most of the plants there exist nowhere else in the world.

Signs that land—and genetic diversity—are under attack appear across the Costa Rican landscape. Everywhere one sees fields hacked out of the forest, almost always a scene of despair. At newly created farms, a few trees stand; many lie fallen and rotting on the ground; others are remembered only by the blackened stumps that fire has not completely destroyed. Crops are planted in irregular plots among the debris. Older farms often become abandoned brush fields that can no longer support any agriculture. Driving along every road, one passes trucks hauling the fat trunks of freshly felled trees.

Costa Rica's steep mountains and heavy rainfall—two factors in its genetic richness—are an equation for erosion even when the heavy hand of progress is not yet at work.[17] "I saw in Honduras, years ago, after the Fifi hurricane, how the hillsides covered with pristine rain forests were scratched, as if a tiger had used his nails to bring down large chunks of forests, exposing the underlaying rock," Jorge León recalls. With the cutting of forests, erosion is all the worse. A 1982 study by the Tropical Science Center reported that 24 percent of the country is moderately eroded and 17 percent severely eroded. Watersheds above virtually every major hydroelectric plant have deteriorated.

"No part of the developing world has been spared" from erosion, the World Resources Institute has reported. "In Africa overgrazing, overfarming, and overcutting—all pushed by rapidly growing populations—have so reduced the productivity of the land that nearly a score of countries are prey to famine whenever the rains fail. In much of Haiti, there is no topsoil left."[18]

With the loss of vegetation to soak up water, the rainy season becomes much more a season of tragic flooding; the dry season becomes much drier. The town of Agua Buena—Good Water—in the south was once known for its springs. Today, water is piped in. Ciudad Neily, not far away, has the opposite problem. When Hurricane Joan's ferocious rains hit the area in 1988, the river running through Ciudad Neily turned into a torrent and, with enormous force, leapt out of its normal channel. I passed through a couple of days later. Homes lay in crumpled heaps; concrete foundations jutted out over wide ditches created by the flood; personal belongings hung from tree limbs, which caught them during the flood. Residents continued to find dead bodies.

Hurricanes are a threat under the best of circumstances. In addition, many Ciudad Neily residents had built too close to the river-bank and ignored official warnings to move. Still, as Jeffrey Leonard among others had previously noted, "Widespread deforestation and destruction of the upstream watersheds . . . have greatly increased annual flooding at the base of the Pacific slope mountains in southern Costa Rica, posing considerable danger to Ciudad Neily."[19]

Farmers' responses to the deterioration of land is typical of farmers everywhere. They work harder. Not far from the Panamanian border, naturalist Luis Diego Gómez and I came upon a farmer and his son hacking away at trees and shrubs with machetes to clear a patch of land on a 50- to 60-degree slope. Not far from them, rain-swollen stream-lets had a few days before cut like a knife through soft soil on a deforested hillside, slicing off tons of earth, which spilled over the road and down the hill onto the farmer's land. A bulldozer that had opened the road was parked off to the side. We climbed down to talk to the farmer, who wore ripped pants and a maroon T-shirt dripping with sweat. He said it would be two years before he could plant on the part of his farm covered by the slide. Meanwhile, he had moved his two cows to another piece of land, where they would be safe from slides, and was clearing this new area to plant beans. He had no help from farm extension agents, he said, but believed that beans would grow satisfactorily as long as he used fertilizer.

When we got back to our chartreuse jeep, Gómez said the farmer was probably wrong: even with fertilizer, beans would be good only for a few years. Gómez was so pessimistic about the stability of the land in the area that he wanted to hurry on to a squatter settlement where we had planned interviews. A heavy rain was expected and another landslide might obstruct the road. That afternoon, when we returned to his home at the Wilson Botanical Garden, we learned that a slide had occurred near the spot where we had talked with the industrious farmer. All traffic was blocked.

Flying back to San José from the south, I saw Costa Rica literally hemorrhaging soil. The plane flew along the coastline. On one side was the land, verdant slopes marred by dark brown gashes. On the other side was water, its deep blue hues interrupted by large brown blotches where the rivers pumped soil into the sea.

These stark images tell what has come to pass and where Costa Rica is heading. Behind them—and the pioneering drive of Don Fidel—is a complex weave of attitudes, policies, and structures interacting internationally as well as nationally. Although in some details Costa Rica is not representative of all developing countries, the trends apply widely.

Traditionally, population growth has been a goal, not a liability. For a family, more children mean more hands to work the land and to take care of parents when they are old. For the government, it means more land in production, more exports, more tax revenue—which is why Costa Rica encouraged the immigration of Italians after World War II to carve settlements out of the forest.

But now population growth is a problem. Costa Rica's relatively advanced social security system has brought a decline in infant mortality and promoted longevity among older people; average Costa Rican life expectancy today exceeds 73 years.

Although a survey has shown that 40 percent of all pregnancies may be unwanted, the strong and conservative Catholic church has not encouraged government-backed family planning programs. Despite church dicta, however, fertility rates did fall—at least until recently, when prosperity evaporated and bad economic times set in. Perhaps because of the old feeling that family security lies in a large family, or perhaps because government budget constraints have curtailed the distribution of contraceptives, those who have fared worst in the economic crisis are those who have had the most children.

Today the country's annual population growth is close to the regional average, about 2.8 percent. At that rate, its 2.5 million population will double in 25 years. And each addition to the population places additional demands on the land for food, for employment, and for a place to live.

The problem is further aggravated by the influx of refugees from countries that do not have Costa Rica's political stability. As many as 200,000 immigrants may have entered from strife-torn Nicaragua, El Salvador, and Honduras to the north, with severe environmental repercussions on land along the border.

Costa Rica, with one of the highest regional population densities on cultivated land, has little room for growth. "The visualization of twice as many people living in Costa Rica, in such a short period of time, with a stagnant economy and an accelerated depletion or deterioration of some of the basic resources such as forests, water, and soil, makes us wonder if the younger generation will not experience as rapid a decline in the quality of life as the ascent that took place between 1960 and 1980," says Carlos Quesada, who heads a government effort to create a national conservation strategy.[20]

Jorge León, the veteran germplasm hunter, tells a story about population growth leading to the destruction of genetic material. He once collected a seed from an avocado tree in a farmer's yard. The seed proved exceptional. But when León went back for more he found the tree was gone. The farmer had cut it down to make room for an addition to his house: his son was getting married. "Many people could tell you the same story," León says.

The same process occurs on a larger scale in cities. As the population grows, more people crowd into the city and, seeking a place to put up homes and businesses, spread onto good farmland on the urban fringes. Rodrigo Gámez thinks that, at current rates, nearly

the entire fertile central valley in which San José sits will be ur-
banized by the end of the century. Valuable genetic sources of
teosinte, the wild relative of corn, have been lost in this way in
Central America. "Numerous species of vegetables, fruits, or
medicinal plants were cultivated around houses in gardens or back-
yards," Gámez says, "but sprawling urbanization and the modern
patterns of consumption are rapidly eliminating these areas, as well
as the cultural traditions that motivated their use."

"The solution," León says, "is to have fewer people. But this is
very difficult. The other solution is to organize the use of land." But
that too runs against tradition. Costa Rica, like other Latin American
countries and like the United States in its frontier days, views land as
being wide open for development and speculation. While urban
growth is a problem, Costa Rica is the one Central American country
in which migration by small farmers and landless peasants into
untamed areas exceeds rural-urban migration.[21]
The government has always encouraged aggressive land use.
Braulio Carrillo, who governed dictator-like in the mid-19th century, promoted coffee production. He made land grants, gave plants
to poor farmers, and decreed that every homeowner plant a few trees
near his house. The introduction of large banana and sugar plantations and of cattle ranches came later. In the typical settlement
pattern that evolved, *campesinos* moved onto unowned forestland and
cut trees to stake a claim. Investors subsequently bought up pieces to
make larger farms. Laws dating from 1888 have allowed these investors to acquire title if they hold the land for 10 years. Under a 1942
law, people who squat on privately owned property for a year acquire
provisional rights that can eventually lead to full title. For years,
people wanting land from the government have invaded ranches and
banana plantations; the government has then compensated them
with land of equal value.[22] Even Costa Ricans who don't think their
country is running out of good land to bring into production admit
to rampant land speculation fever. "Land buying and selling is a way
of life," one businessman responded defensively when asked about
use of natural resources.
Rapid expansion of cattle ranching after World War II went
hand-in-hand with economic and social development. Daniel
Oduber, president of Costa Rica from 1974 to 1978, outlined the

scenario in a television program made by the University of Kentucky Cooperative Extension Service.

> In the first place, malaria was eliminated in the coastal areas, which opened up stretches of free land for Costa Ricans who previously lived in the central highlands. . . . In the second place, a tool appeared that became a problem for us: the American chain saw. The Costa Rican *campesino* was accustomed to working with his family with an ax to clear the forest into farmland, farmland chiefly for maize and beans. So there was a subsistence economy. But with the appearance of the chain saw, a family could deforest 25 to 50 hectares a year [62 to 123 acres]. Everything changed, and the practice of ranching based on maize and beans began, and later ranches were planted with Jaragua pasture grass. . . .
>
> Little by little, a major policy and a large program to create cattle ranches began to spread all over the lowland zones of Costa Rica that had been in forest. And at the same time these ranches were eliminating the small subsistence farmers, who sold their lands to the large ranchers, who sowed more pasture to make ever larger extensions of land for beef cattle.
>
> That began the Costa Rican policy of exporting meat to the United States. I am speaking of the period during the 1950s and 1960s. The result was that Costa Rica converted the new areas—about 2 million hectares, or 40 percent of the national territory—into land for beef cattle. We reached annual exports of 70 million pounds of beef to the United States by 1978. Costa Rica was exporting more beef to the United States than any other country in Latin America.[23]

Ranching made sense when it began in the 17th century. It required large stretches of unsettled land and little labor, just right for a sparsely populated country with large undeveloped spaces. There was no need for sophisticated roads; the cattle could walk to market. But all that has changed today. Costa Rica is running out of land and has plenty of labor. Ranching gives a lower rate of return per acre than does plowing the ground and planting annual crops like beans. Also, cattle are hard on tropical soils; 80 percent of all erosion in Costa Rica takes place on overgrazed pasture land, according to the Tropical Science Center. Unfortunately, old ways are hard to change.

"The cattle industry is the bad guy in Costa Rica," Gonzalo Ramírez says, but the ranchers themselves are hardworking entrepreneurs who, like squatter Don Fidel, have tried to bend the system to their desires—only they are more successful. Ramírez is a former government adviser on cattle and a member of one of the country's leading commercial families; he knows cattlemen well. "They are not dressed in white linen with Panama hats," he says. For their labor and shrewdness, they have acquired large stretches of the best farmland in the country. Many handle intermediary functions like slaughter and transport, and they enjoy political and social prestige of the kind that puts them on bank boards. Cattle ranchers are thus well positioned to capture the benefits of government policies. More than one-third of government agricultural credit— much of it from multilateral development banks—went to cattle farming between 1969 and 1985, according to Jorge León and others.[24] Big ranchers have little incentive to use their land differ- ently. Even with low returns per acre, the large size of their holdings ensures a good income. "If you are a big cattle man," Ramírez says, "you don't give a damn."

According to the Tropical Science Center, Costa Rica ideally would have 44 percent of the land in agriculture: 19 percent in beans, corn, and other annual crops; 16 percent in perennial crops like coffee; and 9 percent in pasture. Instead, only 4 percent is in annual crops while more than three-fourths of the land suitable for annual crops is in pasture.[25] Coupled with this is the unequal distribution of land. According to the 1984 census, 6 percent of the largest holdings sit on 61 percent of the agricultural land; 44 percent of the smaller farms are on 2 percent of the land. Landless *campesinos* looking for a chance to get ahead must typically expand onto marginal land, either on farms that owners want to sell at good prices to IDA or in tropical forests not appropriate for farming.

The best land, Jeffrey Leonard has summarized, is used ineffi- ciently while poor land is used intensely, often with little support from the government.[26] Until they actually get land titles, which can take five or six years, Don Fidel and his fellow invaders are not eligible for credit to buy equipment, fertilizer, or seeds. Many have so little equipment that they cut the enormous trees with axes. Often farmers do not get advice from extension agents. With many people poorer than they were before, Gámez says, "the natural resources in the area are being very rapidly degraded."

Where the government has tried to curb resource depletion, the old exploitative creed persists. Regulations first limited wood exports to boards, rather than cut trees, and now to finished products. Anyone wanting to cut timber is supposed to have a permit. But the chief reason for cutting down trees is not to sell the timber. It is to clear land for farming. If a squatter cannot get a permit, he cuts the trees to make a field and leaves the wood on the ground or burns it. Those who are aggressive enough and can afford a little *chorizo*—a Spanish word for sausage and a Costa Rican word for bribe—can get forestry agents to give them false certificates or simply look the other way. Max Koberg, a Costa Rican businessman who follows the industry, estimates that permits for legal harvesting are issued each year for 400,000 cubic meters of lumber, that 800,000 cubic meters are reported by sawmills, and that 1,000,000 cubic meters are actually cut. Similar calculations are cited by many others.

Reforestation programs favor entrepreneurs with capital. The government has given tax breaks to those who plant trees, a policy that favors large corporations who pay big taxes. To squatters like Don Fidel, however, taxes are not much of an issue. Koberg, who has used government support to plant trees, says incentives have at times been too generous. Moreover, reforestation schemes, founded on the principle of growing trees for commercial sale later, do not necessarily encourage the use of the most appropriate species. Costa Rica knows precious little about many of its native trees, says Rebecca Butterfield, who manages a tree research project for the Organization for Tropical Studies (OTS), which also operates the La Selva Biological Station. Wanting species whose commercial properties are well known, investors frequently use nonnative species of trees acquired from other countries. Environmentalists often complain that these "foreign" trees do not provide natural habitat for native animals and can degrade the soil.

More than domestic urges drive exploitation of resources. In the same way that the watershed dictates what happens in Ciudad Neily, international events shape resource use in Costa Rica.

Costa Rica has always been tied into world markets. Coffee, the first big export, was used to pay not only for manufactured products but also for basic food imports such as wheat flour. The government also used export revenues to buy the first streetlights in Central America. The coffee went to Europe, especially Germany, until World Wars I and II; the United States is now the largest trading partner. Coffee prices have been up and down. From 1955 to 1973, as a coffee grower in the Coto Brus Valley in the south recounted for me, global supplies were high and export prices were low. He and other farmers suffered. But then the Brazilian coffee freeze in 1973 started a trend of global shortages; although not without dips, coffee prices have since climbed and many Coto Brus farmers are prospering again. The recent collapse of the international coffee agreement could, however, cause declines in prices and volume of Costa Rican coffee exports.

The gold rush at Corcovado National Park, driven by forces outside the country, became "a sobering experience" in the vulnerability of land, as Natural Resources Minister Umaña puts it. Corcovado on the Osa Peninsula is one of the best Central American lowland rain forests to have been preserved. For years only a handful of poor miners bothered to search for ore there, not enough to cause significant damage. Then, two events changed the equation in the area. First, foreign-owned banana companies, at odds with local labor unions and fretting over lower world banana prices, pulled out of the area. Large numbers of people were left without work. Second, gold prices soared, from $150 an ounce in 1977 to $700 in 1980. The result was waves of would-be miners rolling into the park. At the high point, the number of gold panners may have reached 1,400, and perhaps more.

The government eventually evicted the gold miners and, in typical Costa Rican fashion of honoring land use, paid them a settlement, writing a compensation law in one day when the miners camped in front of the Congress. By that time, the southern part of the park, where the mining was concentrated, had many fewer animals and, as a report for the government observed, clear rivers and creeks, once full of animal life, had become "liquid deserts."[27] Today, miners continue to slip into the park—and continue to be evicted.

Meanwhile, large companies have begun to mine more extensively on private land elsewhere in the country. They are contaminating water and creating erosion, according to José María Blanco, manager of MINASA, the state-owned mining enterprise. Officials at the Monte Verde Cloud Forest Reserve northwest of San José worry that the deposits of sulfur and gold there make it vulnerable to invasions by would-be miners.

The steep rise in gold prices was symptomatic of a larger set of economic difficulties that created a worldwide recession in the late 1970s. The abrupt rise of oil prices and the rapid fall of prices for other commodities like bananas created a severe crisis for many developing countries, not least of all Costa Rica. In 1977, one metric ton of crude oil cost Costa Rica the equivalent of 26 kilos of coffee sold at world prices. In 1980, Costa Rica had to sell 86 kilos of coffee to buy the same amount of oil; in 1981, it had to sell 130 kilos.[28]

Two factors have exacerbated the problems for Costa Rica, as well as for many other developing countries. The first is the government's domestic policies. Subsidized lending, such as that to cattle ranchers, has not paid off in increased productivity. In addition, during two decades of prosperity, Costa Rica has created one of the largest government bureaucracies per capita in the world. As previously noted, the country has an advanced social security system, as well as an enviable educational system. But for all the good such public spending does, large payrolls for civil servants and inefficiencies in social programs put an enormous drain on government finances.

The second factor exacerbating problems has been mounting indebtedness, which is a case study in interdependence. The oil price hike made some Third World countries much wealthier. As oil-rich countries banked their profits in industrialized countries, commercial bankers were more eager than ever to make loans to other developing countries. Many countries borrowed heavily in hopes of weathering bad times and financing rapid development. Costa Rica's government-guaranteed debt owed to foreign creditors leapt from half a billion dollars in 1975 to more than $3.2 billion in 1983, according to World Bank statistics. At the end of 1986, Costa Rica was indebted to 191 creditor banks in 26 countries. U.S. creditors, which accounted for the largest share of the total, included the giant Bank of America and smaller institutions like First Wisconsin National Bank of Milwaukee.[29]

Compared with Mexico or Brazil, each of which has an external debt in the $100 billion range, Costa Rica has a small debt. As the executive director of the Costa Rican Central Bank has observed, commercial creditors don't put first-team bankers in discussions over

Costa Rican debt. In per capita terms, however, the debt was $1,713 in 1986, more than twice as high as Brazil's. In 1987, the debt equaled three times the total annual exports. Not surprisingly, the country has not kept up with its debt repayments to foreign creditors and by the end of 1988 was in arrears by an estimated $1.1 billion. "We are in a permanent process of rescheduling," says economic consultant Juan Manuel Villasuso, president of *La Tribuna Económica*.

Economic troubles have quickly wiped out many of the gains Costa Rica had made in previous good times. Costa Rica's per capita GNP fell from $1,900 in 1980 to $1,020 in 1983. Costa Rica's literacy and health indicators are among the highest in Latin America, but cuts in public expenditures have slowed further improvements. The Reagan administration, determined to "[preserve] the country as a model of democratic, broad-based development in the region," pumped in large amounts of foreign aid.[30] Coupled with this, the austerity program to cut government bureaucracy and spending helped the economy rebound after 1983. But inflation, which was at 90 percent a year, still hovered around 20 percent by 1988. Per capita GNP, about $1,700 a year, was not back to old levels.

The precise impact of economic problems on the environment is hard to measure. Costa Rica has always used its resources to promote growth and was exhausting its forests before the debt crisis began. But for people like Rodrigo Gámez, steps to nurse the country back to economic health have led to even greater mining of natural resources and destruction of genetic diversity. "Debt," Gámez says, "has forced the country to increase exports on a short-term basis, and to do that you have to go into extensive agriculture. . . . This export increase implies increased deforestation to raise timber exports (while forests remain); intensification of livestock ranching; and development of coffee, banana, cotton, rice, sorghum, oil palm, and other types of higher commercial plantations."

Corporate agricultural practices, Gámez adds, "flatten all the diversity you find there, not only in terms of species but even in topographic diversity. Bulldozers and planners just flatten out everything, and along with that goes not only topographic microclimatic diversity that you require for a particular species but the virtual disappearance of all other variability."

Costa Rican environmentalists often lament new farming practices for coffee. Traditional varieties of coffee grew under large shade trees. These trees provided fruit, fodder, and fuelwood; arrested erosion; and, of course, ensured the existence of a wide variety of tree genes. But new high-yielding varieties of coffee do not need shade. To get maximum production, farmers cut the trees and plant coffee from fence to fence. What is more, the heavy doses of fertilizers and pesticides required by high-yielding varieties damage soil and destroy smaller plants and wildlife that grow among coffee plants.

Debt also has had an impact on government budget resources. Two things are effectively on the table during debt negotiations— debt and natural resources—and debt always takes precedence, says Raúl G. Solórzano, president of the Tropical Science Center. Economist Villasuso concurs: "We must reduce government programs, and some are more difficult to reduce than others. You cut programs with a long-term view. That's environment."

Compelled to adopt austerity measures, Costa Rica has to think twice before it increases the number or training of extension agents or mounts family-planning campaigns. Simply maintaining the status quo is difficult. For several years Silvia Rodríguez, a Mexican sociologist, has observed conditions at the Caño Negro wildlife refuge in the north, a wintering area for U.S. birds. Four people administered and protected the refuge before, she says; now there are two.

Costa Ricans have limited knowledge of which native tree species are best for reforestation and which replanting techniques work best. The forest service has been given responsibility for correcting these deficiencies at a time when the money to support such efforts is limited. The seed bank program, started in 1986, is based in a small building outside San José. Its two employees had a $1,000 research budget in 1988; their refrigerator for storing seeds leaked. Since one of their two vehicles was broken, they shared the working truck with staff from three other projects and thus could not always travel to collect the seeds that were ready for harvesting at experimental plots.

In an ambitious environmental program, the government has put about 26 percent of the country under some some kind of protection: 10 percent of the country is considered protected forests; wildlife refuges account for 2.5 percent; reserves for Indians another 6 percent; and parks, for which the country is best known, 8.5 percent. Some of this land is only nominally protected. Virtually all forest preserves are in private hands and are used for wood supply rather than ecological purposes, says Minister Umaña. The government has not paid for about one-fifth of the parkland; until it is fully paid for, owners have some rights to continued exploitation. Nevertheless, the program is extraordinary by the standards of even industrialized countries; the United States has just over 3 percent of its land in parks.

Protecting the parks has become more difficult as their size has grown and resources have dwindled. José María Rodríguez, deputy director of the National Park Service, discussed the problems as we drove over a bumpy road to a new ranger station northeast of San José. In real terms, the Park Service's 1980 operating budget was just over $1 million; in 1988 it was just under $300,000. Moreover, the number of park staff in late 1988 was 322, down from 409 in 1981. The use of 26 private employees supported by international conservation grants helped a little to offset the problem, but from 1981 to 1988 the areas under park protection increased 150 percent. The new station we visited—actually a rented house in an area with many abandoned farms—was far from the park, which could only be reached on foot or by horse, and the rangers did not visit every day.

"We at the park service feel that the pressure is growing [for invasions by small farmers]," Rodríguez says of the decrease in living standards around the parks. He does not know of any illegal tree cutting yet but notes: "Hunting has increased, probably a lot. It is hard to measure that unless you have sophisticated [animal] census systems. As soon as we turn our backs at places where the frontiers have gone to the park limits, people will come in."

That message was reinforced by Carlos Campos, a union organizer in Guácimo, on the eastern side of the country, who led an eight-day road blockade in 1988 with 2,500 people. If the government does not change policies to help small farmers, he says, they will invade the parks. This might not be good, but he would not be able to stop it: "They have a right to destroy the parks." Luis Diego Gómez, who combines his interest in the environment with strong political sentiments, agrees that the parks are vulnerable. "Just two elections from now, whoever is running will say a million votes makes my day. And there go the parks."

The overuse of fragile, species-rich forestland is repeated in Peru, Thailand, Kenya, and many other developing countries. If the precise details of overexploitation vary, the conclusion is the same. "We are in the mess we are in now because everybody looked short-term," says Carlos Quesada. But how can nations reverse this ingrained historical pattern of discounting long-term costs? With environmental issues transcending borders, answers to this are just as urgent for North Americans as for Costa Ricans. The consequences of not acting fast enough, however, are not easy to calculate. Whereas U.S. bankers can easily size up balance sheets on foreign loans, environmental recordkeeping is still in its infancy.

What Price Diversity?

A poster greets passengers arriving at the San José airport. On it are eye-catching tropical scenes and the words "*Extinción Es Para Siempre*" (extinction is forever). National environmental education programs, which aim to educate Costa Ricans as well as foreigners on the importance of saving the country's natural heritage, are among the best in the Third World. Whatever they may do in practice, squatters like Don Fidel and cattle ranchers boast of the country's natural beauty and of how much they want to save it. The National Park Service had enough clout to annex land belonging to President Arias's uncle when Arias was minister of planning. Entranced by the country, foreigners have stayed. The La Selva Biological Station is one of three field facilities operated by the U.S.-based OTS, a consortium of 54 U.S. and Costa Rican universities that has introduced scientists from all over the world to Costa Rica. And North Americans have started so many enterprises specializing in ecotourism that it is now the third largest source of foreign exchange for the country.

All sorts of reasons are given for Costa Rica's robust conservation movement: its high literacy rate and strong education system; its proximity to the United States, which allows U.S. scientists to visit easily; its long period of economic growth in an earlier era, which gave leaders the luxury of thinking about nature; and its democratic tradition.

"The soil in Costa Rica is a good soil for causes," says Alvaro Ugalde, one of the first two employees at the National Park Service when it was started in 1970, and for 12 years its director. Ugalde, in his mid-40s, has a laid-back look. He comes to a small office he keeps at the Park Service in blue jeans, T-shirt, hiking boots, and turquoise backpack. But as director, he aggressively took up causes opposed by his government bosses. During the revolution that ousted Anastasio Somoza from Nicaragua, Ugalde sent a telegram to the Costa Rican minister of interior demanding eviction of Sandinista guerrillas from one of the parks. Outraged, the minister asked the president to fire Ugalde, but Ugalde stayed in the job and the guerrillas left the park. "It is very easy to make a mess of things," Ugalde says. "A person can knock on the door of the president, . . . [and] newspapers. There is power in the hands of the people in Costa Rica."

But as Don Fidel's battle to survive shows, effective environmental protection embraces problems that cannot be solved merely by creating more parks. The 1987 Brundtland Commission report outlined the central challenge: to meet "the needs of the present without compromising the ability of future generations to meet their own needs."[31] Sustainable development, as the challenge is often called, touches every corner of human activity. In directing the creation of a Costa Rican conservation strategy, Carlos Quesada talks about health, culture, energy, mines, industry, and wildlife. "I cannot point to any of the 20 sectors we have analyzed that is not related to another sector," Quesada says. This array of issues, interacting complexly, is formidable, demanding new methods of recordkeeping, new methods of analysis, and even new ethics—all of which will create new dilemmas.

"We know in general what the problem is," Gámez says. "We don't know the solutions."

One sign of just how much there is to learn is the scant statistical data about the environment. Nineteen eighty-eight was a year of major environmental concerns: drought in parts of Africa, in Argentina, and in Italy, and the nerve-racking hot, dry summer that turned crops deadly brown in the United States. Bangladesh and Sudan experienced floods; Costa Ricans talked of having the rainiest year of the last century. But how much of this is due to deforestation? About this there is scant agreement. Reliable temperature records go back no further than 100 or sometimes 150 years. Extensive meteorological study has occurred only in the last few years.

"The bottom line of the global warming, greenhouse effect issue is that we insult the environment at a faster rate than we understand the consequences," says Stephen H. Schneider, climate expert with the U.S. National Center for Atmospheric Research. If scientists still don't agree on causes and effects, the general public is even more confused. "This is not like economics, where everyone can extrapolate from his household budget to form an opinion on what's happening," writer Bill McKibben has recently observed. "Most of us don't know enough chemistry to begin to assess the contending arguments."[32]

Species loss is equally perplexing. We do not even know how many species exist. Scientists have described 1.4 million species. Estimates of the total number range from 5 million to 30 million, and estimates of the numbers being lost easily move into the arena of wild guesses. Norman Myers has predicted the loss of 1 species an hour, which seems high until compared with the prediction of 17,500 a year (about 2 an hour) made by a group of top U.S. scientists in 1986. A more recent estimate, used by the World Resources Institute, anticipates losses of 100 species a day over the next 25 years. The *Global 2000 Report*, prepared under President Jimmy Carter's administration and released in 1980, projects losses of 15 to 20 percent of all species by the end of the century. That was calculated, however, when estimates of the total number of species was much lower than they are today. Julian L. Simon and Aaron Wildavsky, leading critics of such statistics, agree that species loss is a problem but contend that "better data to estimate extinction rates are needed as the basis for policy decisions."[33]

"Curiously, however, the study of extinction remains one of the most neglected in ecology," Harvard biologist Edward O. Wilson says. As a result of reduced funding possibilities, he adds, the number of systematists looking at humid tropical forests species may actually be dropping.[34]

Some environmental issues seem almost too sublime for quantification. What is the exact loss if tropical forests disappear and North American birds no longer have winter habitats, something that is already becoming worrisome?[35] As the old saying goes, some of the best things in life, like bird watching, are free. On the other hand, those aspects of the environment that have more direct economic implications are hard to value precisely. "Genetic diversity is like oil that the Arabs have under their soil," José María Rodríguez of the National Park Service says. "But it is easy to give a value to oil. It is not easy to give it to genetic material."

Unable to assign economic meaning easily to the environment, traditional economic theory has given little attention to conservation. Until recently, economists have rarely thought about calculating the costs of erosion (for instance, dams will silt up faster; fields will become less productive). "'Intangible' environmental benefits, such as those derived from the preservation of biological diversity, are recognized even less in economic analysis," Robert Goodland and George Ledec of the World Bank have noted. "The irreversible environmental effects of projects or policies are usually treated no differently from more reversible effects."[36] Put another way, economists have given more attention to using natural resources than to husbanding them.

When it comes to appraising the worth of species, a major barrier is that their value and the value of their genetic traits can change dramatically over time. Horses with genes for strength were desired a century ago when farmers used them to plow fields and pull buggies. Those attributes are not important in our motorized age. Plants that would cure AIDS had no value when the disease was unknown. "Although seemingly of limited economic value today, many of those [unknown] organisms are undoubtedly capable of providing useful products to fulfill humanity's modern needs," Gámez says. "For example, how can one predict the potential value of a foul-tasting seed from a rain forest shrub, otherwise known as coffee?"

If we don't know the value of species with any precision, we do know that technology, for all its glories, has not yet devalued tropical forests. Advances have allowed scientists to reproduce synthetically the birth control agent diosgenin found in wild yams or aspirin found in willow leaves. But synthetics can be more expensive than natural products and some genetic properties may never be duplicated in the laboratory. Curare, for example, which the Amazonian Indians use as an arrow poison, produces a muscle relaxant in surgery, but scientists have not been able to reproduce its valuable properties. Moreover, without knowledge of what nature holds in the first place, scientists would have fewer guideposts to tell them what to create synthetically later on.

Nor is it satisfactory to save all the world's germplasm in gene banks. Some seeds cannot yet be stored—for example, those of cacao and coffee. And even when scientists can isolate individual genes, they do not want to "trash the plant," as Karel Schubert at the University of Washington puts it. Plants and animals left in the forest continue to evolve, developing new, useful characteristics along the way. Gene banks, Gámez says, "freeze the process. The plants are no longer exposed to the insect pests and the seasons, and environmental distresses and the natural crosses of selection."

In order to save the individual genes scientists need, entire ecosystems must be conserved. Biologist Dan Janzen uses the expression "living dead" to describe what happens to a lone tree surviving from a once lush tropical forest. No longer part of an interconnected system of animals and plants, which ensures recycling of nutrients and dispersal of seeds, it and its offspring have no secure future. An example of the limitations of smaller systems is Puerto Rico, according to Edward O. Wilson. The island holds fewer species than similar-sized patches of forest in the Amazon basin. The Brundtland Commission noted that conserving one-half of the Amazon rain forest and cutting the rest could reduce precipitation levels to the point where species in the "protected" area would be lost, anyway.

Yet, as with so much else in the environment, there is no agreement on the minimum sizes of ecosystems that should be saved—or on an acceptable rate of species loss. As Simon and Wildavsky note, some species loss is acceptable. "One should not propose saving all species in their natural habitats, at any cost, even if it were desirable to do so, any more than one should propose a policy of saving all human lives at any cost."[37] Others argue, as one Costa Rican put it, that until we know the value, "we can't destroy anything." The Brundtland Commission recommended that, at a minimum, 20 percent of tropical forests worldwide should be protected. Five percent, the commission estimated, is being protected now.

The Conservation Data Center in San José, which is administered from offices of a private, nonprofit Costa Rican organization called Fundación Neotrópica, is doing a sort of genetic census of the national parks to assess precisely how much biodiversity actually exists. This inventory could help determine species loss and eventually optimum park size in Costa Rica. "If you tell me the howler monkey is no longer in Santa Rosa park," says Mario A. Boza, director general of the Fundación Neotrópica, "I can say I don't care because we have it in Corcovado." But the inventory will not be completed soon. "You have to protect first and analyze second, or you will have nothing to analyze," Boza says.

The prospect of open-ended park acquisition makes many people nervous. Without planning limits, conservationists can build empires. Without a clear plan detailing what is needed, park enthusiasts may be unable to ward off developers, as Ugalde did when a group wanted to build a floating hotel along a coral reef. Even among Costa Rican environmentalists, there is no unanimity. "How much can we afford to conserve?" Luis Diego Gómez asks. "A country like ours has reached its limits."

Little wonder then, with all this uncertainty, that sustainable development becomes controversial when environmentalists try to put the concept to work. For one thing, there are no reliable standards for what is—and what is not—sustainable land use. Even a standard as seemingly straightforward as tying sustainability to population density immediately runs into trouble. Only small numbers of people are needed for cattle ranching, which can be far worse for the land than the intense crop farming practiced in many highly populated Asian countries.[38] Costa Rica may exceed the land's carrying capacity today, but with new land use approaches it could get by with even larger populations.

Also little wonder that many seemingly good ideas have unintended consequences. The European Economic Community wanted to ban trade in butterflies from New Guinea until it learned that butterfly farming provided employment and gave local people a reason for conserving the forests. Total world butterfly trade was estimated at $10–20 million in 1983 and rising. Similarly, "the hamburger connection" became a cause célèbre when environmentalists argued that fast food restaurants in the United States imported Latin American beef, thus promoting the clearing of forests to make more ranches. Now some environmentalists dispute the value of boycotting Burger King. For one thing, cattle exports are dropping. But more important, if people cannot sell beef, they will cut the forests to raise some other crop, Dan Janzen argues. Such boycotts, in his view, threaten "the tax and produce base that is picking up the bill for the national parks and other kinds of reserves."[39]

"The threat of losing a working majority of our tropical rain forests has really begun to sink in," commented Jack Hood Vaughn, a committed conservationist who has served widely in the U.S. government, including as assistant secretary of state for Latin America. "The media has caught on fully. Problem is, we don't yet really know what to do about it. Where to start? What kind of resources to marshal? How?"

Vaughn, working with Conservation International, is one of many people who have promoted the idea of debt swaps as a good way to start resolving the tension between the need to repay foreign debt and the need to protect the environment. The debt swap idea was first tried in Bolivia in mid-1987 and within a couple of months was launched in Costa Rica. Swaps can take a number of forms, but Costa Rica's has many typical features.

Although debtor governments are not allowed to buy their foreign commercial bank debt in international markets at a discount, local foundations can. Thus, the Fundación de Parques Nacionales, located in San José and headed by Mario Boza, acquired $5.4 million of Costa Rica's debt (at about 17 cents on the dollar) with the help of the Nature Conservancy, the World Wildlife Fund, and Conservation International, among other U.S. environmental groups. The Fundación then brought the debt to the Costa Rican Central Bank, which in return gave the Fundación local currency bonds worth 75 percent of the face value of the original debt. These bonds mature in five years and, in the meantime, pay the Fundación annual interest. When the swap was completed, the Central Bank had retired part of its foreign debt at a discount and the Fundación de Parques Nacionales had money to help support conservation. The foreign bank had eliminated a high-risk debt from its portfolio.

Costa Rica has since negotiated a four-year, $20 million swap with the Dutch government to support reforestation. In another deal, a creditor bank, the Fleet/Norstar Financial Group of Providence, R.I., "donated" the $254,000 commercial debt owed it by Costa Rica. The bank received a tax break in the United States, and the proceeds were used by Costa Rica to protect land around the La Selva Biological Station. Using foreign contributions, biologist Janzen has masterminded the enlargement of two parks in Guanacaste province, a cattle area in the north. With a goal of $12 million in land and cash donations, the project will eventually cover 280 square miles. Within 300 years, he estimates, the land will be restored to the tropical dry forest state that existed at the time of the conquistadors' arrival, complete with a safe haven for original plant and animal species.[40]

As useful as they are, however, debt swaps have limited value. Small swaps retire only a small amount of debt; large ones retire more debt, but they can also promote inflation by requiring the Central Bank to put a big chunk of money quickly into the national economy. Beyond that, the parks cannot be safe unless the people around them secure a decent living from their land. And the genetic diversity on land outside the parks, which also must be saved, depends on wise farming practices.

"Biologists must understand that people need to eat," says Costa Rican scientist Walter A. Marín. Americans have picked up the refrain. "You could have 100 percent perfect scientific understanding of the problem," says W. Franklin Harris of the Washington, D.C.-based National Science Foundation, which recently completed a study of needed biodiversity research. "But if you don't have the right social and economic factors in place, you are doomed to failure."

Talk has turned more and more to a people approach to conservation, not a parks approach. The land that is most abused, biologists have come to recognize, is public land over which ownership is weakest. Staff at the Tropical Science Center argue for "integrating" people and the land that needs to be protected. "You should not need a national park," says Gary Hartshorn, a tropical forest ecologist at the center. "We should know enough about what land can do and what the people need." Guanacaste National Park has extensive local education programs to encourage people in the region to use the parks and learn about the economic benefits that come from them. At the Monte Verde Cloud Forest Reserve, William Aspinall has plans for butterfly ranching; tourism, which pumps money into the local economy, has already increased.

Land reform that gives plots to smaller farmers who will use land more efficiently than cattle ranchers has become a scientific issue as well as a political and economic one. Conservationists and foreign aid institutions now talk about taking land out of cattle and putting it into other crops, as well as about securing faster land titling for squatters so they can get credit and extension help sooner.

The U.S. Agency for International Development has supported a project to create forest buffer zones around parkland to the north of San José. The $5 million AID grant, combined with $15 million from Costa Rica, addresses one of the major problems behind deforestation: lack of economic incentive for better environmental management of forest resources. Lumber companies typically do not own land and therefore are not inclined to invest in reforestation. They buy logs cheaply from small farmers, who do not have the expertise or capital for commercial forestry and therefore view trees as something to be sold in the process of clearing farmland. The price paid to farmers accounts for only 4.3 percent of the total cost of lumber manufacturing. The AID project would create cooperatives to help farmers acquire land titles, credit and technical advice, and marketing assistance. A related public education and community development program is designed to promote tourism and generally help the community benefit from conservation. The project is seen as a welcome change in foreign aid, which has previously paid little attention to environmental issues.[41]

Success requires overcoming old cultural patterns. Calculations done by the Smithsonian Tropical Research Institute show that rotated use of large tracts of forests can be very profitable. A $1,000 investment in a 2.5-acre track of rosewood would eventually yield $4–6 million of timber. Maturation takes 50 years, but the interim can be manageable if a cooperative has mixed plantations, some of it with fast-maturing trees. The trouble comes in deciding which farmers will plant which trees—and which will have their wood harvested first. It is only natural for farmers to worry about what will happen if their trees are cut first "for the common good" and later the cooperative dissolves. This is particularly the case in Costa Rica, which has a strong heritage of grass-roots action but also pride in self-reliance. Private ownership and independent operation of land is a by-product of the culture.[42] "We are an outdated, agrarian, individualistic country," says economic consultant Mario Vedova.

Costa Rica's efforts to develop new kinds of exports have won praise from AID and the World Bank, both of which have pressed the government to open the economy to trade. An AID-supported investment promotion company with the initials CINDE has set up offices in the United States, Germany, Holland, and Hong Kong. It has encouraged production of nontraditional industrial exports, including baseballs for Rawlings, sweatshirts for Haines, and terry cloth dog diapers ("one of the grossest projects I have ever seen," according to one CINDE employee). On the agricultural side, it has encouraged production of cardamon, shrimp, chayote (a local vegetable), black pepper, macadamia, fruit, and ornamental flowers—crops that did not show up in trade statistics 10 years ago. These crops provide foreign exchange and use land more efficiently.

People like Minister Umaña hope these crops will lead to an integration of industry and agriculture. "If you look at the growth in industry, it's much higher than that of agriculture," Umaña says. "Plus there are other opportunities to tie industry and agriculture [together] in a much more creative way, like agroindustry, like flowers for export. Just one example: Del Monte is going to centralize a good part of their Latin American operations here. They have diversified from banana to pineapple. They are now exploring asparagus and strawberries. Exports of plants and flowers have developed."

Seeing the possible economic advantage, Don Fidel raises annatto, the food-coloring plant being improved at CATIE. Big, ornamental plantations can be seen along the roads. But many farmers are leery. Changing cropping patterns requires capital. While the United States and other industrialized countries have begun to import fresh food during seasons when they cannot raise the crops themselves, Costa Ricans have little experience supplying those tastes. One entrepreneur with dual Costa Rican–U.S. citizenship told me why he quit the shrimp-exporting business: he could never be certain shipments from Costa Rica would reach customers on time. Many cattlemen sneer at the trend toward raising long-stemmed roses and fancy fruits for export instead of cattle. Alberto José Amador, head of the cattleman's association, contemptuously talked about CINDE-type products as he sat in his San José office, which was adorned with cabinets covered with cattle hides: "We export desserts."

Economists are also concerned about exports of agricultural commodities for which international prices can be unstable and global competition stiff. And Rodrigo Gámez worries that in an attempt to appeal to export markets, traditional varieties of plants will be ignored or eliminated and biodiversity will be lost. "Something that is very typical of industrialized countries in their requirements for food is uniformity," Gámez says. "Everything has to look the same; they have to be exactly the same size. No blemish, nothing like that."*

In a world heavily laced with interconnections, Costa Rica can no more easily back away from trade than can the United States. Yet tensions are bound to mount at virtually every level of life. Domestically, redistribution of land—or lack of redistribution—to preserve genetic diversity will create political tensions that must be dealt with one way or the other. Keeping Indian cultures intact to perpetuate valuable knowledge about plants and animals must run up against concerns about whether Indians will benefit more by fully participat-

---

*Similar processes have already taken place elsewhere. Italian, Greek, and Cypriot farmers switched to new wheat varieties after World War II without first saving the traditional varieties. Many of those species are now lost forever.

ing in modern life. More than one Costa Rican mentioned to me that the way environmental problems are addressed may influence the course of democracy in the country.

International tensions over the environment appear in a variety of forms:

- The 1969 war between Honduras and El Salvador started when Honduras deported illegal Salvadoran immigrants back to their greatly overpopulated homeland. The chance of more of such resource wars increases as populations continue to grow. The strains are apparent in figures showing that global population density was nine hectares per person back in 1900 and is likely to fall to two hectares per person in the year 2000.

- Haitians who have streamed into the United States during the 1980s from their severely deforested country have been called environmental refugees. And the recent trend of Costa Ricans illegally entering the United States can also be tied to deteriorating natural resources and loss of work. A San Vito political leader estimates that 120 people have left his small community for the United States since 1980.

- With mountains of garbage, some of it toxic, and no place to put it, European and American companies have begun to look for new dumping grounds. Four or five U.S. municipal garbage companies approached Umaña, the minister reported. Costa Rica turned down the offers, but leaders in other Third World countries have taken the garbage, sometimes quietly. As these activities have come to light, the Organization of African Unity and others have charged industrialized nations with "attack[s] on African dignity" and "toxic terrorism."[43]

Genetic diversity is not exempt from fierce disagreement. One of the most visible controversies is over industrialized countries' commercial use of genes from wild species in the Third World. Foreign companies, Gámez explains, "come here and get a variety of beans or get the wild species of maize recently discovered in Mexico. They take those materials back, and breed them, and improve them, and then they sell them to us. They have a patent. When have we charged them for taking these materials? They are charging us for the seed. They will definitely have no problem in coming here to the country and picking seeds or just pieces of stems or leaves of any species, any medicinal species that we can think of, and then taking that back to the States, Europe, or wherever."

Scientists Come and Go. . .
But Do They Leave Enough Behind?

by Yanina Rovinski

Tropical Costa Rica offers an alluring open-air laboratory for foreign biologists. But while Costa Ricans take pride in the scientific advances made on their soil, they complain of often being among the last to know about them.

Records kept by the Organization for Tropical Studies show that only 5 percent of the scientific articles derived from research carried out at its three field stations in Costa Rica are published in local media, mostly by Costa Rican–based scientists. About 50 percent are indirectly available through foreign publications received by local university libraries. Walter Marín, head of graduate studies at the Biology School of the University of Costa Rica and temporarily director of OTS's La Selva Biological Station, puts the complaint this way: First World scientists "look down on us and say: 'How come you don't know what we have published about Costa Rica? Don't you read scientific magazines?' Theirs is a scornful attitude, implying we only read what we publish ourselves in *Biología Tropical* [a local publication]. That's not the point. We do read the *Journal of Ecology* and the *American Journal of Botany*. But why should we discover by accident that someone did a study on Costa Rica and published it there? They could have informed us, as a mere courtesy to their hosts."

Costa Rican authorities and scientists, conscious of their financial and technical limitations, welcome foreign researchers, who often come with generous funding to study in the country. "The enormous biodiversity of the Third World is at the base of many recent scientific developments," says Gerardo Budowski, an ecologist at the University for Peace in Costa Rica. "It is the raw material for innumerable advances in biology, in medicine, biotechnology. This cannot be overlooked."

But, Budowski says, "the relation of foreign scientists with Third World countries could be a symbiotic relation. The scientist takes what he needs but leaves behind money, or books, or instruments. He trains an assistant or offers him a scholarship. That's the best situation."

"We don't even realize how far scientific development has gone in other places," says Freddy Pacheco, a biologist by training and member of the National University Council. "We only found out about the microchip revolution when we began buying wristwatches with tiny calculators on them. We can't even dream of catching up with the developments in microcomputers, to name just one example."

The private sector in Costa Rica does not play a big role in developing science and technology. Universities have financial constraints. "Out of every 100 colones

The patent issue is an economic disagreement that economics has not solved.[44] Seed companies will not invest money for breeding if

in the universities' budget, only 25 cents go to research," Pacheco says. "This includes the libraries, books, equipment, personnel. You can imagine how much research this can fund."

Just as Alexander von Humboldt and other scientists made contributions to Costa Rican science at the beginning of the century, foreigners help Costa Ricans today. But foreign scientists who do not take the time to share their knowledge voluntarily leave something behind: resentment. "For years, the Caribbean Conservation Corporation has been conducting research about the green turtle here in Costa Rica," Pacheco says. "The CCC had a contract with the Ministry of Agriculture and Livestock to use Tortuguero as a base for its studies. In this contract, they had agreed to keep the ministry informed of their results. I tried to get their reports, and all I found was a memo, written in terrible Spanish, explaining what the project was about." In 1979, Pacheco says, he found an article the scientists published in *American Zoologist*.

At a symposium, Pacheco says, he and his colleagues learned that "the turtles did not migrate all along the Caribbean, as we thought, but that 85 percent of them only went from Costa Rica to Nicaragua. This meant that to protect the turtle we needed to make an agreement with Nicaragua only. It turns out that when Somoza was in power, he had an export business in Corn Islands where they were killing 12,000 to 15,000 turtles a year. Here we did not even allow the poor people of Limón to catch turtle eggs for subsistence. The people at CCC had known this all along and they did not tell us."

Almost everyone has stories of uncooperative foreigners. Marín tells of scientists who contemptuously refuse to comply with Wildlife Department regulations, claiming that these are bureaucratic red-tape and hinder scientific development.

"It is unfair to expect the scientist to share his knowledge out of sheer good will," explains Budowski. "The country is only starting to regulate this, and sometimes the regulations lead to counterproductive situations. Suppose we ask a botanist to leave a copy of his collection behind, and all of a sudden the museum gets 10,000 botanical samples. The museum is not prepared to receive them, mount them, identify them, and put them to proper use. There has to be another way of asking the scientist for retribution." Budowski's suggestions include the payment of a collector's license or a contribution in equipment, publications, and lectures for the museums, the zoos, or universities.

To many Costa Ricans, both logic and justice demand that foreign scientists leave their work behind. "If this is their natural laboratory and they can come and go freely, doesn't it make sense also to keep their tropical database and specimen collections here so others don't have to go round the world looking for them?" Marín says. "What moral justification is there for the fact that someone who wants to study the butterflies of Costa Rica has to go to the Natural History Museum in London?"

they cannot be certain of reaping the rewards. U.S. commercial seed companies have donated seeds to Africa. Monsanto is giving technical support to a Franco-American team experimenting at Washington University with implanting genes for viral resistance into cassava. The project would benefit cassava farmers in Latin America and Africa. But this is not a major trend. Large companies are not charities, and they are generally reluctant to invest in products like cassava that have limited sale in industrialized countries.

By the same token, the ability of developing countries to conserve genetic resources depends in large part on sharing in the profits, but meaningful market values do not exist for wild species. These countries occasionally block exports of germplasm when they have a relative corner on the market—as does India of black pepper and turmeric, Ethiopia of coffee, Ecuador of cacao, Iraq of date palm, and Taiwan of sugar cane. Ironically, these restrictions often hurt other developing countries as much as they do anyone in industrialized countries.

Without solutions that satisfy both developed and developing countries, germplasm will become extinct and everyone will lose. According to people like Jorge León, a moderate voice in the debate, long-term equitable financing of genetic preservation depends on global governmental understandings.

Costa Rica has done a masterly job of selling itself to foreigners. "We are very white, very democratic, and very nice," one economist says, referring to the country's peaceful tradition and large European population. Says a staff member with the MacArthur Foundation, which has donated $2 million to the country, "You can get things done there. Scientists are not interfered with."[45]

Mario Boza of the Fundación de Parques Nacionales, which is managing debt schemes, has become a familiar figure in the U.S. foundation world. In his office is the *Foundation Directory*, a guidebook used in developing grant proposals to U.S. foundations. Having learned that "some people like to see their logo on things," Boza put Coca-Cola's logo on a brochure they helped finance. "I am learning about the secondary markets," he said of his education in managing foreign contributions. "We have to learn how to get a good profit from our money."

Even so, the influx of foreign tourists and scientists and their dollars has caused resentments. Foreign contributions have given the Fundación de Parques Nacionales increasing control over the park system. This irritates the National Park Service, which sees its resources and authority decreasing. University of Pennsylvania biologist Dan Janzen has earned the respect of many Costa Ricans for both protecting their environment and criticizing North Americans for their failure to understand developing countries' point of view. Yet some Costa Ricans derisively call Guanacaste National Park "Janzen's Park." They are uncomfortable with his large role. With all the money he can bring in, one official confessed to me, many Costa Ricans find it difficult to oppose Janzen on policy issues, even when they believe he is dead wrong. Before, there was never a question that Costa Ricans controlled the parks, said one Park Service employee. "The question now is for whom are the parks? For whom are we working?" Some in the country privately criticize fellow Costa Ricans working closely with foreigners as being seduced by international fame.

Without criticizing Janzen, Gámez voices some of the same resentment: "Why are developed countries—industrialized countries—so concerned about the loss of biological diversity when they wiped out all they had? They are asking us to preserve diversity but they are not, in general, conscious of the fact that European culture caused practically the disappearance of I don't know how many thousands of species.

"Our forests are fulfilling a function for the world," Gámez adds. "So it is for everybody's benefit to preserve these forests. But if we cannot cut these forests, or we should not cut these forests, we have to live on something."

Such complaints surface routinely in conversations with people from developing countries, who see a fundamental unfairness in industrialized countries' recent angst over environmental destruction: industrialized nations continue to use disproportionate amounts of resources, such as petroleum, and are far greater polluters (the United States alone produces one-fifth of the gases that cause global warming). Meanwhile, developing countries need their resources simply to meet basic needs. "For the North, the main priority is environment," a Kenya journalist commented to me. "For us, it is food." Latin American Indians, who are respected by many environmentalists because they live in harmony with nature, have expressed similar criticisms about steps to restrict the use of tropical forests. "The environmentalists don't take the inhabitants of the Amazon into account," the vice president of the Confederation of Indigenous Nationalities of Ecuadorian Amazonia told Washington environmentalists in 1989. "They're interested in the butterflies, trees, and animals, but they forget the people."

Brazilians have been particularly vocal. "Brazil refuses to be deterred from the task of incorporating into the world economy and exploiting its resources," one official pledged in 1989. Not until that same year did the Brazilian government agree to accept international funds to protect the Amazon forests, and then the Brazilian president blasted multilateral lending agencies, which have been pressured by special interest groups in industrialized countries to put more emphasis on the environment. "Every time someone in the U.S. says the Amazon belongs to mankind," another Brazilian official said, "it becomes more difficult here to have a rational discussion" about saving national forests.[46]

Minister Umaña downplays concerns about loss of sovereignty, arguing instead that global awareness over the environment gives his country leverage. "The meaning of interdependence is that, if these tropical forests are in developing countries and they are going to be destroyed by economic pressures in these countries, it's the world's responsibility to protect them, regardless of where they are. Our argument is that their best investment can be made here because we have such a high level of diversity per unit area and because we have a good track record and have illustrated that we can deliver, that a dollar here is not going to be wasted. . . . In a futuristic, holistic, global way, that's the way it's going to have to work. That's why we are leaders—because we have been able to attract this attention and people want to help Costa Rica."

Umaña points his finger at the Apollo photograph of the earth on his office wall. That, he says, is "probably the most profound image of the 20th century. It really shows that there are no political boundaries." The world needs a treaty on genetic diversity, he argues. He hopes Costa Rica will host a convention in 1990 that would produce a protocol. "We would like to become a pilot project for 21st-century peaceful society. I mean, that's what it's really all about. . . . We are trying to have our contribution in world events, not by force or by science but by ideas."

As Long As There Is Even One Costa Rica

When, in the middle of the last century, the genius Charles Darwin perceived the way plants and animals evolved—the vision that created the basis for modern biology—he concerned himself little with those species that did not survive. He saw a world overflowing with life. "Hence," he wrote, "we may look with some confidence to a secure future of great length. And as natural selection works solely by and for the good of each being, all corporeal and mental endowments will tend to progress towards perfection."[47]

Today this seems less certain. The lush tropical forests Darwin saw in Latin America, the South Pacific, and Africa are disappearing. Through a natural desire to advance materially, man has overwhelmed nature. Natural selection has given way to voracious consumption. Until very recently, the message industrialized countries have sent to developing nations is that they should make greater use of their resources, not save them.

Now humans must intercede again to arrest the destruction. Modern-day naturalists look for signs that man and nature can remain solvent. "As long as there is even one Costa Rica," Jean-Michel Cousteau has said, "there is hope." Costa Rican environmentalist Gary Hartshorn talks of being locked into being positive. "We really don't have any option except to be optimistic, [but] anyone who looks at it objectively realizes that we are losing. . . . Most countries in Latin America don't have a chance ecologically or economically."

Certainly, public concern over the environment has mounted. In the United States, a 1988 Gallup poll for the National Geographic Society found that 95 percent of the public knew that damage to the ozone layer would have worldwide repercussions. *Time* magazine strayed from its tradition of naming a person of the year in 1988 and declared "Endangered Earth" the "Planet of the Year." Acting on such concerns, the American Institute of Architects conducted a study in 1989 on the use by Americans of building materials from the tropics and the consequences of such use. Los Angeles has embarked on a program to encourage the planting of 2 million trees in the city over five years.[48]

But the public is still not certain how dangerous environmental troubles are. Solutions that suit both industrialized and developing countries remain illusive—for instance, on stepped-up efforts to curtail use of chemicals that damage the ozone. And the more subtle aspects of environmental problems still get inadequate attention. A recent poll found that about three out of every five Americans oppose tougher environmental standards that would eliminate some jobs. The 1984 National Bipartisan Commission on Central America, chaired by Henry Kissinger, called for a multibillion-dollar economic aid program for the region but said virtually nothing about environmental degradation or high population growth rates. According to its budget office, USDA spent only $26.4 million in 1988 on germplasm collection, maintenance, and enhancement, and only $3.4 million on new crop research and development. A small portion of this latter amount applies to Third World varieties.[49]

In defending his own novel theories at the time, Darwin said that "the chief cause of our natural unwillingness to admit that one species has given birth to other and distinct species is that we are always slow in admitting great changes of which we do not see the steps." Perhaps, most fundamentally, the difficulty of solving environmental problems lies in not yet seeing all the steps that make them global issues.

By seeing the inevitability of interdependence, Costa Rica may well be ahead of others. "If I had a negative view about interdependence, I would be in the wrong time," says former National Park Service director Alvaro Ugalde. "Who is independent today? Are you?

"I think the whole planet is caught in this problem" of scarce land and growing numbers of people, Ugalde warns. "If we want to make it to the 21st century, we need to find the other frontier—efficiency and sustainable development."

CHAPTER ■ 3

The Best of Strangers

Along the Kenyan coast, where Africa and Arabia meet, where European colonialists once ruled and European and American tourists now vacation, the blending of cultures is as dazzling as the blue-green Indian Ocean that rolls across the coastal reefs. As in the past, Kenyans strive to gain more from foreigners than they lose. Though relatively successful in that age-old task, Kenya is no longer unusual because of it. As Nancy Morrison explains in the following chapter, countries around the world contend with an ever wider and more intrusive mix of foreign cultures. With high-speed travel, global advertising campaigns, and booming exports of television programming, no country, however mighty or remote, can escape foreign influences. Each nation must instead learn to cope with them.

The cracked concrete dock of Mombasa's Likoni ferry has the look of an international fair. All day long, crowds as diverse as Kenya itself gather to take the quick trip from the coral island of Mombasa to the palm-lined mainland. Plump black Kenyan women swaddle their babies in kangas, the bright cotton prints popular throughout East Africa. Moslem girls in dark veils chatter. Europeans—as Kenyans call all whites, whether American or truly European—inch forward in their air-conditioned cars. And not far off is a new foreign presence. On the channels north of Mombasa, the Japanese have built bridges to speed the trip across the straits.

Kenyans have coped with foreign-engineered change for centuries. The ships of King Solomon and the Queen of Sheba once plied the coast, as did trading vessels from Egypt, Greece, Arabia, India, and China. The soft sounds of Swahili heard along the coast bespeak the fusion of ancient African tongues with the language of Arab traders. A decaying fort at Mombasa's tip marks one outpost of the Portuguese empire that stretched from Brazil to India. The rich smell of curry along Mombasa's streets signals the presence of Indians, who first arrived in force at the turn of this century; the British brought them to build a railroad that linked Mombasa to Lake Victoria, headwaters of the Nile. That same railway transported British colonists' families from "up-country" in Kenya to the coast to enjoy the sea air. Today, the British and U.S. navies call at Mombasa, the major deep-water port on this part of the Indian Ocean. Jumbo jets drop straight out of the European winter, bringing British, American, Italian, German, Scandinavian, and other tourists to the area's white sandy beaches.[1]

It was, and is, a genius of the local Swahili culture to absorb foreigners.[2] Such a skill is especially valuable today, when different people and their cultures throughout the world are coming together as never before. Faster-than-the-speed-of-sound airplanes and transoceanic direct telephone dialing, among other modern marvels, have facilitated the spread of every aspect of culture, from shoe styles to political values. In the meantime, great powers, once so adept at colonizing, now feel that their own cultures are being reshaped by foreigners. The United States, which has traditionally thought of itself as a world unto itself, agonizes about the implications of a new wave of immigration—a wave not from familiar European countries but from regions as diverse as Latin America, the Middle East, Asia, and, of course, Africa.

This new togetherness contains a paradox. As contact with other cultures increases, people's tastes for foreign music, food, and dress may grow. Yet at the same time, people want to protect what is distinctly theirs, as they have always done.[3] One of America's first groups of settlers, the English Pilgrims, left Holland after a brief stay because, among other reasons, they feared their children were becoming too Dutch. Today the Dutch, a country with a long tradition of mastering other languages, worry that their "love affair with English is turning [them] into second-rank Englishmen." It is not that they want to concentrate on their own language now; many Dutch simply want to maintain the old ways of knowing several tongues without any single one dominating.[4]

Even a seemingly carefree cross-cultural activity such as tourism is fraught with tensions and misunderstandings that can sour relations. Yet with growing interdependence in all sectors of society, learning to manage cultural crosscurrents has become an urgent requirement. As business becomes more global, so must businesspeople learn to understand other cultures better. "The best jobs, the largest markets, and the greatest profits," the Southern Governors' Association has concluded, "belong to those who understand the country with which they are doing business."[5] With the ease of traveling, state and local leaders have begun to go abroad more readily to pursue their own foreign policies. Their success— and how they polish or tarnish their nation's image in the world— depends on how much cultural understanding they pack with them and how they greet the foreigners who arrive on their main streets at home. Overall, the challenge for societies and individuals is to make the growing diversity within societies a source of strength: to use it to expand understanding while at the same time keeping foreign ideas from breeding mistrust and divisiveness and eroding national identity.

The Trend Toward Cultural Diversity

Around the world, people are more mobile than ever before. Travel was so limited in the 18th century that the English did not bother to put up signposts and milestones along their bumpy roads. In the last century, Scottish explorer Dr. David Livingstone took months to trek through Africa to reach Lake Victoria, and he died before returning home. Today, U.S. high school students tour the headwaters of the Nile River. The Indians who worked on the British railway that crosses Kenya arrived at Mombasa by boat with one-way tickets; their descendants fly back to India on holiday. A highway has supplanted Asia's ancient silk route, linking remote valleys among the world's highest peaks. Indonesian youths roar through traditional Balinese villages on motorcycles, prowling for nightlife at clubs with a Western beat. Turkish guest workers regularly take the train between West Germany, where they earn their living, and Turkey, which they continue to call home. In Lamu, one of the last outposts of Moslem civilization along the Kenyan coast, Swedish backpackers, international jet-setters, and American Peace Corps volunteers comb the beach.

And just as people are more mobile, so are their cultures. Everywhere visitors go, they spy signs of home. On Nairobi sidewalks, hawkers do a brisk trade in secondhand copies of magazines like *Modern Bride, Washingtonian*, and *Inc*. A Nairobi pharmacy is filled with the soft strains of a Muzak version of the theme from *M*A*S*H*. Crowds in Hong Kong loved *The Godfather*, intrigued by the film's parallels to local Mafia-like Chinese criminal rings. Africans visiting the United States hear Paul Simon's "Graceland" album, which introduced millions of people worldwide to the driving energy of South African music.

Indeed, developing countries increasingly are not only recipients of, but also contributors to, this international mix of cultures. Third World nations are producing and distributing their own television shows, movies, and music. Hong Kong movies are featured on a Washington, D.C., television station. Kenyans tune in to a locally made radio and television soap opera with a birth control message. The techniques used in the program were pioneered in Mexico and subsequently promoted by the New York–based Center for Population Communications-International. The approach has spread to India and soon may be used in Nigeria.[6]

The music industry has taken cultural swaps between the First and Third Worlds one step further by engineering a new pop sound, dubbed "world music," which features the rhythms and energies of developing countries such as Brazil, Nigeria, India, and Caribbean nations.[7] A variant, "world beat," combines Third World music with Western technology and Western sounds. World benefit concerts showcasing Third World performers have carried such music to millions of listeners.

Mainstream recording studios in the United States and other developed countries are spreading the sounds. For instance, Earthworks, an offshoot of British-based Virgin Records, features pop music from southern and western Africa. Island Records has revived its Mango label, which promotes African and Caribbean music. Brazilian music is getting a boost from Polygram and Braziloid, a new label created by the Celluloid recording studio. Small independent record producers are joining longtime champions of

A Few of My Favorite Things

by Wahome Mutahi

At 9:00 on a Saturday night in suburban Nairobi's Jolly Bar, a raucous crowd relaxes after payday by rocking to the driving beat of Michael Jackson's "Bad." Upstairs, drinks flow as fast as the music, but the sound comes not from a jukebox, but from the plucked hide strings of a *nyatti*, an instrument popular around Lake Victoria.

Outside, the musical contest for Kenyans' ears and wallets continues aboard *matatus*, flamboyantly colored communal taxi vans that look like discos on wheels. Drivers compete fiercely for riders with their van's choice of music; the stakes are high because few Kenyans can afford cars. Aboard one high-speed *matatu*, colored bulbs flash to the booming beat of songs like Isaac Hayes's "Love Attack," amplified through megawatt speakers. Aboard another *matatu* that has seen better days, riders hum to a cassette of songs in a tribal language, such as John Ndichu's "Chuchu was Gakunga."

As the competing sounds indicate, Kenya has a musical score to settle. Foreign music is popular and spreading among Kenyans, particularly members of the Westernized middle class. The imported sound is promoted by multinational record companies, most record stores, and many disk jockeys.

But fans of foreign music have drawn fire for neglecting their own music. "Kenyan culture suffers as the nation is bombarded by foreign styles of music and dance—as though Kenyans are incapable of making their own," says Amboka Andere, a television critic with the local daily newspaper, the *Standard*. Some critics charge that the foreign sounds' popularity reflects cultural narrow-mindedness encouraged by years of colonial domination.

Kenyans' musical feelings run deep. "A top executive will go to a club. When he gets a few drinks in him, what he wants to hear is his own music, from his own tribe," says a Kenyan reporter. But when the government tried to substitute local for foreign music on the government-run radio channel several years ago, a newspaper editorial urged, "Stop boring us."

The cultural crosscurrents are reflected in Kenya's postindependence music, which music critic John Kariuki describes as a "deft blend of indigenous rhythms and ethnic music such as Folkways (now part of the Smithsonian Institution, the U.S. national museum system) and Nonesuch.

"People around the world have been listening to American and British music for the past 30 years, very often not understanding the words but enjoying the way people put things together," said Jumbo Vanrenen, who started the Earthworks label. "As Third World artists have access to the same recording studios, it's becoming easier to present their music in a clear way. Language becomes less impor-

---

[imported] ingredients of jazz, rhumba, and twist." As Kariuki explains, "The music draws heavily from around the world. When pop and later soul took over as the mainstream music around the world [in the 1960s], Kenyans were keen to embrace the music of Elvis Presley, Cliff Richard, the Beatles, and Jim Reeves. . . . In the 1970s, soul music . . . firmly established black music, as sounds from Zaire and Dar es Saalem . . . supplied a new source of fusion that has lived until now."

The spread of modern musical instruments and music players throughout Kenya has amplified the rich mixture of foreign and local sounds. Disk jockeys at rural dance halls make their own mix of local tunes, other African music, and foreign funk, blues, reggae, and pop. Jack Wathigo, who has spun records in local dance halls for the last 10 years, explains, "My patrons prefer a good dose of foreign music—mainly from Zaire, West Africa, Britain, and America. Of course, there has to be a measure of Kenyan music, particularly in Kikuyu," the tribal language of many patrons. "Play something from the U.S. or Britain, and the young people become frenzied. Give them reggae and there is no end to the foot-stomping. Yes, they like Kenyan music, but you have to be careful how you strike a [balance] between that and foreign music."

To attract audiences abroad, Kenyan record companies have tried to blend Kenyan music with foreign technology. For instance, British-based Virgin Records collaborated with Kenya's A.I. Records in 1982, producing albums by a Kenyan and Tanzanian group.

The debate between foreign and local sounds has been aired on the Voice of Kenya (VOK), the country's most powerful medium for promoting music. The government-run channel operates two services. Local sounds, as well as music from Kenya's African neighbors, are featured on the Kiswahihi Service. English programming is aired on the other, which caters to the English-speaking local elite and foreigners.

In 1984 and again in 1987, the VOK tried to curb foreign music. Government officials argued that the Kenyan radio channel should feature Kenyan music. Advertisers and the local elite protested vigorously. Even some local music composers tried to get the government on their wavelength. Joseph Kamaru, a veteran composer respected for his ability to tap the rich lore of Kenyan music, said flatly that people would turn off their sets before they'd listen to music they didn't enjoy. "Listening to Kenyan music will not necessarily make [people] fans of local sound or [make them] patriotic."

The VOK eventually reversed its position. But the debate continues. The government recently banned reggae from the VOK, objecting to its revolutionary flavor.

tant. People go for the dance rhythms and the fine quality of people's vocals."

Immigrants no longer leave their culture behind as they once did. "For an Eastern European, to come to America at the turn of the century was a very strong cultural shock," writes Polish journalist Ryzsard Kapuscinski. "His connection to home was cut abruptly. Today, immigrants are living in one place physically, but they are sustained culturally from elsewhere. They can watch Mexican soap operas on TV, or regularly fly back and forth to Mexico on the cheap midnight flight out of Los Angeles International Airport. They can read Korean news at the same time it is being read in Seoul, and can take the daily jumbo jets to Korea."[8]

With this ease of movement, cities in North America have become centers for geographically distant regions. Miami, a mecca for Spanish-speaking immigrants, is now a banking and medical center for Latin Americans generally. Increasing numbers of "yacht people"—wealthy residents of Hong Kong—have begun to set up business bases in other countries before the Chinese Communists take control of the British colony in 1997. Some of these business-people have landed in Vancouver. "We're getting the benefits of their broad economic experience, their incredible array of business contacts around the world," says Michael Goldberg, a University of British Columbia commerce professor. "They're bringing Vancouver into the global economy. It's hard to quantify what that combination of human and financial capital is worth."[9]

Complex cultural interactions between the First and Third Worlds—for better or for worse—occur in every sphere. To cite some trends:

- *Food.* Newly affluent developing countries are adopting Western styles of eating, drinking, and smoking, and thus are suffering increasingly from heart disease and cancer.[10] Meanwhile, many health-conscious U.S. chefs are serving food that is low in fat and high in vegetables, as in Asian cuisines.
- *Sports.* African runners draw cheers in universities across the United States, while viewers around the world watch broadcasts of the Olympics and other sports events. Eastern European training techniques in many sports have become the standards of excellence for athletes worldwide.

- *Education.* More students are studying English in China than in the United States.[11] By the turn of the century, California schools may have more Asian, Hispanic, and other minority students than whites.[12] In 1988, the award for "best teacher in America" went to a Bolivian-born math teacher, Jaime Escalante, who inspired high school students in a heavily Hispanic part of Los Angeles and whose story was dramatized in the 1988 film *Stand and Deliver.*[13] And the winner of that year's national spelling bee sponsored by the Scripps-Howard newspaper chain was a girl whose name most Americans could not spell: Rageshree Ramachandran; the runner-up was Victor Wang.
- *Entertainment.* A television personality with perhaps the world's largest audience lives in the United States. Yue-Sai Kan, a New Yorker born in Guilin, China, brings a glimpse of the outside world to an avid audience of 300 million Chinese each week in "One World," a documentary series that she hosts and produces in the United States and on location.[14] At the same time, the Third World is coming to U.S. audiences, as can be seen from a glance at *Variety*, the New York newspaper that has long covered the entertainment industry. On a recent front page, three out of five stories had a Third World twist: the New York Latino festival; the Brazilian record industry; and overseas funding for films shot in the Philippines, Yugoslavia, and Brazil.[15]
- *Corporate Cultures.* In the Far East, the economic powerhouses of Japan, South Korea, Taiwan, Singapore, and Hong Kong are deriving their energy from a cultural fusion: one that joins the Western idea of competitive markets with Asian ideals of authority, discipline, and community. Japan's highest award for industrial quality is named after J. Edwards Deming, a U.S. industrial engineer whose rigorous methods of quality control were rejected by U.S. manufacturers in the 1950s but seized upon by war-torn Japan in its meteoric rise to industrial prowess. Many Americans now wonder if they should not follow the Japanese example.

In the coming decades, business executives worldwide will have to work with a wider array of cultures. "Managers will have to understand that employees don't think alike about such basics as 'handling confrontation or even what it means to do a good day's work,'" says Harvard Business School professor Jeffrey Sonnenfeld.[16]

The same technologies that permit the spread of culture also become instruments to perpetuate cultural disputes. Take, for example, the furor surrounding the release of Salman Rushdie's novel, *The Satanic Verses*, in early 1989. Iran's fundamentalist Moslem leaders condemned the book as blasphemous and sentenced the author to death. That condemnation outraged many Westerners, who saw the sanctions as violating two central tenets of their own culture: civility and freedom of expression.

Advances in communications and transportation fanned the dispute into a global quarrel. Disputants fired charges and countercharges through the media almost as quickly as they could face-to-face. Rushdie's publisher distributed the offending book worldwide while Moslem immigrants carried protests onto the streets of Europe and the United States. And a sobering realization was that jet travel made the Iranians' death threat credible: an assassin could board a flight in the Middle East and arrive in Britain within hours to hunt for the author.

In another example, about 10,000 direct-dialing long-distance telephone calls were placed daily from China to the United States in mid-1989, helping expose the Chinese to the American way of life. Such long-distance links, combined with television and increased foreign travel and foreign study, have accelerated the drive for market reforms and democracy. When Chinese students poured into the streets in June 1989 to press for greater political freedom, they were offered encouragement and bulletins by facsimile from Chinese students studying at Columbia, Berkeley, the California Institute of Technology, and other U.S. universities.[17]

The clash of values surrounding *The Satanic Verses* and at work in China during 1989 was extreme. But even in countries that seem more open to adopting other cultures, profound differences simmer beneath the surface.

Kenya is one of those countries that have many of the trappings of other societies. On Nairobi's main street, Kenyatta Avenue, Kenya's own yuppies—the Wabenzi, or the "Mercedes Benz tribe"—zip about in their flashy cars. Across town, on the veranda of Nairobi's venerable Norfolk Hotel, once a watering hole of British colonial rule, khaki-clad Japanese and American tourists discuss such topics as computers, new cars, and group liability insurance, while cars and jobs are also the centers of conversation for the coat-and-tie-clad black Kenyan professionals who gather there for a quick Tusker beer after work.

The appearance of sameness, however, is sometimes superficial. Consider the ubiquitous T-shirt. On Nairobi streets, foreign tourists wear T-shirts sporting Swahili slogans while Kenyans wear T-shirts boosting such foreign groups as the Dallas Cowboys, the Jamaica Stars, and even "The Horny Boys' Club." But when a tall young man in Nairobi who wore a jersey promoting the Washington, D.C., football team was asked by Kenyan reporter Ngugi wa Mbugua, "Who are the Redskins?" the man replied, "I do not know . . . nor am I bothered by that. I like the material."[18]

Many businesspeople and diplomats have mistaken a Thai or Japanese for a Westerner because the Easterner wore a Western suit and spoke Western words. "You'll be talking to an educated Indonesian and suddenly you'll realize that he's a mystic," says John H. Sullivan, an expert on Indonesia and former senior official with AID.

As countries converge in their levels of technology and economic development, they often diverge at deeper economic and political levels. A World Bank staffer gave this example:

> When I visited Indonesia on a mission, I used to spend Saturday afternoons in stores that sold inexpensive music cassettes. The other customers there were 14- and 15-year-old Indonesian boys and girls. They were listening to the same tapes as my son in the States. So unlike their parents, who had little or no contact with foreigners and foreign countries, they are the first generation bound together worldwide by common images and experiences. As an economist, I wonder whether Indonesia's economic growth can match Indonesians' growing expectations.

Revolutionary Iran provides an even more striking example. From a studio in Paris, the exiled Ayatollah Khomeini recorded audiocassettes that, distributed secretly in Iran, spread his rallying cry against modernization. The United States, for its part, was shocked at the way Iran turned on Americans.

The forces that bring people together can create new ways of separating them, even within their own societies. For the Kenyans wealthy enough to have access to television, U.S. shows, including "Knots Landing" and "Dynasty," are popular features. Nairobi teenagers even imitate J.J., the gangly youngster on the U.S. situation comedy "Good Times." But in watching television, Kenyans find themselves at odds with their own traditions. In the most well-to-do Kenyan households, children view programs in their own rooms while parents watch their own shows in another part of the house. Modern individualism—and isolation—is a far cry from the communal village life most Kenyans shared a generation or two ago.

The cry of a woman in Nairobi could be the complaint of a resident of Los Angeles. Sitting in her living room, hundreds of miles from her family's home near Lake Victoria, the 40-year-old Kenyan mother of six said, "In the city, everyone is so busy. They have no time for one another. I am shy about meeting my neighbors. We come from different tribes. My next-door neighbor is Sudanese. We do not know each other. I do not know my neighbor opposite." Ruefully, she added, "If my mother heard that, she'd think I was crazy."

As people in the First and Third Worlds try to conserve their own cultures even while drawing into closer contact with one another, they risk becoming the best of strangers. This is in no case more true than with tourism, which brings different cultures face to face and, in the process, poses major threats to the environment and economy as well as to the survival of each nation's culture. Even with centuries of practice, Kenya cannot always blend domestic and foreign forces that crash across its shores into a harmonious whole. But it is trying.

An unmarked door in the lobby of Nairobi's Utalii Hotel opens to a maze of college classrooms. In practice kitchens, Kenya's future chefs perfect their *vol-au-vent* and ravioli, along with African dishes such as goat stew. Down the hall, student tour guides drill French phrases. Across the campus, a professor recreates a German middle-class household. "We follow the German tourists home and see that they are normal working people who have their own home and job and family. They worked hard for their vacation," explains Nathan Munyori, head of the college's tourism program. "They don't want to waste their money." In another classroom, Kenya's budding hoteliers and travel industry workers learn how to cope with what one faculty member calls a British "snob." The idea is "to listen and see whether he's reasonable," says Munyori. "If he is, be polite and fair."

Utalii College is perhaps the most sophisticated tourism and hotel training center in Africa. Organized with the help of Swiss development funds in the 1970s, the program has become "Kenya's brainchild," in Munyori's words, as it aims to boost the ranks of Kenyans in an industry once dominated by foreign investors and managers. To hone their skills, Kenyan students travel to Geneva, Miami, and even Las Vegas. Graduates must pass tests that meet strict international standards. Munyori proudly points to a list of students who passed their exams with flying colors.

The school's extraordinary emphasis on cross-cultural relations is exemplified by the impeccably groomed, unfailingly diplomatic Munyori. Posters of Swiss lakes and Amsterdam decorate his office. "I have traveled quite a bit for tourism conferences and so forth," he says. "I have been to Japan, India, Bulgaria, Czechoslovakia, Spain, Britain, and Canada. I was at a diploma course in tourism training in Salzburg, Austria. But my biggest pride is traveling all over Kenya." Pointing to some animal specimens resting on top of his bookcase, he continues, "My specialty is Kenyan wildlife and animals."

The former conservation education officer for Kenya's National Museum teaches his students to take the same pride in Kenya that he does. Many students become immersed in Kenyan lore, particularly tour guides, who in turn educate foreigners who come to Kenya. "The thinking is, we should not have foreign guides showing Kenya to foreign visitors," Munyori explains. "So we started a tour guide program at government request. The college tries to close the gap between the cultural heritage of [visitors] and the African cultural heritage. . . . We've tried to uplift our own people. They shouldn't think of themselves as being subservient. That starts with respect for themselves. . . . Then they must lift the level of communication" with foreigners.

Teaching students to remain attuned to foreigners while retaining their own inner cultural and personal core is one secret to the program's success in bridging cultures. Students also learn to appreciate cultural differences and treat them sensitively. "Time, for instance, has a different meaning for Europeans or Americans," Munyori explains. "For them, you have to be on time. [But] our own people used to look at the sky and see that it was morning or noontime or evening. It was simply a day."

Utalii's students are taught a shorthand sociology of tourists. One instructor explains differences among foreign visitors this way: "The

American, happily, is a down-to-earth person. The European tourist tends to put on airs. The British wants to be treated like a lord of the past. The Italian wants to pay very little and get a lot. The American will have a high demand for service, but he'll pay for it."

Workers in Kenya's tourist industry graft such knowledge onto a time-honored tradition of hospitality toward guests. Welcoming visitors is also stressed by the Kenyan government. Ads on the state-run television channel encourage Kenyans to greet foreign guests warmly, with the aim of encouraging them to return.

Indeed, Utalii College has raised to a science what many Kenyans do informally and well: quickly size up foreigners, treat them with respect, and benefit from the encounters without being over-whelmed. But behind these cordial greetings and benefits lies a delicate balance. A warm, confident handshake to a foreign guest may not simply be a sign of welcome. It may also be a way to keep a grip on foreign guests. While Kenyans court foreign tourists and investors, they also take care to ensure that outsiders do not take more than they give.

As part of this effort, hotels discourage foreign guests from violat-ing local social standards. Coastal resorts post signs picturing a topless lady encircled in red with a red "X" crossed through her chest. Scantily clad sunbathers are politely but firmly asked to cover themselves.

Kenya's travel industry also coaches foreign travelers in Kenyan ways. On an Air Kenya flight from Nairobi to Mombasa, after a two-hour delay with no explanation, a soothing voice came over the loudspeaker to inform a waiting room full of fidgeting tourists, "Things move slowly at the coast." The punctual Swiss and Germans settled in their seats, aware that they were now moving to a slower clock.

Many Kenyans feel that international hotels and facilities cater exclusively to tourists—an impression compounded by the fact that in the not-too-distant colonial past, blacks were barred from many international hotels. One African hotel manager describes how his restaurant welcomes black Kenyans: "In our restaurant, if I see . . . someone like me, I will direct the waiter to serve the Kenyan first."

The Kenyan government and the private tourism and hotel indus-tries also offer incentives such as travel discounts to promote travel by Kenyans throughout Kenya. Such travel could be a way to promote unity in a country that contains more than 40 different tribes. Today, most Kenyans use their holiday to go to their family farms. But if they visited other parts of the country, says Winfred Maciel, chairman of the Domestic Tourism Council, they'd "eat new foods and meet new people."

While striving to reduce friction with foreigners, Kenya's hotel and tourism industries also try to give Kenyans more economic control. Within the last decade, the majority of management positions have passed to Kenyans themselves, with no decline in the level of tourism and hotel services. Utalii College itself is funded by revenues raised through a fee levied on foreigners' hotel and restaurant bills.

Cultural accommodations will need to be struck throughout the world as the travel boom spreads. Travel and tourism has become the world's largest industry, racking up annual sales of more than $2 trillion and employing more than 100 million people around the world, according to the American Express Company.[19] From 1970 to 1985, the number of overseas visitors to the United States more than tripled to 7.5 million. Similarly, travel to the Third World is soaring; more than 20 million First World tourists visited the Third World in the winter of 1988–89.[20] In the United States, travel and tourism is second only to health services in private sector employment, and international travel ranked as the largest U.S. export in 1987.[21]

From the Seychelles to Indonesia, from Turkey to Mexico, foreign visitors are being wooed.[22] India, for one, has made it easier for foreigners to operate charter airlines and to run their own hotels. The state of Louisiana has tried to boost tourism by giving sales tax rebates to foreign visitors.[23] Even Cuba is trying to entice more travelers, nearly 30 years after the Communists shut down Cuba as an anything-goes playground for foreigners. "We need the money," Rafael Sed, who oversees the tourism drive, told a reporter.[24]

For Third World countries, tourism holds the attraction of turning resources they have in abundance, such as sun and sea, into a lucrative service industry.[25] By 1988, tourism had become the Third World's second biggest earner of foreign exchange after oil, generating $55 billion in earnings. For the rest of the century, spending on international tourism, excluding fares, could grow by as much as 5 percent in real terms. The Third World's share of this should grow even faster.

But the risk looms that, as hard as Kenya and other developing countries try to maintain equilibrium, the balance will swing too far one way or the other. The influx of foreign tourists could be a bonanza, bringing jobs, investment, and much-needed foreign exchange to struggling and often debt-strapped developing countries. Or hordes of tourists could tarnish the local environment and pollute local cultures, turning developing countries into "nations of waiters." Always, as people of vastly different cultures and living standards mix, the good and the bad are tossed together.

Trouble in Paradise?

As the morning breeze stirs the palms, a Kenyan swimming instructor in his 20s wades waist-deep into a blue-green pool. Bronzed German and Italian tourists join him for their daily lesson in water sports. Large Italian men in tiny bathing suits kick in the gleaming pool as the instructor calls out, "*Schnell! Schnell! Uno. Duo.*" The delighted vacationers giggle. A few yards away, a lone American woman in her 30s strolls down the pristine beach. A teenage black Kenyan "beach boy" approaches and propositions her in perfect German. She walks off miffed.

The study in contrasts yields a twofold lesson. Cross-cultural contacts can yield benefits for tourists and their hosts, or they can obliterate the delights that people hope to find in travel. Losses can be as tangible as the coral that travelers break off from fragile reefs for souvenirs, or as intangible as lost innocence among once-gracious locals.[26]

In Kenya and other developing countries, tourism has brought jobs and skills. It has helped lift the level of education, spur the development of a middle class (as Utalii College graduates can testify), and foster greater pride in local culture. Today, tourism remains an attractive option, especially for those developing countries whose industrial exports are being blocked by rising First World protectionism, or whose traditional export commodities have been hard hit by swings in prices and demand. In hopes of earning foreign exchange, the Kenyan government has "invested heavily in developing facilities which make tourism possible, profitable and enjoyable," Mwai Kibaki, former vice president and minister for home affairs, told a Kenyan tourism seminar. But he also stressed that the payoffs from such investments must be great and visible to the citizens.[27]

As Kibaki realizes, tourism also brings with it new problems, as well as difficult political and social choices. It is creating a new kind of global competition among developing countries, not to sell raw materials but to sell scenery. Kenya owes some of its popularity among tourists to other countries' travails—for instance, Israel and Sri Lanka, which have beckoning beaches but have also suffered political unrest.[28] Also, tourism has resulted in environmental damage, such as tropical beaches overrun with high-rise Miami-style hotels; cultural costs, such as crafts shops crowded with cut-rate "airport art"; and personal losses, such as children turned prostitutes to serve free-spending foreign clients.

Successful promotion of tourism in developing countries creates yet another difficult problem of how to share the newfound wealth. That dilemma is expressed by curio dealers who line Mombasa's tourist areas: "We suffer very much because rich men come and park their [tour] vehicles in front of our kiosks and go away even for the whole day thus literally making us their watchmen at the expense of our business," the Coast Petty Traders Association wrote to Mombasa's mayor councillor. To add insult to injury, in the eyes of curio dealers, tour operators steer tour groups away from kiosks and toward those shops that pay guides sales commissions.[29]

In Asian and Pacific countries, a major effort at creating more culturally sensitive tourism was spearheaded in the late 1970s by church and community leaders who were dismayed by sex tours and distressed by damage to local cultures and values. Concerned that industrialized countries controlled too great a share of the industry's profits through foreign holdings of airlines, hotels, and tour groups, they argued that the local jobs that were created were often servile.[30] The drive to make tourism more ethical was taken up by a Bangkok-based group called the Ecumenical Coalition on Third World Tourism, which has devised a brief code of ethics for tourists. The first of 11 precepts urges travelers to "travel in a spirit of humility and with a genuine desire to learn more about the people of your host country." The last precept encourages tourists to "spend time reflecting on your daily experience in an attempt to deepen your understanding."[31]

Culturally sensitive tourism is gaining popularity among American and European travelers. A new kind of travel, called "alternative tourism," emphasizes local spending and simple living. Travelers stay in locally owned lodgings, eat at local restaurants, and employ local guides and group leaders. By the late 1980s, hundreds of alternative tour groups had sprung up in the United States, ranging from reforestation brigades in Central America, to bicycle treks through China, to sojourns on a family farm in Kenya. "Our philosophy is that travel is not just lying on the beach, but also learning about the country whose beach you're lying on," says Bob Guild of Marazul Tours.[32]

But putting such intentions into practice is not always easy. Are travelers wrong, for instance, to turn down a home-cooked Third World meal, knowing that the food will almost certainly make them sick? New York writer Eleanor Schwartz confronted just such an ethical dilemma while traveling in India. She and her companion wanted to see a hilltop temple, but the only route up was a series of steep stairs. They first refused to use bearers; to be carried would turn men into beasts of burden, they thought. But as the women climbed the hill in the monsoon heat, their would-be bearers followed in grim silence. Their guide argued, "Very few tourists come here now. If you do not hire these men, their children will go hungry." The women said they would give them some money for food. "These men are not beggars," the guide replied. Finally the women allowed themselves to be carried, but did so with misgivings that weighed on them as heavily as any load.[33]

Genuine dilemmas also surround efforts to protect Kenya's wildlife—its major tourist attraction, apart from beaches. The bounty of animals draws not only tourists but also poachers, as well as a crescendo of international concern.

Virtually every safari guide can show tourists lions, zebras, wildebeests, and ostriches crossing the sun-soaked savannah of Kenya's Masai Mara game park. But East Africa's roaming herds are threatened. At the turn of the century, big game hunter Theodore Roosevelt rode through Kenya's Athi Plain just outside of Nairobi and marveled, "As we sat over the train's cow-catchers it was literally like passing through a vast zoological garden." Today, travelers on the same route would be lucky to see a score of zebra or wildebeests. Elephants no longer pass by Kenya's capital.[34]

A combination of forces is conspiring against the wild herds. Kenya's population, among the world's fastest growing (thanks, in part, to improved health care), is moving onto lands and next to many game parks where the animals roam. Tourists themselves upset the wildlife, roaming through the game parks in zebra-striped minivans, which gather like mechanized herds around photogenic lions and elephants.

And then there are poachers. The same roads that bring in busloads of tourists also bring in these interlopers—some of whom are from Kenya, and some of whom, evidence suggests, are from Kenya's barren neighbor and longtime antagonist, Somalia. These latter poachers, says Richard Leakey, Kenya's director of wildlife, are "turning Kenya into an economic zone of Somalia."[35]

With their lucrative earnings, thanks to a well-developed worldwide market, poachers equip themselves with AK-47 machine guns. In 45 minutes, they can splay an elephant, hack off the tusks, and flee. A single piece of ivory might be poached in Kenya, shipped through a neighboring African country, cut and polished in Hong Kong, and sold to a Japanese or U.S. businessman on a shopping trip.

Increased demand from the Middle East and East Asia, where local cultures have long prized elephant tusks, rhino horns, and various animal hides, has fueled the tradition of poaching. As elephants and rhino near extinction, the value of their tusks and horns has soared. Ivory and rhino horn have become new international currencies. Collectors and investors are stockpiling. "There's evidence that the price of ivory fluctuates with [the price of] gold," says Mark Stanley Price, head of the African Wildlife Foundation's African operations. "People are using [ivory] as a long-term storable commodity."[36]

Demand for rhino horn suddenly shot up in the 1970s. Esmond Bradley Martin and Chyrssee Perry Martin stumbled on one reason for the increase—in North Yemen, one of the most remote places on earth. In a stroll through a market in Sana'a, the capital of the Yemen Arab Republic, they spotted stacks of horn. Yemenites, newly prosperous from the oil boom, sought a status symbol previously available only to the wealthy: daggers with rhino horn handles.[37] Demand has similarly jumped along the Pacific Rim, where industrial prowess and soaring worldwide trade have enriched residents in major Asian markets such as Hong Kong, Singapore, Taiwan, and Japan.

With the demand for the horns and tusks on the increase, conservationists have stepped up the campaign to protect wildlife. Just as poaching has become a sophisticated international industry relying on advances in technology, transportation, and communications, conservationists rely on both an intricate system to monitor the global trade in endangered species and a worldwide advertising campaign to blunt sales of illegal wildlife products. The African Wildlife Foundation dubbed 1988–89 the "Year of the Elephant" and enlisted celebrities such as movie star Jimmy Stewart to spread the word not to buy ivory.[38] Nairobi has become an international capital for these conservationists, while in capitals around the world, they lobby governments for better wildlife protection. As a result of their efforts, the United States and the European Community have banned all ivory imports.[39] For their part, Kenya, Tanzania, Zaire, Gabon, and Gambia have all called for a worldwide ban on the ivory trade.

Such measures will help shrink the ivory market, but a complete stop to the illegal trade will also require bridging a cultural and economic gulf. A single pair of elephant tusks is worth more than a year's earnings for the average Kenyan; a single rhino horn can fetch up to $15,000 wholesale in the Far East pharmaceutical market. Sustaining each of the 19 black rhinos in the Nakuru wildlife reserve in the Kenyan portion of the Great Rift Valley costs more than $6,000 a year—a sum nearly 20 times the per capita wealth of Kenyans themselves.[40] "As much as I like elephants, people are more important," L. Y. Nda wrote in a letter to the editor of the *Kenya Times*. "What about a little more concern for . . . [deprived] children?"[41]

Many Kenyans have looked upon calls to conserve wildlife much as Americans would view a foreign effort to protect rattlesnakes or rats. Wildlife protection has seemed to be an externally imposed ideal that has best benefited foreign tourists.[42] It has not helped the conservationists' case that foreigners' attitudes toward animals have ranged widely over the years. Among the first foreigners to value Kenyan elephants were Arab traders, who captured slaves to haul tusks to boats on the Indian Ocean. Then came the "great white hunters" and settlers, who killed African wildlife by the thousands. Now some foreigners want to protect Kenya's animals. But Kenyans point out that it is other foreigners—those in far wealthier nations in North America, Europe, the Middle East, Asia, and the Pacific— who are buying the precious animal products.

Recently, both Kenyans and foreign and local conservationists have been advocating the idea of preserving wildlife for profit. With tourism vying with coffee as Kenya's largest earner of foreign exchange, and with wildlife viewing comprising an estimated 40 percent of tourism earnings, the case has strengthened for protecting wildlife on economic grounds.[43] The power of that approach is explained by Leakey, who is also a world-renowned paleontologist and the son of Louis and Mary Leakey, pioneers in the study of the origin of man.

"There are a lot of [Kenyans] who don't get exposed to animals," Leakey notes. "They're city people. Or they're rural people whose only context is to see wildlife either as nothing or as a pest. They've assumed wildlife is for tourists. . . . But everyone is concerned about Kenya's economic growth. When you can put [wildlife] on the level of coffee trees, people can identify with it on an immediate basis."

Preventing poaching has become an issue of national pride as poachers have become more brazen and evidence mounts that some poachers are foreign-backed. Three Somali poachers were charged with the murder of renowned conservationist George Adamson in 1989. Outraged by the outlaw behavior on their territory and worried about losing tourism business, some Kenyans have begun to speak of "poaching as 'sabotage,'" as though poachers were blowing up factories in an industrialized country," says Christopher Gakahu of the New York Zoological Society. In mid-1989 President Daniel arap Moi torched $3 million worth of elephant tusks and reiterated shoot-to-kill orders against poachers.

Several experiments under way in and near the game parks offer local people economic incentives to protect wildlife. In the best developed of these—in Amboseli National Park, in the shadow of Mount Kilimanjaro—new tourist facilities have been built on Masai land; tribesmen have been compensated for lost grazing opportunities caused by migrating wildlife; and local people have gotten better water, roads, and schools.[44] While such incentives are welcome, however, "we would prefer it if there were no national park here," says Jonathan Leboo, the Masai Group Ranch representative and treasurer. "We'd much rather have it as a ranch. But the park is here, and we accept that so long as we are compensated."[45]

Kenyan and foreign conservationists are also trying to educate Kenyans about wildlife protection. At the forefront is Kenya's 20-year-old network of wildlife clubs. On the grounds of Nairobi's museum, in an office decorated with plaques from the Kenyan government honoring the clubs' work, Nathaniel arap Chumo, the director of the Kenyan Wildlife Clubs, explains that the conservation message is just starting to percolate through the general population. But "the lack of interpretive materials" such as guidebooks is slowing the spread of that message, Chumo says. "Tourists can get these things but [must] pay for them. For the ordinary [Kenyan] citizen, with little spending money, there's very little" in the way of books and other media to make the case for wildlife protection. "Even the films we can use are German or English. The emphasis, the tone, is different."

To protect its wildlife treasures, Kenya has set aside more than 8 percent of its land for parks—more than four times as high a percentage as the United States. The question confronting Kenya—a country of farmers, with one of the world's fastest-growing populations—is whether it can afford that kind of park system.

Not all Kenyans agree that protecting wildlife should be a priority in the face of urgent human and social needs. The animals that tourists marvel over and conservationists prize seem to some Kenyan farmers to be a nuisance or a luxury that a struggling country can scarcely afford.

"From the frontier of America to the plains of Africa, there has always been only one winner when the needs of man and animal collide," says journalist David Lamb.[46] Protection of Kenya's wildlife will work only if it makes sense for Kenya's economy and culture.

As Kenya's dealings with wildlife show, moving onto the world stage can have costs as well as benefits. That lesson is also being learned by Kenya's artisans.

This story has a humble beginning. Just outside Nairobi, a potholed road twists eastward and the skyscrapers of the central city recede. For more than a mile, a makeshift city stretches along a crowded valley in a tangle of cardboard, tin, and splintered wood. Mud-caked during Kenya's cold rainy season, dust-dry during the long months of heat, Nairobi's dirt-poor Mathare Valley blends into the earth.

It's a sight that few foreign visitors to Kenya see. Yet foreigners and their tastes are central to the busy workshops and crowded shanties that produce handicrafts. On workbenches in small factories and in their homes, craftsmen and women in Mathare Valley weave handbags, shape sculptures, and fashion jewelry sold around the world.

In the valley and throughout Kenya, the handicrafts trade is booming, thanks to exports and sales to tourists. A small cottage industry has grown into a multimillion-dollar trade for Kenya and a modest staple for many hard-pressed Kenyan handicrafters.

But that success is double-edged. Foreign demand for Kenyan crafts has helped preserve Kenya's cultural heritage. At the same time, however, it has threatened to dilute that heritage and has brought Kenya head-to-head with competitors throughout the Third World.

In the mid- and late 1980s, sales of Kenyan handbags and jewelry jumped. The movie *Out of Africa* popularized Kenyan designs abroad while the Kenyan government aggressively marketed its products. As a sign in the Kenya External Trade Authority proudly proclaims, "The world is our marketplace." Near that plaque hangs a neatly framed proclamation from the city of New York lauding Kenyan products. New York has been good to Kenyan crafts—from swank stores such as Bloomingdale's, which has carried soapstone carvings, to Manhattan sidewalks, where vendors hawk Kenyan bags. Retail clothing companies like Banana Republic have carried Kenyan merchandise in their stores around the country.

Kenyan artisans have busily adapted to growing foreign demand. Kenya's most popular crafts item, in fact, has become the kiondo, the sturdy woven basket used for generations to carry vegetables. Now women weave the baskets into handbags, briefcases, and even backpacks. From earth tones, the palate of kiondo colors has expanded into a rainbow of hues.

Such adaptations to foreign tastes and markets seem to have generally benefited both buyers and sellers in the case of the kiondo. "Our weavers like special orders" that deviate from traditional styles, says Jisaidie Cottage Industries' Lucy Mwenje. When filling special requests for custom colors and designs, producers know that their work will sell, she adds.[47]

But the danger of producing cut-rate "airport art" lurks for many other Third World crafts. The sorry effects of commercialization are spreading to crafts centers such as Bali in Indonesia, where producers offer two lines: crowd-pleasing knockdowns and finely crafted designs for more discerning customers. Sales to foreigners are "a buyers' market," argues the South Pacific Peoples Foundation in a report on the social, economic, and cultural costs of tourism. "Consequently, quality is often sacrificed for quantity. In addition, originality, too, falls by the wayside."[48]

The challenge is to preserve tradition and build upon it. Intricately carved wooden doors, the products of a centuries-old tradition of fine craftsmanship, were virtually stripped from Kenya's coastal buildings by foreign tourists and antiquities dealers before the Kenyan government placed a preservation order on them.[49] In recent years, demand from tourists has helped revive the wood-carving tradition along the coast, and Kenya's hotels have spurred the demand by featuring wooden furniture made with traditional designs and materials.[50] Beautiful doors in the old style of the coast grace a prominent office building in Nairobi.

The souvenir and crafts shops in Nairobi "used to be more junky," says Philip Leakey, a former assistant minister for tourism and wildlife, and brother of Richard Leakey, director of wildlife. "Some of them are quite tastefully presented now."

One pioneer in upgrading Kenyan and African crafts is Alan Donovan, an American who came to Nigeria in 1969 as a relief worker for AID. Donovan went on to open one of Nairobi's most fashionable crafts stores, African Heritage. His cofounder was Kenya's former vice president, Joseph Murumbi, a prominent art collector who shares Donovan's concern about preserving authentic African art. "It is a tragedy that so few Africans appreciate their own culture and their own past," says Murumbi.[51] African Heritage now carries two lines: traditional and contemporary crafts. In addition, the shop's fashion shows helped launch the careers of such international models as Iman and Khadija Adam, a former Miss Africa. Thus, the shop has become a profitable way to teach Africans and foreigners about African art while revitalizing the Kenyan art market through exports.

Kenya shares its hopes for handicrafts with many other Third World countries, and its very success has led to cutthroat competition with rivals in the developing world. Raphael Omusi of the Kenyan National Chamber of Commerce and Industry neatly summarized the problem: "Most of the African countries are fighting for the same market" for some crafts. As he spoke, Kenyan exporters eager to boost overseas sales crowded the lobby outside his office to seek advice; while waiting, they leafed through copies of *Czechoslovakian Heavy Industry*, *British Trade News*, and *Trade Opportunities in Taiwan*.

Growing foreign competition haunts crafts producers like Mathare Valley's Jisaidie Cottage Industries, which in fact has centers throughout Kenya. Like many crafts cooperatives that dot Kenya, Jisaidie was founded to promote its members' products while protecting their profits. "We want to cut out the middleman . . . who is out to make a huge profit," says Barnabus Kimomge, who manages the export department for the Mathare Valley center. "Our aim is not to make a profit, but to make sure the person making the basket can feed her entire family."

The most complex machine in Jisaidie's Mathare Valley workshop is a jigsaw. Workers hand-file puzzle pieces. Then they hand-dip them in paint, carefully collecting the drippings to use again. Men who cannot read or write make wooden maps and alphabet puzzles bound for schoolchildren. Women in simple cotton frocks craft high-fashion jewelry.

Jisaidie Industries places a premium on teaching its members employable skills. Above the buzz of saws and the whirr of old Singer pedal-type sewing machines, a manager in the woodworking department explains, "We encourage [workers] to use their hands" so they can perfect skills for other jobs. "We may be forced to lay them off. Then they will have no paycheck."

Kenyan producers may be adapting too well. As one exporter says, "Some of my customers don't want the quality to be too good. They think [the woven handbags] are more 'African' if they're rough." Similarly, a Bolivian cooperative that hand-made sweaters became so proficient that buyers in developed countries started to think the garments were made by machine. To keep the appeal of their products, knitters started to drop the occasional stitch.

Pressure on the Kenyan crafts industry has intensified as foreign competitors throughout the Third World have copied Kenyan designs. Within a few short years after Alan Donovan introduced his line of "jungle jewelry," for instance, craftsmen in Haiti, Mexico, the Philippines, India, Hong Kong, and China had pirated the designs. Kenyan bags have been copied by workers in the Philippines and other countries. "Kenya now appears to be on the hit list of countries to be copied," says Andrew Wanyandeeh of the Kenyan External Trade Authority.

To protect their designs, then, Kenyan craftsmen and women may soon have to adapt something else from abroad, a technique from the developed world: design patents.

Bridging the Cultural Divide

Eight thousand miles from Nairobi, in Washington, D.C., craftsmen of another sort promote Kenya's interests in the United

States. American lobbyist Dennis Neill and his Washington government relations firm craft strategies to help the Kenyan government win friends and influence key American government officials, journalists, and citizens. Neill is known as "the one who buys the sandwiches" during the long meetings when members of Congress, their aides, and lobbyists hammer out foreign aid legislation.

An evergrowing web of interests binds Americans and Kenyans. The Kenyans need economic resources for development. The United States regards with favor Kenya's relatively democratic institutions and burgeoning market-oriented economy. It also views Kenya as a strategic ally that provides a military jumping-off point to the Persian Gulf and the Horn of Africa. Neill's company explains the intricate workings of the American political system to key Kenyans and the Kenyan system to Americans, and it steers Kenya's requests for U.S. foreign and military aid and other matters through Congress, the White House, and the Pentagon. Kenya received $58 million in U.S. aid in 1988.

Neill founded Neill and Company in 1981. Since then, the firm has assembled a team of experts to help foreign clients grapple with a variety of concerns. Partner Les Janka, for instance, worked for the Reagan White House, the National Security Council staff, and the Defense Department, where he specialized in Near Eastern, African, and South Asian affairs. Neill himself was a former senior official with AID, where he helped shepherd the U.S. foreign aid budget through Congress.

Key to the tasks Neill and his firm perform is understanding the diverse cultures of the parties involved. His government clients alone come with an imposing array of histories and interests. On a given day, Neill bounces intellectually from Egypt to Jamaica, from Morocco to Guinea. And true to the nature of interdependence, his client list also includes nongovernmental entities—multinational giants such as the General Electric Company and the Washington, D.C.-based international satellite group, Intelsat, which itself has 114 members—with their own cultures and global interests.

Neill and others who represent foreign governments and businesses are not unique. Such lobbying has grown into a flourishing business in recent years. More than 100 developing countries, from the tiny Pacific islands of Micronesia to giant Brazil, are tapping Washington lobbyists, lawyers, and public relations specialists. The jobs of these specialists range from clipping newspaper articles about the client country, to arranging White House luncheons, to buying U.S. tanks, to influencing trade and investment legislation.[52] And this is not just a Washington phenomena. When Brazilians wrote their new constitution, ratified in 1988, representatives for petroleum companies such as ARCO, Texaco, Exxon, and Shell were nearby, objecting to the proposed nationalization of foreign-owned gas stations. And more than 200 foreign consultants have gone into business in Brussels, where scores of rules are being drafted to bring about unification of the European Community in 1992.

"Foreign agents," as people like Neill are called, owe their jobs to interdependence and the urgent need for countries to communicate effectively with each other. While tourism and other getting-to-know-you activities seem to be simple leisure pastimes, understanding other countries' cultures is a vital component of any national strategy. Governments formerly entrusted such work to their own diplomats; the wide range of connections today, however, has created the need for a new class of intermediary—a person whom the client may not consider as patriotic as a native son but who has the specialized knowledge needed to work within the alien system. Thus, the Kenyans tend to hire Americans for work in Washington, and American businesses tend to hire Brazilians for work in Brasilia.

Countries often seek help from Americans because "something has gone wrong"—for example, Congress has cut their foreign aid, Janka explains. "Or a new government takes power" and wants to cultivate Washington ties. In addition to Neill, the Kenyans have retained the Alexandria, Va., public relations firm of Black, Manafort, Stone, and Kelly in part to help counter American concerns over poaching and other lawlessness in parks, which could harm tourism trade.[53] Trade issues in Washington are particularly critical to developing nations such as Brazil, Mexico, Hong Kong, Singapore, South Korea, and Taiwan, whose exports to the United States have jumped. Some countries use Washington specialists in a long-term strategy to avoid crises and actively promote their causes in the United States.

Growing competition among developing countries is adding to the demand for Washington representation. As U.S. foreign and military aid is trimmed, as trade privileges to developing countries are cut, and as trade restrictions increase, developing countries "try to get in first" to Washington policy-making circles by working with U.S. lobbyists, says Janka. Some foreign countries even employ several different Washington firms to gather additional information and cover their political bases.

From the firm's standpoint, striking the balance between these interests is tricky. Neill must avoid seeming to take sides among his many clients. "We can represent Latinos and Africans and Asians. But we might have a problem" representing different African countries, Janka explains. Especially delicate is the task of protecting the national sovereignty of foreign clients—along with that of the United States. The Kenyans' sensitivity on sovereignty, for example, runs high on such issues as their military significance to the United States. "You've got to stick up for [foreign countries'] sovereignty. But as an American, you're stupid if you compromise your own," says Neill, a native of Missouri. "Our clients have to respect us as Americans. Our value to them is that we grew up with American attitudes and grew up with this system."

As with other intercultural activity, foreign agents' actions have created tensions in both America and developing countries. U.S. lawmakers such as Sen. John Heinz (R-Pa.) worry that lobbyists—in particular, those promoting foreign trading partners—work against U.S. interests. "It's hard to find a former U.S. trade negotiator who does not now represent foreign interests in Washington," said Rep. Richard Gephardt (D-Mo.).[54] Foreign agents already are required to register with the U.S. government under a 1938 law that was originally passed to control Nazi propaganda. Heinz and others want to tighten those registration requirements. Moreover, some lawmakers want to bar U.S. government officials from trading on their knowledge of the U.S. system by leaving government service and immediately representing foreign governments.

For their part, many developing countries are troubled by the basic openness of the U.S. political system, in which many interests, foreign as well as domestic, can lobby on their own behalf. Some outsiders regard lobbying in the United States as a way to circumvent the system. "We view it as organized corruption," says one African member of Parliament. And Janka reports, "We had one Asian country tell us that if they had to go to [their] Parliament and ask for $250,000 to pay us, there'd be no chance [of approval]. The attitude is, 'Why do we have to pay to convince the Americans to like us and trust us?'" Adding to their unease about employing foreign lobbyists in foreign countries, many developing countries adhere to policies of nonalignment with either the East or West. Any attempt to lobby in another country, they fear, will seem to violate their arm's-length relationship.

"Most of the contracts we get come after long, protracted negotiations," Neill explains. "Another client recommended us to Kenya. The Kenyans checked us out and checked us out and checked us out."

In light of such sensitivities at home and abroad, Neill takes great care in his own work. He stresses, "We have a rule. . . . We only represent clients whose interest is in getting closer to the United States, not in being confrontational. . . . Everything we do, we do openly. Everyone knows who we are and what we are doing." Neill is "very good at staying away from trying to justify things that [Americans] would find hard to justify," says a U.S. reporter who has seen him in action in Congress.

As the web of contacts between First and Third World countries thickens, productive relationships are coming to depend on how well countries learn to be—if not the best of friends—then, at least, the best of strangers. That's a lesson being learned by Kenyan officials who must deal with the U.S. political system. Initially "amazed" by some aspects of American political culture, says Neill, they are learning to adapt. Much of Neill's firm's work with Kenyans involves making U.S. ways seem less strange and helping Kenya avoid unpleasant American surprises.

To avoid stumbling blindly into an interdependent future, people must constantly monitor how they are seen in other countries. Consider the case of former U.S. president Jimmy Carter, who sought to enliven a public greeting of Mexico's president by joking about a stomach malady Americans have nicknamed "Montezuma's Revenge." Americans may have chuckled at Carter's joke. Mexicans seethed.[55] With cross-cultural contacts increasing through travel, business, movies, food, sports, and the like, risks worse than embarrassment lurk for those who are unprepared; dangers range from culture shock to alienation to hostility to racism.

Interdependence demands a clear-eyed view of foreigners, and that requires healthy skepticism about common assumptions, which are more often myth than truth. One such assumption holds that, through close interaction, people will automatically understand one another better; travel, it is said, broadens the mind. But many tourists adroitly avoid exposure to other cultures. Entire tour packages are devoted to seeking out the familiar, as tourists rush from international airports to international hotels through well-worn circuits of sights. One study of a popular resort in Sousse, Tunisia, "found that 90 percent of the tourists claimed they had come for 'the sun, the beach, the sea, and the palm trees,' and only 10 percent professed any interest in Tunisian society and history. The tourists spent an average of 22 hours a day inside the hotel complex, and 65 percent did no sightseeing at all."[56]

Even when people of different cultures get to know one another better through increased cultural exchanges, they may not like one another better. A troubling example can be found in the friction that flares between the United States and Japan. Americans' ties with the Japanese have never been closer. Thanks to business deals and increased travel, as well as to a burst of books, articles, videos, and films—all part of an explosion of cultural and commercial exchanges—Americans have more information than ever about Japanese culture. In some cases, such new information has fueled Americans' belief that, through trade inequities and economic expansionism, Japan poses a serious danger to America's well-being. A prominent American journalist, James Fallows, who has lived in Japan as part of a cultural exchange, caused a furor in 1989 on both sides of the Pacific by urging the United States to contain Japan, as America sought to contain the Soviet Union during the cold war. A 1989 *Washington Post*–ABC News public opinion poll showed that nearly half of those Americans surveyed believe that Japan is a bigger threat to the United States than the Soviet Union.[57]

And the Japanese, who are traveling to the United States in record numbers, sometimes retain their unflattering stereotypes of Americans. A Japanese tour director who lives in San Francisco cautioned a group of Japanese tourists newly arrived in his adopted city, "Don't trust anyone. People steal passports here. Don't even trust Japanese people who live here. Some have been living here too long—they will steal, too."[58]

Faced with a profusion of foreign influences, people around the world are responding to cultural interdependence with similar nationalistic anxieties. The U.S. debate about the foreign "buying of America" finds surprising parallels in Kenya's policies of boosting Kenyan management and control. Even the rhetoric is similar. Some Kenyans remain wary of foreign control (as well as of economic control by Kenyans of Asian descent) decades after the country's independence from British colonial rule. Meanwhile, in America, some members of Congress have accused Japan of turning the United States into a colony that supplies Japan with raw materials while serving as a market for Japanese exports.

Such cultural insecurity is long-standing, even in open societies like the United States. "When [Thomas] Jefferson offered the young [American] nation his personal library (which was to be the foundation of the Library of Congress), it contained so many foreign-language books (including numerous 'atheistical' works of Voltaire and other French revolutionaries) that some members of Congress opposed its purchase," observes Daniel Boorstin, former head of the Library of Congress.[59]

Today, U.S. conservative activist Phyllis Schlafly sounds like officials from the Kenyan Ministry of National Guidance and Political Affairs in warning against the dangers of foreign pollution. Schlafly has criticized any teaching about other countries that promotes "the error of equivalence—that is, the falsehood that other nations, governments, legal systems are identically equivalent to our own and entitled to equal respect." For its part, the Kenyan Ministry censors foreign films and videos that it deems dangerous or immoral. The list of offensive films includes *Nude Jell-o Wrestling Special* and *The Year of Living Dangerously*.[60]

In trying to gain more than they lose as their own culture interacts with others, Kenyans send mixed signals to outsiders. On the one hand, Kenya welcomes foreigners, depending heavily as it does on foreign tourism and international aid. The country is banking on an open, outward-looking economy to support its rapidly growing population. Interest in things foreign is keen among the elite of educated, urban Kenyans. "I get yelled at if I don't bring in my *Newsweek*," says an American who works in Nairobi.

Yet for all their interest in foreigners and foreign help, Kenyans also maintain their distance from outsiders. The government's official foreign policy is one of nonalignment with either the West or the East. A domestic economic policy of "Kenyanization" aims at decreasing foreign economic control and increasing control by Kenyans, particularly blacks. Tensions sometimes flare between black Kenyans and Kenyans of South Asian descent. Meanwhile, Kenyan government officials periodically chastise domestic and foreign journalists for spreading propaganda about Kenya. The concern with Kenya's foreign image is "obsessive," says one Kenyan journalist, who refuses to be quoted because he is being monitored by the government.[61]

Kenya broke from British colonial rule only 25 years ago. Much as the 25-year-old United States borrowed from the superpowers of its day—Britain and France—to fashion something uniquely American, so do some Kenyans pick and choose among a range of foreign influences to fashion their own identity in the modern world. But in today's interdependent age, contacts between Kenyans and foreigners occur far more quickly, intensely, and unavoidably than they did between Americans and the rest of the world in the early 19th century. While it is still true that in Kenya large sections of the population have virtually no direct contact with foreigners, such isolation is changing—fast. In the middle of the Great Rift Valley, in an area as desolate as central Nevada, a Japanese rental car filled with American tourists slows as three male Kenyan teenagers, dressed in T-shirts and chinos, moonwalk, Michael Jackson–style, along the side of the Italian-built road. One teenager hoists a boom box—an oversized radio popular among U.S. teenagers—on his shoulder. The Americans look on in amazement. The Kenyans wave.

Interdependence is forcing a widespread reexamination of group identities, as is seen in the worldwide debate over English, which has become the international language of business and science. When Japanese and French businesspeople meet, they're likely to switch to English to converse. The language is so strong a global link that the Aga Khan, spiritual leader of millions of Ismaili Moslems, stresses that English and science are two keys that developing countries need to enter the modern world. Yet millions of English speakers from Jamaica to India to Malaysia prefer their homegrown variant of English that captures the rhythms and meanings of their local lives. In the United States, to guard against what they view as a threat to the American way of life by Spanish speakers and other immigrants, 16 states had declared English their official language by mid-1988.[62] In Kenya, lawmakers periodically discuss whether to switch the official language of parliamentary debate from English to Swahili.

The new perplexities of cultural interdependence will demand new skills. Adaptability is key to the strategy of one French girl of North African heritage. "I've opted for French nationality," she told a reporter. "But it's not a question of being either French or Maghrébine. I'm both," she said, ". . . as and when it suits me."[63]

Similarly, discernment among cultures and self-confidence about one's own is also the preferred strategy of one young Kenyan who works in the U.S. embassy in Nairobi. "We see America's problems. We see your drugs. Maybe America doesn't have all the answers. We can pick and choose" among a range of foreign ideas and influences.

The subtleties of extracting the best from strangers in an increasingly pluralistic world are nicely captured by the flap in the United States about foreign athletes. To produce winning seasons—as well as alumni checks—some U.S. college sports teams have become heavily foreign. "I think it deprives [us of] opportunities for American kids," says a track coach at a midwestern university. "We had one woman runner from Long Island. She ran really well—and she came in 14th" in a field dominated by foreign athletes who ran for U.S. schools. "She was discouraged. I think it sours these people on college sports."

But Kenyan Hillary Tuwei, a star runner at the University of Richmond in the early 1980s, turned that viewpoint on its head. "American runners who criticize schools for bringing in foreign athletes on scholarship look at things pretty narrowly. For years, [runner] Craig Virgin used to complain about it. He doesn't anymore. Maybe he knows that running against people like Henry Rono [a Kenyan from Washington State] in college gave him an opportunity to run against the best. Now, he's the world cross country champion. Maybe it wouldn't be that way if he'd just run against Americans all the time."[64]

Increasing contacts between the First and Third Worlds will bring new challenges and complications. Coping with a borderless world will require people to pack new strategies in their intellectual and emotional baggage. Like the souvenirs visitors bring home, cultural encounters may offer a mixed bag of surprises, disappointments, and delights.

If This Is to Be a Revolution

When the French Revolution burst forth, the word *revolution* was used to describe circular motion such as the stars make; it had yet to acquire its modern political meaning: to turn out the old order for something entirely new. "The French did not have much of a political vocabulary before 1789," one historian has noted, "because politics took place at Versailles, in the remote world of the king's court."[1] In the heady days of *liberté, égalité et fraternité*, which nurtured modern ideas of freedom and nationalism and spawned the guillotine and the word *vandalism*, the French experimented with everything. The revolutionary calendar, which designated the year the monarchy fell as Year One, lasted only until 1805. The metric system, decreed in 1795, spread worldwide.

Global interdependence is often described as revolutionary. Certainly it operates in the same exhilarating, harsh, and confusing way, complete with missteps and dumb luck. But the more important parallel with the French Revolution is that the real meaning of interdependence and the precise direction in which it is heading are unclear. As the foregoing chapters show, we do not know how to calculate the rough dimensions of the change—to measure trade in services or to tally the number of species lost annually or to gauge the extent to which foreign influences reshape other cultures. We do not know how to manage these connections. We know so little that in time we may find that the term *interdependence* is not even the best one—though the idea of revolution is likely to remain.[2]

This book has presented three profiles of interdependence—economic, environmental, and cultural. It has shown how complex these connections can be. These final pages do not promise the answers to the problems raised in the chapters. They do, however, try to highlight common, overarching trends that are likely to endure; and they suggest mechanisms for American problem solving.

What Next?

Where will the future take us? How can we discriminate those factors with long-term salience from those destined to wander into historical cul-de-sacs? Often the trends are as murky for us as they were for the French at the height of the revolution.

What of the future role of raw materials, for instance? New products like fiberglass cables and computer chips do not require raw materials to the extent that traditional products do. "The raw materials in a semiconductor microchip account for 1 to 3 percent of total production cost; in an automobile their share is 40 percent. . . . Fifty to 100 pounds of fiberglass cable transmit as many telephone messages as does one ton of copper wire," says Peter F. Drucker.[3] The consequences could be catastrophic for developing countries, one-fifth of whom depend on one or two raw materials for over half of their export earnings. Yet raw material imports during the past years have been up, not down. What's more, new "raw materials" may become marketable. Perhaps countries like Costa Rica will find ways to treat its genetic wealth like a commodity.

To what extent will business continue to go abroad? Automation could make low-wage rates in developing countries less attractive and could prompt companies to bring manufacturing plants back to the United States, as discussed in chapter 1. On the other hand, to what extent will developing countries like India design robotics? To what extent will workers around the world join together to demand equitable distribution of work? And what about the other nonwage-related reasons that business goes abroad? Businesses see many developing countries as promising new markets. They set up factories overseas so they can better gauge and satisfy local tastes and so they can sidestep trade barriers.[4]

The list of such questions can go on and on, with experts differing violently about precisely how events will coalesce. Still, amid the welter of uncertainties, some factors stand out as clear trends.

Permeability. National borders have lost—and will continue to lose—meaning as barriers. This is not to say that black lines will disappear from maps or that national governments cannot—or should not—exert control over their frontiers. It *is* to say that nations will find it progressively more difficult to do so.

Concern over terrorism, among other things, has prompted more nations to require visas for entry. World Bank employees who work in developing countries applied for more than three times as many visas in 1988 as in 1985. But visas and other traditional border mechanisms are from another age; they have limited utility. The U.S. Congress passed a tougher law in 1986, designed to keep out illegal immigrants. But enforcement has been difficult, and some experts believe that border crossings from Mexico remain at old levels.[5]

What border patrol can keep Costa Rica's environmental problems away from the United States? Kenya's government tries to regulate foreign influences, but it cannot stop them. Saztec's data entry operation is just one example of how information flows across borders without passing through traditional customhouses. The Philippine government prohibits foreigners from owning newspapers, but Filipinos lament that their newspapers are filled with ads placed by foreign advertising agencies such as J. Walter Thompson.

As borders become more porous, with businesses coming and going easily, national loyalties become impossible to assess. Which company do you help, laments one American diplomat charged with promoting U.S. companies overseas, "when Airbus, owned by a consortium of European governments and using U.S.-made Pratt & Whitney engines, is competing against Boeing using Rolls Royce engines?"

It may be, as some have speculated, that the concept of the nation-state is becoming anachronistic. "The nation-state is becoming too small for the big problems of life, and too big for the small problems of life," Daniel Bell has observed.[6] Whether or not this is true, national governments can no more easily block their borders than a person can hold back a stream of water with his hands.

Pluralism. More countries play a global role; more groups within nations play global roles.

Gov. Ray Mabus of Mississippi observed at an April 1989 governors' trade conference that states have assumed a larger part in foreign policy: "In order for us to prosper, it is almost necessary for us to look at ourselves as nation-states." On the business side, not just giant companies have multinational interests. The trend has filtered down to companies smaller than even the modestly sized Saztec. Sometimes companies just use overseas labor or materials; sometimes they only sell their products abroad. Either way, they have become global actors.

Third World countries and their citizens face more constraints than industrialized countries. Even so, interdependence has given relatively weak actors relatively greater power and significance. A group of terrorists not only can capture world attention but also can influence political decisions by governments. The weakness of a nation is more likely to become a setback for everyone. If a country's environment deteriorates, for instance, the loss can be global. If a developing country, out of desperation, seeks to attract foreign investment by eschewing pollution controls on manufacturing, it can not only damage commonly used resources such as air and water but also set in motion a competitive struggle that compels other countries to neglect their environment—a kind of self-destructive leveling process.[7]

First World–Second World–Third World classifications, still an important part of political rhetoric, are becoming obsolete. The Eastern bloc countries—part of the Second World—have begun to act more independently as the Soviet Union has loosened its grip. As acknowledged at the beginning of this book, the Third World is anything but homogenous; some developing nations are progressing much faster than others. The Paris-based Organization for Economic Cooperation and Development, made up of the most powerful industrialized nations, has not formally admitted fast-growing Singapore, Taiwan, Hong Kong, South Korea, Malaysia, and Thailand into its ranks. But it has begun to explore ways to involve them in OECD dialogues on trade and investment.[8]

As part of pluralism, new affiliations will coalesce around special interests. Western Europe's plans for a more unified market in 1992 have stirred African, Pacific Rim, and Latin nations to contemplate the creation of their own economic alliances. "Either we change with the times or the clock of history will forever be set back," declared Carlos Menem of Argentina at an October 1989 meeting of Latin heads of state. Australia, Canada, Brazil, Argentina, Hungary, Thailand, and other smaller food-exporting nations have already formed the Cairns Group to enhance their strength in food trade negotiations with the United States and the European Community. Dr. Russell Mittermeier of the World Wildlife Fund has suggested the creation of a new grouping of nations along the lines of the G7, or Group of Seven, made up of the seven countries with the world's largest economies. This new group, which he labels the M7, would consist of Brazil, Colombia, Mexico, Zaire, Madagascar, Indonesia, and Australia, seven "megadiversity" nations that together account for more than one-half the world's total estimated genetic resources. Although such a group may not take shape soon, Brazil joined with seven other South American countries in 1989 to form the Amazon Pact, whose purpose is to resist "foreign meddling in rain forest preservation." As these examples suggest, countries will find themselves allies on one set of issues and opponents on others.[9]

Increased vulnerability and tension. With borders more permeable and the number of actors proliferating, nations are bound to feel increasingly under siege and defenseless. More than ever, the world will be prone to frustration and misunderstanding. "Interdependence is not the equivalent of peace and justice," a task force on citizen education wisely concluded more than a decade ago. "In fact, it may lead to peace and justice no more than nuclear deterrence has led to disarmament."[10] Studies show that some of the bloodiest wars in the last 150 years have erupted between nations with strong trading ties (e.g., Japan and the United States in 1941) and that since 1945 there have been more civil wars than interstate wars.[11]

The more countries come together, the more differences they must resolve. In a possible foretaste of the future, European unification has forced the 12 countries involved to agree on permissible levels of lawnmower noise and safety standards for baby rattles. But agreement has not been possible for the configuration of electrical plugs; the cost of standardization is too high. Something as simple as a consumer complaint becomes difficult when many countries are involved, as a young American learned when he found a bug in a Coke he purchased in Japan. Coca-Cola's Atlanta headquarters told him to contact the Japanese office; and the Japanese, he discovered, did not have a tradition of responding well to consumer complaints.[12]

Concern about North-South conflict has obscured the increase in South-South tensions. Developing countries' trade with each other increased by more than 50 percent between 1970 and 1986. Imbalances in that trade can cause the same kind of quarrels that have dominated U.S.-Japanese relations in recent years.[13] As it is, developing countries fiercely compete with each other. To entice foreign investors, they offer special tax breaks. Costa Rica is effectively competing for international funds to maintain its environment. The more funds it gets, the less will be available for other nations with valuable genetic resources. The Kenyans worry that once they have a good idea for a handicraft, another country quickly copies it.

Despite all the concern about superpowers racing to acquire arms, the greater danger lies in developing countries acquiring nuclear arsenals but not necessarily the fail-safe mechanisms to guard against mistakes. Obvious fault lines run between countries like Pakistan and India—traditional rivals that are developing nuclear technology.

The United States cannot escape these three trends. Its borders will be more permeable. It, too, will confront more actors, inside and outside the country. It will feel more vulnerable. Americans are entangled in the paradox of interdependence: they must pay more attention to their foreign relations but they have less ability to determine outcomes.

The paradox lies at the foundation of an intense debate over the future of American power and strength. On one side are those who note, as Yale University historian Paul Kennedy has, the "imperial overstretch": "that is to say, decision-makers in Washington must face the awkward and enduring fact that the sum total of U.S. global interests and obligations is nowadays far larger than the country's power to defend them all simultaneously." On the other side are people like former secretary of state George P. Shultz, who decries "the declinists" as "false prophets" and maintains, "Our democracy holds the potential for resilience and rejuvenation in the face of any challenge."[14]

The United States does have advantages that suit it well in coping with interdependence and remaining a world leader. At the same time that its traditions of self-sufficiency are a liability, its relatively open society is a major asset. In a world where trade is growing in importance daily, the United States in recent years has been a leading proponent of free trade. In a world where people and ideas move easily, the United States has a long tradition of pluralism. It has assimilated foreigners for decades. No country gives more freedom to its press.

Economically, the nation has a strong technological base and is producing new jobs faster than Western Europe. The dollar lost some standing after 1971 when the Nixon administration dropped the government's pledge to back it internationally with gold. Still, if the dollar now fluctuates with other currencies, it remains the chief world currency and accounts for about three-fourths of all international banking transactions.[15]

The English language, the language of the United States, is the dominant world language. In 1972, Lester Brown reported that 44 countries considered English an official language. In the mid-1980s, according to *A Geolinguistic Handbook*, that number increased to 57 countries. Of the 180 delegates, observers, and heads of agencies that receive documents at the United Nations, 117 list English as their language of preference. French, the second most popular language, is listed 39 times.[16]

Americans may be prepared to embrace a new, broader view of their relations with the world. According to a recent survey, 62 percent of the public consider the country's economic power more important than its military power in determining its influence; only 22 percent think military power is more important. "America may be on the verge of a landmark debate challenging historic definitions of national security," the pollsters conclude.[17]

Still, there are reasons to worry that the United States may turn inward. "People don't feel comfortable with large units, with globalism, or even with national society," public opinion analyst Daniel Yankelovich has commented.[18] If Paul Kennedy and George Shultz disagree about the U.S. decline, they concur that looking inward will only accentuate Americans' weakness. "Still-powerful 'escapist' urges in the American social culture," Kennedy has commented, "may be understandable in terms of the nation's 'frontier' past but [are] a hindrance in coming to terms with today's more complex, integrated world and with *other* cultures and ideologies."[19]

Thus, in one sense, the biggest question of all is what the United States should do to marshal its strengths?

What the United States Can Do

Harold H. Saunders and Michael Shuman are two people with revolutionary ideas for coping with interdependence.

Saunders is hardly the kind of person one thinks of as a revolutionary. He is a quiet, retired foreign policy bureaucrat who started his government career after earning a doctorate in American Civilization at Yale. He worked on the National Security Council (NSC) and in the State Department, ending his career as assistant secretary of state for Near Eastern and South Asian affairs. He is now a visiting fellow at the Brookings Institution.

The idea Saunders uses to capture the new kind of diplomacy needed in an interdependent world is hardly one that would inflame people, put them in the streets, or topple governments. Nor is that what Saunders wants. Instead of single, sweeping, dramatic solutions, he wants a process that will permit steady progress on a wide range of problems. His word for dealing with interdependence is *relationship*.[20]

Saunders sees a world in which ubiquitous foreign connections create a never-ending stream of issues that must be managed. It no longer pays to bring all one's power to bear on one problem and solve it. Although a government might succeed, power politics, with its traditional emphasis on force, can create animosity and obstruct dialogue on the other issues that flow relentlessly. Governments, Saunders believes, must develop long-term relationships that permit "continuous interaction."

Crucial to this approach is thinking of relationships in terms of the full range of U.S. interests, the other country's interests and the motivations behind them, and the ways in which both sets of interests intersect. Negotiation, Saunders says, "depends more on political leaders working to change the political environment than on the skills of negotiating teams in finding technical solutions." The approach is less like chess, with a winner and a loser, than like a teeter-totter, on which both sides try to keep the relationship in play. Less crisis oriented than traditional approaches, it allows people to think in terms of "we," which brings a higher level of maturity to the relationship. "Peace," Saunders says, "is never made today. It is always in the making."

Michael Shuman is another kind of revolutionary. He is young enough to be Saunders's son and has no experience inside government. He is brash, among other things suggesting that states enact their own state neutrality acts, "which would put the Oliver Norths of the world out of business, once and for all." After graduating with a law degree from Stanford University, he and two friends founded the Center for Innovative Diplomacy, of which Shuman is currently president. Among its initial projects, the center organized conferences for peace and produced *Having International Affairs Your Way: A Five-Step Briefing Manual for Citizen Diplomats.*[21]

Whereas many traditional policymakers decry citizen activities as muddling U.S. foreign policy, Shuman thinks local activism is essential. Citizen diplomacy, he says, gives expression to views that are excluded by elite policymakers. Conducted in the open, it avoids the problem of secret decision making, which has led to some of the greatest foreign policy blunders in the past. Citizen diplomacy is efficient because local action is necessary to deal with such problems as global competitiveness. Finally, he says, citizen activists are less likely to provoke wars. Localities do not have military power as one of their resources. They must use persuasion. "Local people are experts in nonviolent conflict resolution," Shuman says.

The federal government, he continues, should be a traffic cop, monitoring what citizens do but not getting in their way. The one exception is its responsibility to maintain the military; and in that case, the national government should not be able to deploy troops without local sanction.

Shuman has a five-year goal: the creation of offices for international activities in 100 cities. These cities would play a major role in foreign policy formulation on such diverse issues as Third World economic development and human rights. The mechanisms would include making agreements with other countries, lobbying the federal government, and creating local international education programs. Shuman's 50- to 100-year goal is grander still: a United Nations of cities that would make international law.

Saunders and Shuman are two examples, among many, of Americans looking for ways of managing interdependence. Shuman's organization is still a place of dreams. Saunders's ideas also have yet to be embraced by a foreign policy apparatus nurtured on "realist" theories of power and by a public that wants swift solutions no matter how complicated the problems. But if their specific approaches prove to be false starts, many ideas they advocate seem indispensable. Not the least of these, in the words of Saunders, is that "we have to start with the premise that we will do business differently."

Doing business differently does not mean abandoning self-interest. The underlying premise of this book is that the United States and every other nation has as its foremost obligation to advance its own interests. Almost two decades ago, economist

Richard Cooper put the proposition this way with regard to trade: "How to keep the manifold benefits of extensive international economic intercourse free of crippling restrictions while at the same time preserving a maximum degree of freedom for each nation to pursue its legitimate economic objectives."[22] The same task applies to all aspects of interdependence: how to maximize the good and minimize the bad.

The difference suggested herein is that the United States cannot pursue its self-interest through traditional approaches. New approaches are required. These approaches must take into account that the list of U.S. foreign interests is growing faster than ever before. They must look beyond short-term gains and seek long-term security. And they must recognize that nations cannot insulate themselves from the rest of the world but must learn how others see the world.

The role of multilateralism. The United States was the prime mover in the establishment of multilateral institutions after World War II. "We have come to recognize that the wisest and most effective way to protect our national interests is through international cooperation," U.S. Treasury Secretary Hans Morgenthau said at the 1944 Bretton Woods Conference that led to creation of the International Monetary Fund and the World Bank. "This is to say, through united effort for the attainment of common goals. This has been the great lesson of contemporary life, that the peoples of the earth are inseparably linked to one another by a deep, underlying community of purpose."[23]

Yet the United States has only reluctantly embraced multilateralism. After centuries of hearing George Washington's injunctions against entangling alliances, the public has been deeply distrustful of the concept of global partnership. President Woodrow Wilson failed in his campaign to have the United States join the League of Nations, and the country was one of most strongly protectionist nations during the depression of the 1930s. Ronald Reagan's administration came to office with little enthusiasm for multilateral institutions, including the development banks Morgenthau helped create. When President Reagan left office, U.S. dues were fully paid to only 10 of the 46 international bodies in which it participates.

This is the wrong time for such an attitude. The United States does not have the power to determine unilaterally the rules governing the mounting number of global transactions in commerce, culture, and environment. It must find a new style of diplomacy with a long-term perspective, one that is based on persuasion and global consensus building. Two economists have put the proposition this way: "If world traders are to be analogous to Londoners trading with Yorkshiremen, then we need something analogous to English law courts and police to define property rights and enforce contracts. We have no such world authority and have failed repeatedly at even modest attempts to institute one."[24]

Although much needs to be done to create effective multilateral approaches, world institutions are already making valuable contributions. In 1988, the United Nations played lead roles in peace-keeping activities in the Middle East, Afghanistan, and South Africa. The International Atomic Energy Agency ensures that commercial nuclear material is not diverted for military purposes; the UN Environmental Programme has led efforts to reach agreements on protecting the earth's atmosphere; and the World Health Organization is justly credited with eradicating smallpox and controlling other diseases.[25]

The benefits of multilateral approaches can be subtle. Multilateral decision making brings the weight of more countries to bear on a problem. It shields individual countries from opprobrium if the measures must be harsh. Even when international meetings seem to produce more talk than action, they provide a setting for quiet diplomacy, a place in which people can learn each other's point of view. In this way, the multilateral banks have promoted not only development but also resolution of political differences. The World Bank played the lead role in resolving the Indo-Pakistani dispute over the development and division of the Indus River Basin, which culminated in a 1960 treaty. The greatest legacy of the Marshall Plan to help Europe at the end of World War II, according to many of the policymakers involved, was not the economic recovery, which was inevitable, but the pattern of cooperation it nurtured among European nations that participated. From the beginning, those nations were expected to decide collectively how the program should work.

Multilateralism should not be confined to working through established international bodies like the UN. In its broadest sense, multilateralism means finding cooperative strategies for solving global problems. Some organizations may only be needed for a short time. Some may exist without a formal office building or secretariat.

To establish the necessary relationships, the United States will have to bow to others' wishes at times. This does not mean that Americans should sacrifice their interests or that the country must submit its decisions to an international referendum. Saunders uses the concept of common security to describe the new challenge. U.S. security depends on other countries feeling secure.

The importance of thinking internationally. Nations have different perspectives on any international issue (see box). To anticipate what other nations will do and what their interests are, and to know what

Seeing Them, Seeing Us

by John Maxwell Hamilton

"Being poor is hard work," observes Alejandro Roces, a flamboyant Filipino newspaperman with a knack for articulating how Americans misunderstand the Philippines.

Americans mistakenly equate poverty with laziness, says Roces, who attended the University of Arizona after World War II and is now president of the *Manila Times*. But poor Filipinos, often just children, spend hours in the hot sun weaving in and out among the vehicles waiting at stoplights in Manila. The youngsters hawk cigarettes or simply beg. The money they earn puts food on their families' tables.

Roces's insight points to a larger truth. The world is more closely knit, but that only means it is all the more imperative to understand how people can see the same thing in a different way. As close as the United States and the Philippines have been, the examples of different national perspectives span every aspect of their relations:

- In 1987 the Philippines ranked 26th among U.S. trading partners. The United States ranked 1st among the Philippines' trading partners. Not surprisingly, Filipinos pay more attention to the U.S. economy than the other way around.

- When Americans think about the origin of Acquired Immune Deficiency Syndrome (AIDS), they think of Africa. Some of the earliest evidence of the disease has been found in African blood samples. But when Filipinos think about the origin of AIDS, they think of the United States. American military personnel and tourists are thought to have brought the disease to their islands.

- To many Americans, U.S. military bases in the Philippines stand for security, an outpost for the American fleet. To many Filipinos, the bases they have to offer, Americans must learn to understand other countries' points of view. Unfortunately, the United States is not doing a good job of preparing its citizens for this task.

Just as basic skills such as reading and writing have slipped (thus making the United States less competitive globally), so have Americans taken a complacent attitude toward international basics. Typical high school seniors have acquired most of their international education by the time they are 14, educator Richard Wood has noted. Time and again surveys show that U.S. students have more

---

stand for insecurity. Military installations are likely targets for American enemies. An accident on a nuclear-powered ship could injure Filipinos.

- Americans argue that the bases and military personnel stationed in the Philippines pump money into the local economy. But, Roces points out, communities near the bases are full of brothels and drug dealing. Can such social disruptions, he asks, be considered "an economic success"?

- The United States thinks of itself as a Philippine benefactor. President William McKinley described the U.S. role there as one of "benevolent assimilation." Filipinos think of themselves as an American colony.

When the United States wrested control of the Philippine islands from the Spanish, it instituted a farsighted education system that brought literacy to vast numbers of Filipinos. But schools taught American history over Philippine history, and students sang the U.S. national anthem before class, not their own.

Many Filipinos have come to see this approach as more pernicious than if the United States had engaged in outright oppression. Says journalist Adlai Amor, "The United States made the Philippines an experiment in colonization and you succeeded quite well."

Examples of such misunderstandings occur among virtually all countries. On the subject of AIDS, one survey found that black Africans think white men are the chief propagators of the disease. While Texans "Remember the Alamo," Mexicans remember their heroes who died defending Mexico City from U.S. Gen. Winfield Scott.

Despite their different perspectives, Americans typically find Filipinos outgoing and friendly. As Roces says, reality is more complex than black and white feelings. A common Filipino lament, for instance, is that they want their own culture but prefer consumer goods from the United States.

These complicated perceptions tell Americans something about Filipinos and also something about themselves.

"You Americans are really lazy," a Filipino confided to me over a beer one afternoon. "You only work five days a week. We will work seven days a week if we have a chance."

trouble today than in the past finding their way around world maps. A survey of Indiana University freshmen revealed that only one-quarter knew that citizens of England speak English.[26] In contrast, a Kenyan mother of eight told Nancy Morrison that schoolchildren in her country learn "where the Great Lakes are, where Niagara Falls is. We can find New York and Seattle on a map. By the time you are 14 or 15, you know these things."

Although Americans have an advantage because their language is spoken widely, this is no excuse for eschewing the language skills necessary to penetrate other societies. Indeed, *not* developing those skills puts the United States at a distinct *dis*advantage. Yet only one out of six elementary schools offers foreign language courses; only one student in five leaves high school with more than two years of language study. According to a 1986 Southern Governors' Association report, the U.S. foreign service is the only one in the world a person can enter without fluency in a foreign language.[27]

Americans have been highly innovative, but they have not been good "fast followers," learning to adapt other people's ideas and techniques. Sixty-one percent of U.S. business schools do not offer any international courses. The National Science Foundation recently reported that inadequate language training and inadequate study-abroad programs for faculty, students, and professionals have prevented American engineers from learning about and using technological advances made by other countries.[28]

Schools should study units on world culture and history, but as the National Governors' Association recommended in 1989, international perspectives should also be incorporated into existing courses. The governors also suggested that the states sponsor programs for businesses on international trade, reinforcing the important idea that everyone needs to know about the world. The Commission on National Challenges in Higher Education made a similar point in January 1988, arguing that international education must also reach into "professional schools, particularly those concerned with law, public policy and business."[29] Because interdependence cuts across virtually every aspect of life, art, biology, journalism, medicine, engineering, information services, hotel management, and virtually every other schoolroom subject has an international perspective.

The U.S. government must provide more resources for effective international education. Although the federal deficit requires budget cuts, not every sector of government spending should suffer. One cause of the budget deficit is the inability of Americans to compete internationally. It makes sense, then, for the government to spend in ways that will produce more competitive citizens.

The solution to good formal education does not rest solely at the federal level. Effective international education must begin in communities. School boards in every city and county must insist that their schools truly educate young people. News media must do a better job of showing that foreign events have an impact on the community—and that better elementary and secondary education is essential.

Behind educational shortcomings is both Americans' traditional go-it-alone mentality and their fears that their culture will be diluted by outside influences, the sentiment captured in the previous chapter on Kenya. These feelings are ironic for the United States, which, more than most countries, is culturally derivative. American culture is an amalgam of other cultures—and becoming more so. By not explaining these influences to young people, we cannot be said to have educated them as to what is unique about the United States.

The need to rethink government structure. U.S. government structures took shape at a time when foreign affairs were foreign, not woven throughout the fabric of American domestic life. As a result of these outmoded structures, it has become increasingly difficult to coordinate national trade policy. The difficulties surfaced vividly during tough U.S.-European Community negotiations on beef exports in 1989, when the Texas commissioner of agriculture, Jim Hightower, tried to make a separate deal with the Europeans. Nor is the wide range of environmental ties abroad well coordinated. "The state of play of the U.S. government's activities relating to biological diversity, pesticide use, and global warming illustrates the fragmented lines of authority, oversight, and coordination on international environmental matters," Maurice Williams of the Overseas Development Council has written. "In addition, except where U.S. domestic interests are directly involved, many line domestic agencies have neither the budget nor the mandate to address these concerns."[30]

The chapters in this book have pointed to areas in which the U.S. government must devote more attention—for instance, tropical biological research. But the big first step is for the government to create mechanisms for assessing international connections and for managing them.

On the assessment side, some work has already been done. President Lyndon Johnson called a White House Conference on International Cooperation in 1965. Its 5,000 representatives, drawn from virtually every corner of American society and organized in committees, made numerous recommendations for strengthening UN peace-keeping activities, establishing a world weather watch, and harmonizing aviation regulations with those of other countries.[31]

Some of those recommendations have been acted on, but the effort came at a time when the United States was distracted by the war in Vietnam. Today, many of the issues of interdependence—for instance, illegal immigration, loss of trade competitiveness, global spread of diseases (e.g., AIDS)—are foremost in the public mind. The need currently is to get a clear picture of all the connections that are taking shape, to see them as multidimensionally as possible.

Any number of approaches could be taken to develop such a picture. One possibility is for the president to direct every government department and agency to carry out an inventory of its foreign connections. No bureau of government would be exempt. This interdependence assessment would look especially at the ways in which foreign decisions affect the business of that particular agency and of the American constituency it represents. The emphasis would not be on statistics, but on analysis of the trends and their implications.

For obvious reasons, the State Department would not list its foreign policy agenda; rather, it would look at the ways in which its work meshes and clashes with that of states and localities. To help achieve this kind of understanding, the State Department might consider giving a higher priority to an existing program—the detailing of senior diplomats to governors as advisers for a year or two. The diplomats acquire a better picture of local foreign affairs and, in the process, add critical expertise to state staffs that are still learning how to deal effectively with other countries.

An interdependence assessment is a potentially powerful technique for refashioning American views of foreign affairs. But such an effort will amount to little without developing management structures to ensure that policymakers routinely factor interdependence into their thinking. One of the most intellectually adventurous ideas along these lines was the Aspen Institute's National Commission on Coping with Interdependence, convened in the mid-1970s. "Foreign policy is not a subject matter for government decision-making," it concluded; "it is rather an aspect of every important government decision." To erase the line between domestic and foreign affairs, the commission suggested that the domestic council that then existed in the White House should become the Council on Interdependence.[32]

It may be too soon for such a council. But it is not too early to expand the mandate of the NSC. At a minimum, a new position should be created for an NSC deputy assistant to the president for interdependence, equal to the current deputy but with different duties. The new deputy and his small staff could coordinate within the NSC and widely throughout the federal government. This NSC office would monitor local foreign policy activities and, on occasion, coordinate policy issues with officials whose actions could support or undercut national policy.[33] Properly managed, this interdependence mechanism could help ensure the plotting of future trends and discussion of the steps to deal with them.

In a related change, Congress should create a joint committee on interdependence. This committee would have no legislative authority. Like the joint economic committee, it would encourage the Senate and the House of Representatives to explore issues in ways that cross normal committee jurisdictional lines. The Foreign Affairs committees in the House and Senate could also create subcommittees to monitor and facilitate local foreign policy-making—an approach that could make assignments on those committees more appealing to members of Congress.

If This Is to Be a Revolution . . .

For every complex problem there is always a simple solution, H. L. Mencken once observed, and it is always wrong. The recommendations above are only first steps. The public and its leaders must do much more to size up and manage their way through the interdependence revolution, which is full of uncertainties and potential missteps. Clearly, this is not an easy task for any country, but least of all for the United States.

The United States never had a revolution like the French did, in which an entire system was overturned. In the so-called revolutionary war, Americans merely sought independence from a foreign power whose essential values they accepted. Yet the United States has always extolled its ability to adapt, to be flexible, to improvise. It has congratulated itself on not fearing sweeping change.

Interdependence confronts Americans with an opportunity to test these values. Americans can watch themselves be overtaken by events—or they can respond creatively and achieve a real global leadership role. The choice was phrased by German chancellor Otto von Bismarck in a different age: "If this is to be a revolution, we should rather make it than suffer it."

NOTES

Introduction

1. Sen. John Warner, *Congressional Record*, 101st Cong., 2d sess., February 22, 1989.
2. C. Northcote Parkinson, *Parkinson: The Law, Complete* (New York: Ballantine, 1988), p. 17.
3. Richard Halloran, "Panel Finds Less Support for U.S. Troops Abroad," *New York Times*, August 7, 1988.
4. Commission on Integrated Long-Term Strategy, *Discriminate Deterrence* (Washington, D.C.: U.S.GPO, 1988), p. 19.
5. Felix Rohatyn, "Restoring American Independence," *New York Review of Books*, February 18, 1988, p. 8.
6. For historical background, see Stan Steiner, *Fusang: The Chinese Who Built America* (New York: Harper and Row, 1979), pp. 46–47, 56; A. Gary Shilling, Op-Ed, *Wall Street Journal*, March 10, 1975; Anthony Sampson, *The Money Lenders: Bankers in a Dangerous World* (Philadelphia, Pa.: Coronet, 1981), pp. 54–55; Richard N. Gardner, ed., *Blueprint for Peace: Being the Proposals of Prominent Americans to the White House Conference on International Cooperation* (New York: McGraw-Hill, 1966), p. 325; Alfred W. Crosby, *Ecological Imperialism: The Biological Expansion of Europe, 900–1900* (Cambridge, England: Cambridge University Press, 1986), p. 5; *Trends and Characteristics of International Migration Since 1950* (New York: United Nations, 1979), pp. 1–4; Fernand Braudel, *The Structures of Everyday Life: Civilization and Capitalism 15th–18th Century* (New York: Harper and Row, 1979), pp. 37–38, 43; Gabriel G. Nahas, "The Decline of Drugged Nations," *Wall Street Journal*, July 11, 1988; Paul Kennedy, *The Rise and Fall of the Great Powers: Economic Change and Military Conflict from 1500 to 2000* (New York: Random House, 1987), p. 81.
7. Keynes quoted by Art Pine, "Interdependence: It's Not Entirely a Plus," *Wall Street Journal*, June 27, 1983.
8. Simon S. Kuznets, *Modern Economic Growth: Rate, Structure, and Spread* (New Haven, Conn.: Yale University Press, 1966), pp. 312–313; Peter J. Katzenstein, "International Interdependence: Some Long-Term Trends and Recent Changes," *International Organization* 29 (Autumn 1975): p. 1032.
9. Geoffrey Barraclough, *An Introduction to Contemporary History* (New York: Penguin, 1967), p. 50.
10. Paul Scott Mowrer, *Our Foreign Affairs: A Study in National Interest and the New Diplomacy* (New York: Dutton, 1924), pp. 72, 308–309.
11. Erich Marcks quoted in Barraclough, *Contemporary History*, p. 53.
12. Braudel, *Structures of Everyday Life*, p. 427; Gary M. Walton and Ross M. Robertson, *History of the American Economy* (New York: Harcourt, Brace, 1955), p. 61.
13. Richard McKenzie, "The Global Economy and Government Power," Formal Publication Number 90 (Center for the Study of American Business,

Washington University, St. Louis, March 1989), pp. 12–13; "Designing a Yardstick for Computer Speed," *Wall Street Journal*, March 13, 1989; John Burgess, "The Battle for Long-Distance Dollars," *Washington Post*, December 27, 1988.

14. Richard W. Stevenson, "Hollywood Takes to the Global Stage," *New York Times*, April 16, 1989.

15. Joan R. Dassin, "The Brazilian Press and the Politics of *Abertura*," *Journal of Interamerican Studies and World Affairs* 26, 3 (August 1984), pp. 387, 405; Clyde H. Farnsworth, "Developing Nations Benefit as Service Exports Grow," *New York Times*, September 4, 1989.

16. Richard N. Cooper, "Economic Interdependence and Foreign Policy in the Seventies," *World Politics* 24 (January 1972): p. 162; Riad Tabbarah, "Prospects of International Migration," *International Social Science Journal* (1985): p. 430.

17. Demetrios G. Papademetriou, "International Migration in a Changing World," *International Social Science Journal* 36, 3 (1984): pp. 417–418.

18. Benjamin J. Cohen, *In Whose Interest? International Banking and American Foreign Policy* (New Haven, Conn.: Yale University Press, 1986), p. 29.

19. C. Michael Aho and Marc Levinson, *After Reagan: Confronting the Changed World Economy* (New York: Council on Foreign Relations, 1988), pp. 6, 141; John M. Hennessy, "The World Catches Takeover Fever," *New York Times*, May 21, 1989.

20. James P. Sterba, "The Manhole Cover Is a Thing of Beauty to Howrah, India," *Wall Street Journal*, November 29, 1984; *Kiplinger Washington Letter*, December 30, 1988.

21. Michael Stewart, *The Age of Interdependence: Economic Policy in a Shrinking World* (Cambridge: Massachusetts Institute of Technology, 1984), p. 20.

22. "The Missile Trade Launch Mode," *U.S. News & World Report*, July 25, 1988, pp. 32–38; Richard M. Weintraub, "India Tests Mid-Range 'Agri' Missile," *Washington Post*, May 23, 1989.

23. Eric Margolis, "Asia Worries About Gandhi's Military Complex," *Wall Street Journal*, May 2, 1988.

24. Charles William Maynes, "America's Third World Hang-Ups," *Foreign Policy* 71 (Summer 1988): p. 117.

25. Michael H. Shuman, "Dateline Main Street: Local Foreign Policies," *Foreign Policy* 65 (Winter 1986–87): p. 154.

26. Louis Uchitelle, "U.S. Businesses Loosen Link to Mother Country," *New York Times*, May 21, 1989; Michel Crozier, "Structural Evolution in Industrialized Societies," in *From Marshall Plan to Global Interdependence: New Challenges for the Industrialized Nations*, ed. Lincoln Gordon (Paris: Organization for Economic Cooperation and Development, 1978), p. 38.

27. Report of the Bilateral Commission on the Future of United States–Mexican Relations, *The Challenge of Interdependence: Mexico and the United States* (Lanham, Md.: University Press of America, 1989), p. 30.

28. James Brooke, "Inside the East Bloc's African Outpost," *New York Times*, January 13, 1985.

29. Barraclough, *Contemporary History*, pp. 42, 50, 54.

30. Herbert Feis, *Europe the World's Banker*, quoted in Cohen, *In Whose Interest?* p. 18.

31. Kennedy, *Rise and Fall of the Great Powers*, pp. 149, 245, 327–328; Kuznets, *Modern Economic Growth*, pp. 312–313; Katzenstein, "International Interdependence," p. 1032; James Chace, "A New Grand Strategy," *Foreign Policy* 70 (Spring 1988): p. 12.

32. *Workforce 2000: Work and Workers for the Twenty-first Century* (Indianapolis, Ind.: Hudson Institute, 1987), p. 6; different statistics can be found in Kennedy, *Rise and Fall of the Great Powers*, p. 432.

33. C. Fred Bergsten, "The United States and the World Economy," *The Annals of the American Academy of Political and Social Science* 460 (March 1982): pp. 11–20.

34. James R. Donald, "World and U.S. Agricultural Outlook," U.S. Department of Agriculture (USDA), December 1, 1987, p. 11; Pat Choate and J. K. Linger, *The High-Flex Society: Shaping America's Economic Future* (New York: Alfred A. Knopf, 1986), p. 53.

35. David Wessel, "Buying Foreign; Despite Foreign Dollar," *Wall Street Journal*, February 9, 1988.

36. James J. MacKenzie, *Breathing Easier: Taking Action on Climate Change, Air Pollution, and Energy Insecurity*, World Resources Institute monograph (n.d.), pp. 14–15.

37. Bergsten, "The United States and the World Economy," pp. 11–20; Gabriel Kolko, *Confronting the Third World: United States Foreign Policy 1945–1980* (New York: Pantheon, 1988), p. 228.

38. Benjamin M. Friedman, "The Campaign's Hidden Issue," *New York Review of Books*, October 13, 1988, p. 26.

39. Kennedy, *Rise and Fall of the Great Powers*, p. 358.

40. Craig Forman, "Idyllic Switzerland Discovers Its Idyll Is Turning Prosaic," *Wall Street Journal*, July 25, 1989.

41. Anthony M. Solomon, "Restoring American Independence: An Exchange," letter to the editor, *New York Review of Books*, May 12, 1988.

42. Friedman, "The Campaign's Hidden Issue," p. 27.

43. William Celis III, "Protectionist Bills May Come Before Congress," *Wall Street Journal*, December 24, 1988.

44. William Schneider, "Conservatism, Not Interventionism: Trends in Foreign Policy Opinion, 1974–1982," in *Eagle Defiant: United States Foreign Policy in the 1980s*, ed. Kenneth A. Oye, Robert J. Lieber, and Donald Rothchild (Boston, Mass.: Little, Brown, 1983), p. 45. For a contrasting view on public opinion, see Daniel Yankelovich and Larry Kaagan, "Assertive America," *Foreign Affairs* 59 (1981): p. 709.

45. Thomas L. Hughes, "The Twilight of Internationalism," *Foreign Policy* 61 (Winter 1985–86): pp. 25–48.

46. Wlodzimierz Aniol, "Global Problems: An Ecological Paradigm," *Coexistence* 25 (1988): p. 213.

47. On the nature and definition of interdependence, see Mark J. Gasiorowski, "Economic Interdependence and International Conflict: Some Cross-National Evidence," *International Studies Quarterly* 30 (1986): pp. 23–38; Robert O. Keohane and Joseph S. Nye, Jr., *Power and Interdependence: World Politics in Transition* (Boston, Mass.: Little, Brown, 1977) pp. 8–9; Richard Rosecrance and Arthur Stein, "Interdependence: Myth or Reality?" *World Politics* 26 (October 1973): p. 2.

48. A path-breaking example is Richard N. Cooper, *The Economics of Interdependence: Economic Policy in the Atlantic Community* (New York: McGraw-Hill, 1968).

49. Robert O. Keohane and Joseph S. Nye, Jr., *"Power and Interdependence Revisited," International Organization* 41 (August 1987): pp. 725–726. See also R. J. Barry Jones, "The Definition and Identification of Interdependence," in *Interdependence on Trial: Studies in the Theory and Reality of Contemporary Interdependence,* ed. R. J. Jones and Peter Willetts (London: Francis Pinter, 1984).

50. John Mauro, "Readers Care," appendix, in John Maxwell Hamilton, *Main Street America and the Third World,* 2d ed. (Cabin John, Md.: Seven Locks Press, 1988).

Chapter 1

1. Tyler's prediction is a common one; for example, see "Information Technology: Unshackling European Companies," *International Management* 42, 2 (February 1987): p. 23. See also John Elkington and Jonathan Shopley, *The Shrinking Planet: U.S. Information Technology and Sustainable Development* (Washington, D.C.: World Resources Institute, 1988), p. 7.

2. Clement Bezold and Robert Olson, *The Information Millennium: Alternative Futures* (Washington, D.C.: Information Industry Association, 1986), p. 2-2.

3. Pat Oddy, "British Library Catalogue Conversion," British Library *Newsletter,* June 1987, pp. 4–6.

4. U.S. Department of Commerce, International Trade Administration Office of Service Industries, *A Competitive Assessment of the U.S. Data Processing Services Industry* (Washington, D.C.: U.S.GPO, 1984), p. 23.

5. Peter Dicken, *Global Shift: Industrial Change in a Turbulent World* (New York: Harper and Row, 1986), pp. 302–304.

6. *World Development Report 1987* (New York: Oxford University Press, 1987), p. 46.

7. U.S. Congress, Office of Technology Assessment (OTA), *International Competition in Services: Banking, Building, Software Know-how* (Washington, D.C.: GPO, 1987), pp. 91–92.

8. Christopher J. Chipello, "Losing Ground: Foreign Rivals Imperil U.S. Firms' Leadership in the Service Sector," *Wall Street Journal,* March 21, 1988.

9. William James Stover, *Information Technology in the Third World: Can I.T. Lead to Humane National Development?* (Boulder, Colo.: Westview Press, 1984), p. 67.

10. For background on the Philippine situation, see government papers: "Telecommunications Development Conference," New Delhi, February 22–26, 1988, and "National Telephone Development Plan," typewritten, n.d.; see also "Electronics and Telecommunications: 1987–1988," a booklet by the Philippine Electronics and Telecommunications Federation. General background on developing countries can be found in Robert J. Saunders, Jeremy J. Warford, and Bjorn Wellenius, *Telecommunications and Economic Development* (Baltimore, Md.: Johns Hopkins University Press, 1983), pp. 4–5.

11. Independent Commission for World-Wide Telecommunications Development (Maitland Commission), *Report—The Missing Link* (Geneva: International Telecommunications Union, 1985), p. 57.
12. For a discussion of Brazil, see United Nations Centre on Transnational Corporations, *Transborder Data Flows and Brazil* (New York: United Nations, 1983).
13. Elkington and Shopley, *The Shrinking Planet*, p. 29.
14. Philippine National Computer Center study, 1987, pp. 2–5.
15. Jonathan D. Aronson, "The Service Industries: Growth, Trade and Development Prospects," in John W. Sewell, Stuart K. Tucker et al., *Growth, Exports, and Jobs in a Changing World Economy*, Overseas Development Council (New Brunswick, N.J.: Transaction, 1988), p. 108.
16. Robert Schware, "Software Industry Development in the Third World: Policy Guidelines, Institutional Options, and Constraints," *World Development* 15 (1987): pp. 1255–1256.
17. Farnsworth, "Developing Nations Benefit."
18. J. Steven Landefeld, "International Trade in Services: Its Composition, Importance and Links to Merchandise Trade," *Business Economics* (April 1987): p. 26.
19. OTA, *International Competition in Services*, pp. 221–222.
20. OTA, *International Competition in Services*, p. 61.
21. Bruce Stokes, "Beaming Jobs Overseas," *National Journal*, July 27, 1985, pp. 1726–1731.
22. OTA, *International Competition in Services*, pp. 63–65, 341–342.
23. Peter Robinson, "From TDF to International Data Services," *Telecommunications Policy* (December 1987): p. 373.
24. Vin McLellan, "Computer Systems Under Siege," *New York Times*, January 31, 1988; John Burgess, "Race to Secure Computers Threatens Free Exchange of Data," *Washington Post*, March 4, 1989.
25. OTA, *Intellectual Property Rights in an Age of Electronics and Information* (Washington, D.C.: U.S. GPO, 1986), pp. 6–7.
26. Daniel Southerland, "Piracy of U.S. Software in China Is Big Problem, Commerce Officials Warn," *Washington Post*, January 14, 1989; Eduardo Lachica, "Trade Thievery: U.S. Companies Curb Pirating of Some Items But By No Means All," *Wall Street Journal*, March 16, 1989; *OTA, Intellectual Property Rights*, p. 228.
27. Evelyn Richards and John Burgess, "New U.S.-Soviet Computer Links Raising Questions About Security," *Washington Post*, February 10, 1989.
28. U.S. Congress, House Subcommittee on Government Information and Individual Rights, *International Information Flow: Forging a New Framework, H. Rept. 96-1535*, 96th Cong., December 11, 1980, p. 31.
29. Alejandro R. Roces, *Fiesta* (Philippines: Vera-Reyes, 1980), pp. 11 and 27.
30. David A. Ricks, *Big Business Blunders: Mistakes in Multinational Marketing* (Homewood, Ill.: Dow Jones-Irwin, 1983), pp. 76–77, 81.
31. Joseph N. Pelton, "International Telecommunications Competition in the Age of Telepower," *International Journal* 42 (Spring 1987): pp. 253–254; also 1987–1988 Intelsat annual report.
32. Karl P. Sauvant, *International Transactions in Services: The Politics of Transborder Data Flow* (Boulder, Colo.: Westview Press, 1986), p. 21.
33. For background on GATT negotiations, see Ronald K. Shelp, "Trade in Services," *Foreign Affairs* 65 (Winter 1986–87): pp. 64–84; Chakravarthi

Raghavan, "The U.S. Drive to Bring Services into GATT: A Rollback of the Third World," *Development and Peace* 7, 2 (Autumn 1986): pp. 22–29; various articles in Sewell, Tucker et al., *Growth, Exports, and Jobs*; J. Michael Finger and Andrzej Olechowski, ed., *The Uruguay Round* (Washington, D.C.: World Bank, 1987). On migration, Maria Alcestis Abrera-Mangahas, *Filipino Overseas Migration: Focus on 1975–1986* (Quezon City: Social Weather Stations, Inc., June 1987), p. 4; Stuart Auerbach, "GATT's Global Stakes: Issues Are Complex, Crucial in Montreal," *Washington Post*, December 4, 1988.

34. John Markoff, "American Express Goes High-Tech," *New York Times*, July 31, 1988.

35. OTA, *Automation of America's Offices, 1985–2000* (Washington, D.C.: U.S. GPO, OTA-CIT-287, December 1985), pp. 213–214.

36. Peter Drucker, "Low Wages No Longer Give Competitive Edge," editorial, *Wall Street Journal*, March 16, 1988.

37. Abrera-Mangahas, *Filipino Overseas Migration*, p. 8.

38. Norman Bodek, "A Letter to Members," *DEMA Newsletter*, March 1988, p. 6.

39. Bezold and Olson, "The Information Millennium," pp. 2–21.

Chapter 2

1. Jerry Payne, "Costa Rica Specializes in Own Kind of Happiness," *Indianapolis Star*, September 11, 1988.

2. Gerald O. Barney, *The Global 2000 Report to the President: Entering the Twenty-First Century*, vol. 2, *The Technical Report* (Washington, D.C.: U.S. GPO, 1980–81), pp. 328–331.

3. Edward C. Wolf, "Avoiding a Mass Extinction of Species," in *State of the World 1988*, by Lester R. Brown, William U. Chandler, Alan Durning et al. (New York: Norton, 1988), p. 108.

4. For good discussions of diversity issues in Costa Rica, see Rodrigo Gámez, "Threatened Habitats and Germplasm Preservation: A Central American Perspective" (unpublished, May 1988). Estimates of tropical countries' comparative advantage in genetic diversity can be found in numerous sources, including Catherine Caufield, *In the Rain Forest* (New York: Alfred A. Knopf, 1985), pp. 59–60.

5. Crosby, *Ecological Imperialism*, p. 75.

6. Steven C. Witt, *Biotechnology and Genetic Diversity* (San Francisco: Californian Agricultural Lands Project, 1985), p. 15. For another set of estimates on increases in food production, see Robert and Christine Prescott-Allen, *Genes from the Wild: Using Wild Genetic Resources for Food and Raw Materials* (London: International Institute for Environment and Development, 1983), p. 9.

7. Donald L. Plucknett, Nigel J. H. Smith, J. T. Williams, and N. Murthi Anishetty, *Gene Banks and the World's Food* (Princeton, N.J.: Princeton University Press, 1987), p. 111.

8. For an excellent study of genetic material for agriculture, see Plucknett et al., *Gene Banks*. On Iltis's work, see Arthur Fisher, "Preserving a Diverse Lineage," *Mosaic* 13, 3 (May/June 1982): pp. 46–52; David Tenenbaum,

"Seeking Teosinte," *Wisconsin Alumni* (May/June 1988): pp. 18–21. See also Richard Huttner, ed., *Amaranth: Modern Prospects for an Ancient Crop* (Washington, D.C.: National Academy Press, 1984); E. P. Cunningham, "The Significance of Biological Diversity in Livestock Production" (unpublished paper, Economic Development Institute, World Bank, May 17, 1988); Caufield, *In the Rain Forest*, pp. 228–229; OTA, *Technologies to Maintain Biological Diversity* (Washington, D.C.: U.S. GPO, 1987), p. 53; *Bioprocessing Technology* 8, 8 (August 1986): p. 3; Rural Advancement Fund International, "Biotechnology and Natural Sweeteners," *Development: Seeds of Change* 4 (1987): pp. 33–34.

9. World Commission on Environment and Development (hereafter the Brundtland Commission), *Our Common Future* (New York: Oxford University Press, 1987), p. 155. For discussions of how wild species are used as food and medicine and in industry, see Noel Grove, "Quietly Conserving Nature," *National Geographic* (December 1988): pp. 824–828; Margery L. Oldfield, "Tropical Deforestation and Genetic Resources Conservation," *Studies in Third World Development* 14 (December 1981): pp. 277–345; Edward C. Wolf, *On the Brink of Extinction: Conserving the Diversity of Life*, Worldwatch paper 78, June 1987; E. O. Wilson, ed., *Biodiversity* (Washington, D.C.: National Academy Press, 1988); Prescott-Allen, *Genes from the Wild*; Norman Myers, *A Wealth of Wild Species: Storehouse for Human Welfare* (Boulder, Colo.: Westview Press, 1983); Boyce Rensberger, "Scientists See Signs of Mass Extinction," *Washington Post*, September 29, 1986; "Just What the Witch-Doctor Ordered," *Economist*, April 2, 1988, pp. 75–76; Eugene Linden, "The Death of Birth," *Time*, January 2, 1988, pp. 32–34; Christine and Robert Prescott-Allen, *The First Resource: Wild Species in the North American Economy* (New Haven, Conn.: Yale University Press, 1986); Larry Tye, "As Stakes Rise, Plans Emerge for Preserving the Forests," *Boston Globe*, April 10, 1989; *Bioprocessing Technology* 8, 8 (August 1986): p. 5; William Booth, "Combing the Earth for Cures to Cancer, AIDS," *Science* 237, August 28, 1987, pp. 969–970.

10. Patricia Morris, *New African*, April 1988, pp. 28–29.

11. Myers, *A Wealth of Wild Species*, p. 91.

12. Joel B. Smith and Dennis A. Tirpak, eds., "The Potential Effects of Global Climate Change on the United States," draft of Environmental Protection Agency report to Congress, October 1988.

13. Plucknett et al., *Gene Banks*, p. 15; Steve Nadis, "Return of the Potato Famine?" *Technology Review* (May/June 1986): pp. 11–13; Norman Myers, "Environment and Security," *Foreign Policy* 74 (Spring 1989): pp. 23–41.

14. Gary Hartshorn et al., *Costa Rica: Country Environmental Profile, A Field Study* (Tropical Science Center and USAID, 1982), p. 28; "Natural Resource Management in Costa Rica: A Strategy for USAID," internal AID paper, December 1987, pp. 12, 45, 49; H. Jeffrey Leonard, *Natural Resources and Economic Development in Central America* (New Brunswick, N.J.: Transaction Books, 1987), pp. 117, 143; Janet Brown, "U.S. Policy in the 1990s: International Cooperation for Environmentally Sustainable Development," World Resources Institute paper for Michigan State University Conference on Cooperation for International Development, May 15–18, 1988, p. 4.

15. Sandra Postel and Lori Heise, "Reforesting the Earth," *State of the World: 1988*, pp. 83–100.

16. The Brundtland Commission, *Our Common Future*, p. 149; "The Race to Save Wild Rices," *The IRRI Reporter*, March 1989, p. 1.
17. Leonard, *Natural Resources and Economic Development*, pp. 135–136; Hartshorn, *Costa Rica: Country Environmental Profile*.
18. Brown, "U.S. Policy in the 1990s."
19. Leonard, *Natural Resources and Economic Development*, p. 136.
20. Carlos A. Quesada, "Population-Development-Resource and Environment Linkages: A Costa Rican Perspective," unpublished paper. Also on population, see Leonard, *Natural Resources and Economic Development*, pp. 37–41.
21. Leonard, *Natural Resources and Economic Development*, p. 44.
22. Hartshorn, *Costa Rica: Country Environmental Profile*, pp. 28–30. For a basic history of the country, see Richard Biesanz, Karen Zubris Biesanz, and Mavis Hiltunen Biesanz, *The Costa Ricans* (Englewood Cliffs, N.J.: Prentice-Hall, 1987).
23. From the video "Central America: On the Horns of a Dilemma," produced by Britt Davis and James Lindenberger, with support of the University of Kentucky.
24. Sheldon Annis, "Costa Rica's Dual Debt: A Story about a Little Country That Did Things Right," draft case study for the World Resources Institute, June 1987.
25. Hartshorn, *Costa Rica: Country Environmental Profile*, pp. 5–6, 54.
26. Leonard, *Natural Resources and Economic Development*, pp. 101–102, 107.
27. D. H. Janzen et al., "Corcovado National Park: A Perturbed Rainforest Ecosystem," unpublished report to the World Wildlife Fund, 1985.
28. Leonard, *Natural Resources and Economic Development*, p. 59.
29. *World Tables* (Washington, D.C.: World Bank, 1987); *Taxes International*, February 15, 1988.
30. "USAID/Costa Rica Strategy Update," USAID document, March 1988, p. 2.
31. The Brundtland Commission, *Our Common Future*, p. 8.
32. Stephen H. Schneider, "Doing Something about the Weather," *World Monitor* (December 1988): p. 37; Bill McKibben, "Is the World Getting Hotter?" *New York Review of Books*, December 8, 1988, p. 9. See also Philip Hilts, "Some 'Greenhouse' Effects: Pestilence, Super-Storms?" *Washington Post*, December 8, 1988.
33. *The Global 2000 Report*, vol. 2, pp. 328–331; Rensberger, "Scientists See Signs of Mass Extinction"; World Resources Institute and International Institute for Economics and Development, *World Resources: 1988–89* (New York: Basic Books, 1988), pp. 92–93, and "Agriculture, Forestry, Biological Diversity," World Resources Institute fact sheet (draft, June 1989); Ariel E. Lugo, "Estimating Reductions in the Diversity of Tropical Forest Species," in *Biodiversity*, pp. 58–70; Julian L. Simon and Aaron Wildavsky, "On Species Loss, the Absence of Data, and Risks to Humanity," in *The Resourceful Earth: A Response to Global 2000*, ed. Julian L. Simon and Herman Kahn (New York: Blackwell, 1984), p. 175.
34. E. O. Wilson, "The Current State of Biological Diversity," *Biodiversity*, pp. 13–14.
35. William Booth, "Tropical Forest Loss May Be Killing Off Songbirds, Study Says," *Washington Post*, July 26, 1989.

36. Robert Goodland and George Ledec, "Neoclassical Economics and Principles of Sustainable Development," *Ecological Modelling* 38 (1987): p. 19. A discussion of these issues will be found in David Pearce, "Economists Befriend the Earth," *New Scientist*, November 19, 1988.

37. Simon and Wildavsky, "On Species Loss," p. 181.

38. Diana M. Liverman, Mark E. Hanson, Becky J. Brown, and Robert W. Merideth, Jr., "Global Sustainability: Toward Measurement," *Environmental Management* 12, 2 (1988): pp. 133–143.

39. "The Vanishing Jungle," *Economist* (U.K.), October 15, 1988, p. 13; National Research Council Report, *Butterfly Farming in Papua New Guinea* (Washington, D.C.: National Academy Press, 1983); Norman Myers, "The Hamburger Connection: How Central America's Forests Become North America's Hamburgers," *Ambio* 10, 1 (1981): pp. 3–8; D. H. Janzen, "Buy Costa Rican Beef," *OIKOS* 51, 3 (1988): pp. 257–258.

40. William O. McLarney, "Guanacaste: The Dawn of a Park," *The Nature Conservancy Magazine*, January/February 1988, pp. 11–15; Marjorie Sun, "Costa Rica's Campaign for Conservation," *Science*, March 18, 1988, pp. 1366–1369.

41. For criticism over the lack of attention paid to these environmental issues by foreign aid institutions, see Leonard, *Natural Resources and Economic Development*, p. 187.

42. The project is described in USAID project identification document 515–0243; on Smithsonian Tropical Research Institute's estimates, see Philip J. Hilts, "Tests Debunk Some Old Ideas About Stomaching Spicy Foods," *Washington Post*, December 19, 1988.

43. On resource wars, Arthur H. Westing, ed., *Global Resources and International Conflict: Environmental Factors in Strategic Policy and Action* (New York: Oxford University Press, 1986); James Brooke, "Waste Dumpers Turning to West Africa," *New York Times*, July 17, 1988; James Brooke, "African Nations Barring Toxic Waste," *New York Times*, September 25, 1988; Frank Barton, "The Merchants of Death Switch to Africa," *Daily Nation*, December 6, 1988; Blaine Harden, "Africans Turn to Hostages in Battle Against Foreign Waste," *Washington Post*, July 16, 1988.

44. Plucknett, *Gene Banks*, pp. 32–40, 80; Prescott-Allen, *Genes from the Wild*, pp. 68–69; Witt, *Biotechnology*, p. 103.

45. Steve Tripoli, "Costa Rica Halts Assault on Its Fragile Tropical Forest," *Christian Science Monitor*, January 4, 1989.

46. Marlise Simons, "Brazil Agrees to Accept Aid to Save Rain Forests," *New York Times*, February 5, 1989; Mac Margolis, "Amazon Nations Back Brazil on Rain Forest," *Washington Post*, March 9, 1989; Larry Tye, "Traveling and Helping the Land," *Boston Sunday Globe*, April 9, 1989.

47. Charles Darwin, *The Origin of Species* (New York: Colliers, 1909), p. 506.

48. "Green Politics Can Hurt," *Financial Times*, May 4, 1989; "The Talk of the Town," *New Yorker*, February 13, 1989.

49. On poll, see Richard Morin, "Polls Show Public Wants Cleanup, but Will It Pay?" *Washington Post*, June 18, 1989. For references to environment in Kissinger report, see *Report of the National Bipartisan Commission on Central America* (January 1984), pp. 16, 79–80; Michael Weisskopf, "Reagan Aide Blocks 'Greenhouse' Rule," *Washington Post*, January 11, 1989.

Chapter 3

1. Mohammed Amin and Duncan Willetts, *The Beauty of the Kenyan Coast* (Nairobi: Westlands Sundries, Ltd., 1986). For descriptions of Mombasa and the Kenyan coast, see *Insight Guides: Kenya* (Hong Kong: APA Publications Ltd., 1988); "In the Beginning, an 'Island of War,'" *Kenya Export News* (July 1987): pp. 16–23; Mary Battiata, "Swept Away in Mombasa," *Washington Post Magazine*, March 15, 1987; George Sunguh, "Mombasa's Past Today," *Msafiri*, n.d., p. 42.

2. James Allen, former curator of the Lamu Museum, cited in Joan Karmali, "Living History," *Msafiri*, n.d., p. 36.

3. Crosby, *Ecological Imperialism*, p. 143.

4. Ronald va de Krol, "Dutch Fearful of Losing Knack for Languages," *International Herald Tribune*, February 24, 1988.

5. *Cornerstone of Competition*, Southern Governors' Association, Advisory Council on International Education, Washington, D.C., July 1986.

6. Sheila Rule, "To Cut Births, Kenya Turns to TV Show," *New York Times*, June 14, 1987; Loretta McLaughlin, "Soap Opera with Social Messages," *Boston Globe*, February 14, 1983; David O. Poindexter, "Soap Opera for the Betterment of the Masses," *1987 Almanac, The Annual of the International Council of NATAS*, pp. 115–121.

7. Richard Harrington, "When Music Takes the World View," *Washington Post*, June 3, 1988.

8. Ryzsard Kapuscinski, an interview conducted by Nathan Gardels in *New Perspectives Quarterly* (Summer 1988), cited in *Utne Reader* (March/April 1989): p. 105.

9. David Clark Scott, "Hong Kong's Migrant Millionaires," *World Monitor* (May 1989): p. 42.

10. Robin Herman, "Diseases of Affluence," *Washington Post*, Health section, January 3, 1989.

11. Statistics from the Chinese embassy, Washington, D.C.

12. National Clearing House for Bilingual Education, Washington, D.C.

13. Jay Mathews, *The Best Teacher in America* (New York: Henry Holt and Co., 1988).

14. Jonathan Kolatch, "A. U.S. Host Takes China on a TV Tour of the World," *Asian Wall Street Journal*, February 16, 1987; Edward Reynolds, "She's the Most Popular TV Person in the World," *National Examiner*, January 20, 1987; Dori Jones Yang, "Guess What They Watch in China on Sunday Nights?" *Business Week*, January 19, 1987.

15. *Variety*, August 20, 1986.

16. Carol Hymowitz, "Day in the Life of Tomorrow's Manager," *Wall Street Journal*, March 20, 1989.

17. Laurent Belsie, "News Trickles Back to China via Student Faxes," *Christian Science Monitor*, June 12, 1989; Michael Gartner, "Up Freedom! Faxes to the Rebels, Gunfire Via Cellular Phone," *Wall Street Journal*, June 8, 1989; Claudia Rosett, "Miss Liberty Lights Her Lamp in Beijing," *Wall Street Journal*, May

31, 1989; Arthur Unger, "Rather's Coup in China," *Christian Science Monitor*, June 5, 1989.

18. Ngugi wa Mbugua, (Nairobi) *Daily Nation*, December 7, 1988.
19. David Churchill, (London) *Financial Times*, April 17, 1989.
20. United Nations estimates, cited in "Third World Tourism: Visitors Are Good for You," *Economist* (U.K.), March 11, 1989.
21. Laetitia Yeandle, Rosalind Kelly, Larry and Margaret Lasch, "The English Traveller in the 1500s and 1600s," *Europe* (January/February 1985): p. 40; *Tourism Facts*, prepared by the Travel and Tourism Government Affairs Council, January 1989.
22. Jim Bodgener, "Turkey's Services Stumble in Tourism Race," (London) *Financial Times*, November 1, 1988; Brook Larmer, "New Leader Pins Hopes on Tourism," *Christian Science Monitor*, January 18, 1989; "Potential of Tourism Appeals to Ethiopians," *Washington Times Insight*, October 31, 1988.
23. Barbara Crossette, "India Loosens Travel Policies to Woo Tourists," *New York Times*, April 9, 1989; Alan Sayre, "Louisiana Plans Tax Rebates for Foreign Tourists," *Washington Post*, July 9, 1988.
24. Joseph B. Treaster, "Can Cuba Be Fun Again? Yes, but No Sex Please," *New York Times*, September 1, 1988.
25. "Third World Tourism: Visitors Are Good for You."
26. For discussions of the economic, social, and cultural costs and benefits of Third World tourism, see Fred P. Bosselman, *In the Wake of the Tourist: Managing Special Places in Eight Countries* (Washington, D.C.: Conservation Foundation, 1978); Lloyd E. Hudman, *Tourism: A Shrinking World* (Columbus, Ohio: Grid Inc., 1980); Emanuel de Kadt, *Tourism: Passport to Development*, joint World Bank–UNESCO study (Oxford University Press, 1979); John P. Lea, *Tourism and Development in the Third World* (New York: Routledge, 1988); Ron O'Grady, *Tourism in the Third World* (Maryknoll, N.Y.: Orbis, 1982); Louis Turner and John Ash, *The Golden Hordes: International Tourism and the Pleasure Periphery* (London: Constable, 1975).

    For discussions on tourism in Kenya, see Philipp Bachmann, *Tourism in Kenya: A Basic Need for Whom?* European University Studies, series 10: *Tourism*, vol. 10 (Berne: Peter Lang Publishers, 1987); "Kenya's Tourism Boom: Triumph of the Nyayo Era," *Executive* (Nairobi), October 1988; Nicholas Harman, "The Overcrowded Minibus," *Economist*, June 20, 1987, p. 12; Ministry of Tourism and Wildlife, *Tourism Market Report 1986*, Nairobi, Kenya.

    For discussions of the costs and benefits of tourism along the Kenyan coast, see Amin and Willetts, *Beauty of the Kenyan Coast*; Battiata, "Swept Away in Mombasa"; Lorna P de L Hayes, "Coast Tourism: An Overview," *Executive* (Nairobi), October 1988; Joseph Okoth Nyangi, "Garbage Dumping Along Beach Hotels Alarming," letter to the editor, (Nairobi) *Standard*, November 28, 1988; "Hard on the Sell," *Financial Review*, November 21, 1988; Rik, "The Magic of Malindi," *Msafiri*, n.d., pp. 44–45; George Sunguh, (Nairobi) *Daily Nation*, November 16, 1988; *A Study of Tourism in Kenya, with Emphasis on the Attitudes of Residents of the Kenyan Coast*, conducted on behalf of the Swiss Development Corporation, Institute for Development Studies, University of Nairobi, 1982.
27. "Future Growth Vital, Says Kibaki," *Kenya Export News*, May 1982.

28. "Kenya's Tourism Boom"; Laura Blumenfeld, "Israel All Out to Repair Tourism Damage," (London) *Financial Times*, March 3, 1989.

29. "Not Fair, Say Curio Men," *Kenya Hotelier and Caterer* (September/October 1988).

30. Medea Benjamin and Andrea Freedman, *Bridging the Global Gap: A Handbook to Linking Citizens of the First and Third Worlds* (Cabin John, Md.: Seven Locks Press, 1989), p. 13.

31. Arthur Frommer, "Ethical Travel: Does Tourism Cause More Harm Than Good?" in *New World of Travel 1988*, by Arthur Frommer (New York: Prentice Hall Press, 1988). See also *Contours*, the quarterly newsletter of the Ecumenical Coalition on Third World Tourism, Bangkok, Thailand; James T. Yenckel, "Fearless Traveler," *Washington Post*, January 1, 1989.

32. Benjamin and Freedman, *Bridging the Global Gap*, p. 19.

33. Eleanor N. Schwartz, "A Reluctant Burden," *New York Times*, March 12, 1989.

34. Roosevelt cited in David Lamb, *The Africans* (New York: Random House, 1987), pp. 290–291. For articles on the extent of poaching in Kenya, see "Elephant Slaughter in Kenya," (Nairobi) *Weekly Review*, September 9, 1988; "Too Much to Bear," (Nairobi) *Financial Review*, November 7, 1988; Jane Perlez, "Tourism Joins Kenyan Game as Imperiled," *New York Times*, April 23, 1989; Jane Perlez, "Only Radical Steps Can Save Wildlife in Kenya, Leakey Says," *New York Times*, May 23, 1989; Sheila Rule, "In Kenya, Man and Beast Compete for Free Land," *New York Times*, August 2, 1987.

35. For how roads to the game parks affect poaching, see Mark R. Stanley Price, letter to the editor, (Nairobi) *Weekly Review*, September 16, 1988.

36. See Ginette Hemley, "International Wildlife Trade," in *Audubon Wildlife Report, 1988/1989*, ed. William J. Chandler (San Diego, Calif.: Academic Press, Inc.), pp. 337–374; "The Ivory Trade Threatens Africa's Elephants," African Wildlife Foundation, Washington, D.C., n.d.; "Monitoring Wildlife Trade— The Traffic Network," World Wildlife Fund factsheet, n.d.

37. Chryssee Perry Martin, "Black Rhinos: An Uncertain Future," in *Safari Diary—Kenya*, ed. Kathy Eldon (Nairobi: Kenway Publications Ltd., 1987).

38. "Poaching Threatens Africa's Elephants: Americans Urged to Stop Buying Ivory," press release, African Wildlife Foundation, Washington, D.C., May 11, 1988. See also "The Elephants and the Ivory," editorial, *Washington Post*, April 25, 1989; Robert M. Press, "Africans Back Ban on Ivory Sales," *Christian Science Monitor*, April 26, 1989.

39. "President Announces U.S. Ban of All Elephant Ivory Imports," *Washington Post*, June 6, 1989; "EC Bans Import of Ivory," *New York Times*, June 11, 1989; David S. Hawkins, "For the Elephants' Sake, a Quick Ban on Ivory," *New York Times*, June 11, 1989.

40. Christian Tyler, "Stopping Evolution's Clock," (London) *Financial Times*, April 8–9, 1989.

41. *Kenya Times*, November 17, 1988.

42. Clifford D. May, "Preservation for Profit: New Strategies to Save African Wildlife," *New York Times Magazine*, September 12, 1982; Neil Henry, "Preserving Paradise in Kenya," *Washington Post*, September 4, 1989. See also A. H. Harcourt, H. Pennington, and A. W. Weber, "Public Attitudes to Wildlife and Conservation in the Third World," *Oryx* 20, 3 (July 1986).

43. Tyler, "Stopping Evolution's Clock." See also Kathleen Kouril, "Making Wildlife Protection Pay in Africa," *Wall Street Journal*, August 5, 1988.

44. George Ledec and Robert Goodland, *Wildlands: Their Protection and Management in Economic Development* (Washington, D.C.: World Bank, 1988), pp. 99–100.

45. May, "Preservation for Profit," p. 154.

46. Lamb, *The Africans*, p. 294.

47. Two other Kenyan crafts industries, soapstone and figurine carving, were never anything *but* commercial. They started solely for foreigners and experts. Over the years, the most talented artists have upgraded designs, which lesser-grade craftsmen copy in commercial quantities. See Joan Karmali, "Creating an Image," *Msafiri*, n.d., pp. 33–35; Tony Troughear, "Kamba Carving: Art or Industry?" *Kenya Past and Present*, Kenya Museum Society, Issue 19 (1987): pp. 15–25.

48. "Tourism in the Pacific Islands," excerpts from the South Pacific Peoples Foundation, September 1987, in *Contours* 3, 4 (December 1987): p. 17.

49. *The Old Town Mombasa: An Historical Guide* (Mombasa: Friends of Fort Jesus, 1987), p. 12.

50. "Malindi Handicrafts Popular Exports," *Kenya Export News*, October 1988, p. 9. For more on the wood-carving tradition, see Sheila Unwin, "Dhow Trade Chests," *Kenya Past and Present*, pp. 34–43.

51. For articles on African Heritage, see Juliet George McCleery, "African Heritage Exports More Than Art," *Museum Store*, The Museum Store Association (Winter 1986): pp. 29–33; "The Art of African Heritage," *Kenya Hotelier and Caterer* (November/December 1987): pp. 20–23; "Bagfuls of Adventure," *Kenya Export News*, May 1982, p. 21; "African Heritage 15th Anniversary: The Beauty in Art, Culture," (Nairobi) *Weekly Review*, February 5, 1988; "Jewelry Past and Present," *Msafiri*, n.d., p. 28; "A Veritable Treasure Store of Africana," *Kenya Export News*, October 1984, p. 12; "Where to Buy Jewelry for Export," *Kenya Export News*, August 1988, p. 11.

52. Figures from the U.S. Office of Foreign Agents Registration, Washington, D.C.; for background on trade lobbying by newly industrialized countries, see Bruce Stokes, "Developing Countries Join the Big Leagues in Washington Trade Lobbying," *National Journal*, January 25, 1986.

53. Neil Henry, "Kenya Burns Tusks to Dramatize Effort to Wipe Out Ivory Trade," *Washington Post*, July 19, 1989.

54. Gephardt cited in "Free Trade in Politicians," *Economist*, May 6, 1989.

55. David M. Alpern with Thomas M. DeFrank, Lars-Erik Nelson, and Washington bureau reports, "Feeling Helpless," *Newsweek*, February 26, 1979; Peter Goldman with Eleanor Clift, "Scolding in Mexico," *Newsweek*, February 26, 1979; Dom Bonafede, "Bad News from Abroad," *National Journal*, February 24, 1979; Miroslav Ambrus, "President Carter's Visit to Mexico," BBC World Broadcast, February 17, 1979.

56. Benjamin and Freedman, *Bridging the Global Gap*, p. 14.

57. *Washington Post*-ABC News Poll, February 14, 1989, cited in Hobart Rowen, *Washington Post*, April 23, 1989; James Fallows, "Containing Japan," *Atlantic*, May 1989, pp. 40–48; see also Peter Riddell, "Signs of Strain in the Pacific Friendship," (London) *Financial Times*, May 31, 1989.

58. Daniel Burstein, "Yen and the Art of Package Travel," *Condé Nast Traveler* (May 1989), p. 131. For a description of less superficial U.S.-Japanese cultural exchanges, see Phyllis Ellen Funke, "When in Japan. . .," *Washington Post*, June 4, 1989.

59. Daniel Boorstin, *The Republic of Technology: Reflections on Our Future Community* (New York: Harper and Row, 1978), p. 3.

60. "Subversion by Cassette," *Time*, September 11, 1989, p. 80.

61. "Nassir Warns Press: 'Be Mindful of Nation's Future,'" *Kenya Times*, November 21, 1988; Naphtaly Otieno Awiti, *Standard*, November 28, 1988; Sammy Masara, "Counter Anti-Kenya Slur, Journalists Told," *Standard*, November 15, 1988.

62. Zita Arocha, "1980s Expected to Set Mark as Top Immigration Decade," *Washington Post*, July 23, 1988.

63. Jennifer Monahan, "Bridging the Cultural Divide," (London) *Financial Times*, March 11, 1989.

64. "Tuwei Elude," (Richmond) *Times-Dispatch*, May 4, 1980; see also John Markon, (Richmond) *Times-Dispatch*, April 29, 1982.

Conclusion

1. Robert Darnton, "What Was Revolutionary about the French Revolution?" *New York Review of Books*, January 19, 1989, p. 3. See also Simon Schamn, *Citizens: A Chronicle of the French Revolution* (New York: Alfred A. Knopf, 1989), pp. 619 and 829. Hannah Arendt elaborated on the meaning of revolution in *On Revolution* (New York: Viking Compass, 1969), chapter 1. She notes that the first *political* meaning of revolution was to mark the "return to a preordained order. Thus, the word was first used not when what we call a revolution broke out in England and Cromwell rose to the first revolutionary dictatorship, but on the contrary, in 1660, after the overthrow of the Rump Parliament and at the occasion of the restoration of the monarchy" (p. 36).

2. For an argument that the term simply does not work, see John MacLean, "Interdependence—An Ideological Intervention in International Relations?" in *Interdependence on Trial*, ed. Jones and Willetts, p. 130.

3. Peter F. Drucker, "The Changed World Economy," *Foreign Affairs* 64 (Spring 1986): p. 773. A farsighted discussion of raw materials is presented by Raymond F. Mikesell, "The Changing Demand for Industrial Raw Materials," in Sewell, Tucker et al., *Growth, Exports, and Jobs*.

4. Louis Uchitelle, "Trade Barriers and Dollar Savings Raise Appeal of Factories Abroad," *New York Times*, March 26, 1989.

5. Pauline Yoshihashi, "Employer Sanctions and Illegal Workers: Many Contrive to Find a Way Around the Law," *Wall Street Journal*, May 26, 1989. For a different view, see Brooke A. Masters, "'87 Law Cut Illegal Immigration," *Washington Post*, July 20, 1989.

6. Daniel Bell, "The World and the United States in 2013," *Daedalus* (Summer 1987): p. 13.

7. The issue about the environment being threatened as countries compete for capital is made in John B. Cobb, Jr., and Herman E. Daly, "Free Trade Versus Community," in their forthcoming book, *For the Common Good* (Boston, Mass.: Beacon Press). For an argument that developing countries are relatively more dependent than others, see Mark J. Gasiorowski, "The Structure of Third World Economic Interdependence," *International Organization* 39 (Spring 1985): pp. 331–342.

8. Hobart Rowen, "Larger Nations Opening Doors to Four Evolving 'Asian Tigers,' " *Washington Post*, April 8, 1989.

9. "The Other Group of Seven," *Economist*, June 4, 1988.

10. Saul H. Mendlovitz, Lawrence Metcalf, and Michael Washburn, "The Crisis of Global Transformation, Interdependence, and the Schools," in *Education for Responsible Citizenship: The Report of the National Task Force on Citizen Education* (New York: McGraw-Hill, 1977), p. 192.

11. John Lewis Gaddis, "The Long Peace: Elements of Stability in the Postwar International System," *International Security* 10 (Spring 1986): pp. 111–112.

12. Robert J. McCartney, "Europe Seeks an Economy of Scale," *Washington Post*, March 19, 1989.

13. See table in Sewell, Tucker et al., *Growth, Exports, and Jobs*, p. 214.

14. George Shultz's comments found in "Recommended Reading," *Washington Post*, January 11, 1989. Background on this important debate can be found in Kennedy, *Rise and Fall of the Great Powers*, pp. 514–535; Paul Kennedy, "Can the U.S. Remain Number One?" *New York Review of Books*, pp. 36–42; Friedman, "The Campaign's Hidden Issue," p. 28; Edward Mortimer, "The Proper Role for Top Nation: Foreign Affairs," *Financial Times*, February 28, 1989; Joseph S. Nye, Jr., "Understating U.S. Strength," *Foreign Policy* (Fall 1988): p. 72; Nye and Keohane, *Power and Interdependence*, p. 231.

15. Cohen, *In Whose Interest?* p. 29.

16. Lester Brown, *World Without Borders*, rev. ed. (New York: Vintage, 1973), p. 271; Erik Gunnermark and Donald Kenrick, *A Geolinguistic Handbook* (Sweden: Joterna, Kungalv, 1986). UN figures from interview with Angel Santillana, chief of Distribution Section, Publishing Division, Department of Conference Services.

17. Marttila and Kiley, Inc., *Americans Talk Security* (Boston, Mass., April 1988), pp. 43–45; see also *Old Doctrines vs. New Threats: Citizens Look at Defense Spending and National Security*, Roosevelt Center for American Policy Studies monograph, April 1989; and World Policy Institute Survey, *Defining American Priorities* (June 1989).

18. Robert C. Nelson, "An Interview with Daniel Yankelovich," *Kettering Review* (Fall 1988): p. 44.

19. Kennedy, *Rise and Fall of the Great Powers*, pp. 514–535.

20. For background on Saunders's views, see his unpublished manuscript, "An Historic Challenge to Rethink How Nations Relate," March 8, 1989; Harold H. Saunders, *The Other Walls: The Politics of the Arab-Israeli Peace Process* (Washington, D.C.: American Enterprise Institute for Public Policy Research, 1985); Harold H. Saunders, "The Arab-Israeli Conflict in a Global Perspective," in *Restructuring American Foreign Policy*, ed. John D. Steinbruner (Washington, D.C.: Brookings Institution, 1989).

21. For background on Shuman's work, see Gale Warner and Michael Shuman, *Citizen Diplomats: Pathfinders in Soviet-American Relations—and How You Can Join Them* (New York: Continuum, 1987); Shuman, "Dateline Main Street," pp. 154–174; Michael Shuman, "Put Ollie in State Prison," *Bulletin of Municipal Foreign Policy* 2, 3 (Summer 1988): pp. 2–4.
22. Cooper, *Economics of Interdependence*, p. 5.
23. Hans Morgenthau, quoted in speech by Nicholas Brady at Department of State, March 10, 1989.
24. Cobb and Daly, "Free Trade Versus Community."
25. Richard Gardner, "Practical Internationalism," *Foreign Affairs* 66 (Spring 1988): pp. 827–845.
26. Richard Wood, "For Americans, the World Is Terra Incognita," *Christian Science Monitor*, February 28, 1989; Bonnie Brownlee, "Main Street America Asks Students to Give International Perspective," *Journalism Educator* 43, 3 (Autumn 1988), p. 17.
27. Edward B. Fiske, "The Global Imperative," *New York Times* education supplement, April 9, 1989; *Cornerstone of Competition*, Southern Governors' Association, p. 18.
28. Tom Peters, "Closed Minds Can't Open Markets," editorial, *U.S. News & World Report*, March 3, 1986; Barbara Vobejda, "U.S. Students Called Internationally Illiterate," *Washington Post*, November 22, 1986; National Academy of Engineering, *Strengthening U.S. Engineering Through International Cooperation: Some Recommendations for Action* (Washington, D.C., 1987): p. 6.
29. *America in Transition: The International Frontier*, report of the National Governors' Association, 1989; Commission on National Challenges in Higher Education, *Memorandum to the 41st President of the United States* (January 1988): p. 1.
30. Maurice Williams, "U.S. Coordination of Economic and Development Cooperation Policies," in Overseas Development Council's report, *U.S. Development Cooperation and the Third World: Issues and Options for the 1990s*, Washington, D.C., 1988, p. 9.
31. For background on the conference, see Gardner, *Blueprint for Peace*.
32. Adam Yarmolinsky, "Organizing for Interdependence: The Role of Government," Interdependence Series No. 5, Aspen Institute for Humanistic Studies, 1976.
33. Some of these ideas are found in Robert H. Johnson, "Managing Interdependence: Restructuring the U.S. Government," Overseas Development Council development paper, February 23, 1977. The need for involving a broad range of expertise in foreign policy planning is underscored by Jessica Tuchman Mathews, "Redefining Security," *Foreign Affairs* 68 (Spring 1989): p. 176.

INDEX

A. C. Nielsen, 54
Adam, Khadija, 146
Adamson, George, 143
Afghanistan, 167
Africa, 7, 55, 125, 128, 129, 168;
  biological resources, 80, 81, 82,
  83, 85, 87, 118; environmental
  concerns, 92, 93, 106, 121; trade,
  16, 17, 118, 160. *See also* Kenya
  and other individual countries
African Heritage, 146
African Wildlife Foundation, 142
Aga Khan, 154
Agua Buena, 93
Aho, C. Michael, 10
AIDS, 18, 87, 168, 169
A.I. Records, 129
Algeria, 7
Alviar, Fides, 71
Amador, Alberto José, 114
Amazon basin, 88, 109, 120
Amazon Pact, 161
Amboseli National Park, 143
American Airlines, 38
American Express Company, 69, 137
American Institute of Architects, 121
American Journal of Botany, 116
"American Junk," 66, 67
American Telegraph & Telephone
  (AT&T), 8, 52
American Zoologist, 117
Amor, Adlai, 169
AMR, 38
Andere, Amboka, 128
Angola, 14
Apo Hiking Society, 66, 67
Appalachian Computer Services, 38
Aquino, Benigno, 71
Aquino, Corazon C., 48;
  government of, 49, 52
Argentina, 14, 106, 160–161
Arias Sanchez, Oscar, 77, 80, 105
Arthur Anderson Inc., 42, 54
Asia, 7, 9, 81, 83, 110, 125, 127, 139,
  141. *See also* individual countries

Aspen Institute, 172
Aspinall, William, 112
Association of American
  Universities, 65
Athi Plain, 140
Australia, 4, 30, 87, 160–161

Bagtas, Eduardo, 44, 45, 47
Banana Republic, 145
Bangladesh, 106
Bank of America, 101
banking, global, 10, 14–15, 22, 42,
  69, 101–102, 111, 163
Barbados, 38, 48
Barraclough, Geoffrey, 4, 15
Barras, Gary, 39
Bell, Daniel, 159
Bell, Peter, 8
Bergsten, C. Fred, 16
Berne Convention for the
  Protection of Literary and
  Artistic Works, 64
Berry, John, 58–59, 73
Bilateral Commission on the Future
  of United States–Mexican
  Relations, 14
Biología Tropical, 116
biological imperialism, 81
Bismarck, Otto von, 174
Black, Manafort, Stone, and Kelly, 149
Blanco, José María, 100–101
Bledsoe, Bob, 41
Bloomingdale's, 145
Bodek, Norman, 33, 38, 72
Boeing Services International, 39
Bolido, Erlinda, story by, 70–71
Bolivia, 48, 111, 147
Boorstin, Daniel, 153
Booz-Allen and Hamilton, Inc., 41
Borneo, 80, 92
Bortnick, Jane, 69
Boza, Mario A., 109, 118
Bray, Dorothy, 87–88
Brazil, 7, 13, 91, 100, 131; biological
  resources, 79, 80, 81, 87, 120;

foreign debt, 14, 101, 102, 111; information revolution, 9, 48, 55, 65, 68; music industry in, 127, 128, 131; trade, 149, 160–161
Bretton Woods Conference, 166
Brewbaker, James, 83
British Data Protection Act, 63
British East India Company, 3
British Library General Catalogue, 36–37
Brown, Lester, 20, 163
Brundtland Commission. *See* World Commission on Environment and Development
Brundtland, Gro Harlem, 87
Brussels, 149
Budowski, Gerardo, 116, 117
Burger King, 110
Bush, George, 17
Bushkin, Arthur A., 61
Bustamante, Jorge, 10
Butterfield, Rebecca, 99

Cable & Wireless, 52
Cairns Group, 160–161
Campos, Carlos, 104
Canada, 68, 160–161
Caño Negro wildlife refuge, 103
Caribbean Conservation Corporation (CCC), 117
Caribbean Data Services (CDS), 38, 53
Carnegie Endowment for International Peace, 19
Carrillo, Braulio, 96
Carter, Jimmy, 107, 151
Castro, Fidel, 13
CD-ROM technology, 73
Celluloid Records, 128
Center for Innovative Diplomacy, 14, 164–165
Center for Population Communications–International, 127
Central America. *See* Latin America
Centro Agronómico Tropical de Investigacíon y Enseñanza (CATIE), 84, 86, 114
Charles II, king of Naples, 3
Chile, 4, 85

Chilote Indians, 85
China, 6–7; biological resources, 82, 89; cultural diversity and, 131, 140; information revolution, 38, 48, 64, 132; trade, 16, 89, 125, 147
Christian Science Monitor, 27–28
Chumo, Nathaniel arap, 143–144
CINDE, 113, 114
Ciudad Neily, 93
Coast Petty Traders Association, 139
Coca-Cola, 118, 161
Colgate Palmolive Company, 14
Colombia, 8, 161
Commission on National Challenges in Higher Education, 170
communication networks: global banking and, 42; international, 50–53, 55–57, 59; private, 40–42; technology of, 28, 41–42, 50–53, 56, 60, 69, 73, 141, 158; United States and, 8–9
communications technology: copyright protections, 63–64, 68; data entry industry, 32–40, 59, 69–72, 73; economic constraints and, 49–53; emerging problems, 60–65, 69–72; expertise in, 49–50, 53–57; manufacture of, 28, 50, 158; privacy and, 58, 62–64, 68; Third World and, 7–13, 28–29, 50, 52, 53–57, 60–62, 64–72, 158; threat to jobs, 55, 69–72, 158; trade in, 28, 49–50, 54–55, 60, 61, 65
Communist National People's Army (Philippines), 65
competition for markets, global, 13, 114, 131, 139, 149–150, 161–162; crafts industries and, 145, 146–147; data entry companies and, 33, 44–57, 72; economic constraints, 49–53; labor factors, 14, 28, 38, 44, 45, 47–48, 49, 57, 69, 72; political factors, 48, 49; technical expertise, 49–50, 53–57; U.S. and, 14, 16–17, 18–19, 56, 57, 152, 169, 171, 172. *See also* trade, foreign
Computer Accounting Services, 31

computers, 28, 34, 41, 45, 49–50, 54,
    55, 56, 59–60, 63
Conference Board, 10
Conservation Data Center, 109
Conservation International, 110, 111
Conway, James, 39, 45, 46–47, 52, 53
Cooper, Richard, 166
copyright protections, 63–64, 68
Corcovado National Park, 100, 109
Costa Rica, 115, 159; agricultural
    production, 90, 96, 97, 98, 100,
    102–103; biological resources,
    loss of, 78, 89, 91–92, 95–101,
    102–103, 115, 119; cattle
    ranching, 96–98, 101, 102, 110,
    112, 114; coffee production, 96,
    98, 100, 101, 102–103;
    conservation efforts, 78,
    103–104, 105–106, 108–113;
    crops endemic to, 82, 84, 86, 87;
    deforestation in, 21, 78, 91–92,
    93, 97, 99, 102–104, 112;
    development, 89–94, 95–99,
    100–101, 102–104, 106, 110;
    domestic policies, 96–97, 101,
    103–104; economic problems,
    95, 101–102, 103; foreign
    contributions to, 118–119, 162;
    foreign debt, 78, 101–102, 103,
    110–111; foreign scientists and,
    116–117; genetic diversity of, 78,
    79–80, 92, 102, 109, 111, 114,
    119, 120, 162; gold mining,
    100–101; Indians, 86, 114–115;
    land (re)distribution, 98,
    112–113, 114; national character,
    77, 78, 94–95, 105, 113, 118;
    population growth, 78, 94–96,
    97, 110; protected reserves
    (includes national parks), 78,
    103–104, 109, 111, 112, 119;
    reforestation, 91, 92, 99, 103,
    111, 112–113; soil erosion,
    92–94, 98, 107; Spanish
    settlement of, 80–81, 91;
    squatters, 89–91, 96, 98–99, 112;
    tropical forests, 77–78, 100, 119;
    world trade and, 97, 100, 101,
    102, 110, 113–114
Costa Rican Central Bank, 101, 111

Côte d'Ivoire, 91
Council on Foreign Relations, 10
Council on Interdependence, 173
Cousteau, Jean-Michel, 121
Crosby, Alfred W., 81
Cu, Emmanuel B., 31, 32, 44, 48
Cuba, 13, 88–89, 137
cultural diversity, 9, 125–134, 159;
    cultural identity, threats to,
    65–67, 125–126, 133–134, 135,
    145–146, 152–155; tensions
    from, 132–134, 151, 161–162,
    168–169; understanding,
    importance of, 148, 149
Cyprus, 114n

Danish West Indies, 15–16
Dar es Saalem, 129
Darwin, Charles, 121, 122
data entry industry, 27, 30, 32–33,
    34, 39, 54; communications
    technology and, 32–40, 59,
    69–72, 73; competition for
    markets, global, 33, 44–57, 72;
    low–wage labor in, 38, 44, 47–48,
    57, 69–72; offshore facilities,
    38–40; services trade and, 28,
    60–61. See also Saztec
Data Entry Management
    Association (DEMA), 33
debt, foreign, 3; debt swaps,
    110–111; Third World, 10,
    14–15, 22, 49, 78, 101–102, 103,
    110–111; United States and, 2, 3,
    14, 15, 17, 22
defense issues, 2, 11–13, 14, 88, 148,
    150, 162, 163
Del Monte, 113–114
Deming, J. Edwards, 131
Denmark, 4, 86
Department of Labor and
    Employment (Philippines), 71
developing countries. See Third
    World
DIALOG, 50, 57
Directory of Online Databases, 34
disease: AIDS, 18, 87, 168, 169, 172;
    genetic resistance to, in tropical
    species, 82, 83, 85, 89, 118;
    global interdependence and, 3,

83, 87–89, 108, 130, 167;
medicinal benefits of plant
species, 87–88, 92, 108
Doloroso, Cora, 71
Dominican Republic, 38
Donovan, Alan, 146, 147
Dowd, Chris, 35, 73
Drucker, Peter F., 70, 158
drugs, illicit, 4, 18, 19
Dun & Bradstreet, 55
"Dynasty," 134

Earthworks, 128
Economist, 42
Ecuador, 92, 118
Ecumenical Coalition on Third
World Tourism, 139
Edward III, king of England, 3
Egypt, 13, 125
El Salvador, 48, 95, 115
environmental concerns, 17, 20,
110–111, 159, 161, 171; chemical
pesticides, use of, 20, 85, 171;
conservation efforts, 78,
105–106, 108–113, 119–120;
costs of, 107–108; global
warming (greenhouse effect), 13,
88, 106, 119, 121–122, 167, 171;
international tensions over, 115;
land use, 96–101, 110; plant and
animal species, loss of, 78, 88–89,
91–92, 100, 103, 107–109, 114,
121; population growth, 78,
94–96, 97, 140, 144; soil erosion,
92–94, 98, 107; tourism and, 139,
140–142; tropical biology
research, spending on, 79,
116–117, 122, 171; tropical
deforestation, 21, 78, 81, 91–92,
93, 97, 99, 102–104, 106, 107,
109, 110, 121, 115, 121; waste
disposal, 18, 115; wildlife,
protection of, 140–144
Equidata, 39, 45, 46
Escalante, Jaime, 131
Ethiopia, 82–83, 85, 118
Europe (Western), 6, 9, 17, 18, 56,
62, 81, 87, 100, 160, 161, 162, 167
European Community, 11, 142, 149,
171

European Economic Community,
110, 160–161

facsimile (fax) machines, 28, 36, 53, 63
Fallows, James, 152
farming, advances in, 81–83,
102–103
Fatherhood (Cosby), 66
fiber optic cables, 8, 28, 52, 53
First Wisconsin National Bank of
Milwaukee, 101
Flaminia, La, 89–91
Fleet/Norstar Financial Group
(Providence, R.I.), 111
Florentine Academy of Science, 4
Folkways, 129
Ford Motor Company, 40
Foundation Directory, 118
France, 4, 9, 15–16, 154, 157
Fraser, Alan, 29–35, 44, 45, 46, 48,
52–53, 54, 55, 69, 73
French Revolution, 157
Friedman, Benjamin M., 17
Fundación Neotrópica, 109
Fundación de Parques Nacionales,
111, 119

Gabon, 142
Gakahu, Christopher, 143
Galapagos Islands, 85
Gallup poll (1988), 121
Gambia, 142
Gámez, Rodrigo, 80, 82, 86, 95–96,
99, 102, 106, 108, 114, 115–116,
119
Gandhi, Rajiv, 69
Garcia, Mercedes F., 52
gene banks, 83–84, 103, 108
General Agreement on Tariffs and
Trade (GATT), 10, 68–69
General Catalogue (British Library),
36–37
General Electric Company, 28, 63,
148
General Motors, 30
genetic material: agricultural
benefits, 81–86; collections of, in
gene banks, 83–84, 103, 108;
commercial benefits, 82, 84–85,
87; conservation of, 108–109,

118, 122, 162; disease resistance in, 82, 83, 85; diversity of, in tropics, 82–83, 84–89, 107, 120; genes, 81–82, 83; importance of, 81–89, 107, 108; Indian cultures and, 85–86; loss of, 86, 87, 95–96, 118; medicinal benefits, 87–88, 92, 108, 118; patents for, 115–118; sources of, in Third World, 82–88, 161; techniques for using, 83

Geolinguistic Handbook, A, 163

Gephardt, Richard (U.S. Rep.), 150

Germany, 4, 16, 100, 113. *See also* West Germany

germplasm. *See* genetic material

global interdependence: English language and, 46, 67, 131, 154, 163; growth of, 5–6, 13–15; history of, 2–5; implications of, 19–22, 157–162; local participation in, 13–15, 159–160; money flow, 8, 10, 22; permeability of national borders, 159; pluralism, 159–161; Third World and, 6–7, 9, 10–13, 22, 54–55, 64–72, 97, 100, 101, 127–134, 148–151, 158, 159, 160, 161–162; United States and, 5, 15–23, 64–72, 162–174; vulnerability of nations, increased, 161–162; Washington lobbyists for foreign governments, 147–151. *See also* banking, global; communication networks; communications technology; competition for markets, global; cultural diversity; debt, foreign; defense issues; disease; drugs, illicit; environmental concerns; immigration; information revolution; investment, foreign; stock market; tourism; trade; tropics

Global 2000 Report to the President, 78, 107

Globo, 9

Godfather, The, 127

Goldberg, Michael, 130

Gómez, Luis Diego, 93, 94, 104, 109–110

"Good Times," 134

Goodland, Robert, 107–108

Gorbachev, Mikhail, 7

Gosiengfiao, Victor, 68, 69

"Graceland" (Simon), 127

Great Britain, 3, 57, 80, 125, 126, 154; influence in Africa, 125, 127, 129, 153, 154; information revolution, 57, 58, 59; trade, 3, 4, 15–16

Great Rift Valley, 142, 154

Great Depression, 15, 166

Greece, 114n, 125

Grenada, 38

Griffith, W. Patrick, 38–39

Guanacaste National Park, 112, 119

Guanacaste province, 111

Guild, Bob, 140

Guzmán, Rafael, 85

Haiti, 38, 48, 93, 115, 147

Harris, W. Franklin, 79, 112

Hartshorn, Gary, 112, 121

Having International Affairs Your Way, 165

Heinz, John (U.S. Sen.), 150

Helsinki (Finland) National Library card catalogue, 28, 39–40

Hightower, James, 171

His Way (biography of Frank Sinatra), 66

Hitachi, 31–32

Holland, 15–16, 79, 111, 113, 126

Holz, Frank, 54

Honduras, 92–93, 95, 115

Hong Kong, 7, 113, 130, 131, 160; cultural diversity in, 127; trade, 11, 141, 147, 149

Hughes, Thomas L., 19

Humboldt, Alexander von, 117

Hungary, 160–161

IBM, 29, 30, 41–42, 50

Iltis, Hugh, 84–85

Iman, 146

immigration, 95, 115; illegal, 72, 115, 159, 172; to United States,

4, 9–10, 18, 71–72, 83, 88–89, 115, 125, 159, 172
Inc., 127
India, 6–7, 91, 147, 158, 167; cultural diversity and, 125, 127, 137, 140; defense issues, 11–13, 162; information revolution, 9, 38, 41, 48, 57, 64, 68; trade, 10, 69, 118, 125
Indiana University, 170
Indianapolis Star, 77
Indonesia, 20, 79, 92, 127, 133, 145, 161
INFOLINK, 58–60, 62, 63, 72
Information Control Inc., 33
information flow, 8, 49, 64–65, 159
Information Industry Association (IIA), 34
information revolution: copyright protections, 63–64, 68; cultural identity, threats to, 65–67; emerging problems, 60–65, 69–72; global banking, 42; global flexibility, 34–43; information flow, 8, 49, 64–65, 159; low costs of, 36, 40–42; low–wage labor, 28, 30, 38, 47, 49, 57, 69–72, 158; offshore capabilities, 38–40; policy issues, 58–72; privacy and, 58, 62–64, 68; services trade, 28, 42–43, 60–62, 68–69; speed of information transmission, 36, 38–39, 40–42; technical expertise, 49–50, 53–57; technology of, 8, 28, 36, 38–39, 41, 42, 50–53, 55–56, 59, 63, 69, 73, 141, 158; Third World and, 53–57, 64–72. *See also* communication networks; communications technology; data entry industry; Philippines; Saztec; service industries
Institute of Advanced Computer Technology (IACT), 71
Instituto de Desarrollo Agrario (IDA), 89–90, 98
Intelsat, 68, 148
International Atomic Energy Commission, 167
International Monetary Fund, 60, 166

International Resource Development Inc., 63
International Telecommunications Union, 51, 56
Introduction to Contemporary History (Barraclough), 4
investment, foreign, 10, 15, 19, 55, 111, 113, 117–118, 135, 160
Iran, 13, 132, 133
Iraq, 11, 118
Ireland, 7, 52, 83
Island Records, 128
Israel, 139
Italy, 4, 106, 114n

Jamaica, 38, 52
Janka, Les, 148, 149, 150
Janzen, Daniel, 87, 109, 110, 111, 119
Japan, 2, 17, 125, 131, 161; competition for markets, global, 18, 56, 57; trade, 4, 11, 16, 141, 152, 153; and the U.S., 6, 11, 57, 152, 153, 161
Jefferson, Thomas, 153
Jisaidie Cottage Industries, 145, 146–147
Johnson, Lyndon, 172
Joson, Theresa U., 45
Journal of Ecology, 116
J. Walter Thompson, Inc., 159

Kamaru, Joseph, 129
Kan, Yue-Sai, 131
Kapuscinski, Ryzsard, 130
Kariuki, John, 128–129
Kennedy, John F., 6
Kennedy, Paul, 16, 162, 163
Kenya: competition for markets, global, 139, 145–146; crafts industries, 144–147, 162; cultural identity, threats to, 128–129, 133–134, 135, 145–146, 154; domestic economic control, efforts to increase, 135, 137, 152–153; foreign influences in, 125, 127, 128–129, 132–134, 152–154, 159; lobbyists for, in Washington, 147–151; military significance to the U.S., 148, 150; music, 128–129; poaching,

141–142, 143, 149; population
growth, 140, 144, 153; tourism,
125, 134–144, 145–146, 149, 153;
trade, 138–139, 142–143,
144–147; wildlife, protection of,
140–144
Kenya External Trade Authority,
145
Kenya Times, 142
Kenyan Ministry of National
Guidance and Political Affairs,
153
Keohane, Robert O., 20
Keynes, John Maynard, 4
Khomeini, Ayatollah Ruholla,
133
Kibaki, Mwai, 138–139
Kimomge, Barnabus, 146–147
Kiplinger Washington Letter, 10
Kissinger, Henry, 122
"Knots Landing," 134
Koberg, Max, 99
Korean War, 13

La Selva Biological Station, 77, 80,
99, 105, 111
labor: immigrants in work force,
9–10, 69, 70–72; low-wage, 14,
28, 30, 38, 41, 44, 47–48, 49, 57,
69–72, 158; threat of
communications technology to
jobs, 55, 69–72, 158; training, 54;
unrest, 47–48
Lagman, Augusto C., 39, 49, 57
Lamb, David, 144
Lambie, David, 37
Lamu, 127
Landefeld, J. Steven, 60
Latin America, 7, 118, 140;
biological resources, 78, 80–81,
82, 83, 87, 91, 96, 119–120, 121;
emigration from, 9, 88–89, 95,
115, 125, 159; trade, 110, 160.
See also individual nations
League of Nations, 166
Leakey, Philip, 146
Leakey, Richard, 141, 143
Lealand, Conrad, 29, 37, 39
Leboo, Jonathan, 143
Ledec, George, 107–108

Ledesma, Kuh, 66
Leggett, Dan, 35
León, Jorge, 84, 93, 95, 96, 98, 118
Leonard, Jeffrey, 93, 98
Levinson, Mark, 10
Livingstone, David, 126
LMI, 33, 35
Lorenzo, Erlinda, 45, 71

Mabus, Ray, 159–160
MacArthur Foundation, 118
Maciel, Winfred, 137
Madagascar, 79, 80, 87, 92, 161
Madeira, 81
*Main Street America and The Third
World* (Hamilton), 22
Malaysia, 84, 160; Yellow Pages, 39
Malmö (Sweden) fire department,
28, 63
Marcos, Ferdinand, 48, 49, 52, 65,
71
Marcus, Sidney, 60
Margolis, Eric, 11–13
Mariel boatlift (1980), 88–89
Marín, Walter A., 112, 116, 117
Marshall Plan, 167
Martin, Chyrssee Perry, 141
Martin, Esmond Bradley, 141
Martinique, 38
Marx, Karl, 28
Masai Mara game park, 140
M*A*S*H, 127
Mathare Valley, 144, 146–147
Mattel toy company, 48
Maynes, Charles William, 13
Mbugua, Ngugi wa, 113
McKibben, Bill, 106–107
McKinley William, 169
Mencken, H. L., 173
Mendez, Fidel, 89–91, 98–99, 114
Menem, Carlos, 160
Mexico, 127, 147, 151, 159, 169;
biological resources in, 80, 85,
115, 161; data entry facilities in,
38, 48; foreign debt, 14, 101;
low-wage labor in, 14; trade, 10,
149
Meyer, Kent, 35, 40, 67
Middle East, 125, 141, 167
MINASA, 101

Mittermeier, Russell, 161
Modern Bride, 127
Moi, Daniel arap, 143
Monsanto, 118
Monte Verde Cloud Forest Reserve, 101, 112
Morgenthau, Hans, 166
Morocco, 87
Mountain Bell telephone system, 27
Mowrer, Paul Scott, 5, 6, 15
multilateral agencies, 120, 166–168
Munyori, Nathan, 134, 135
Murumbi, Joseph, 146
Mutahi, Wahome, story by, 128–129
Mwenje, Lucy, 145
Myers, Norman, 88, 107

National Academy of Sciences, 65
National Aeronautics and Space Administration (NASA), 79
National Bipartisan Commission on Central America (1984), 122
National Cancer Institute, 87
National Commission on Coping with Interdependence, 172–173
National Computer Center (Philippines), 49, 56–57, 64
National Geographic Society, 121
National Governors' Association, 170
National Park Service (Costa Rica), 104, 105, 119
National Science Foundation, 112, 170
National Security Council, 173
Nature Conservancy, 111
Nda, L. Y., 142
Neill and Company, 148
Neill, Dennis, 148, 149, 150, 151
New African, 87–88
New Guinea, 110
New York Times, 14
Newsweek, 153
Nicaragua, 14, 77, 95, 117
Nigeria, 91, 127
Nixon, Richard M., 162–163
Noble, Kenneth, 48
Nonesuch, 129
North Atlantic Treaty Organization installations, research on, 63
North Korea, 13

North Yemen, 141
Northwest Placement, Inc., 71
Norway, 4, 63
Nude Jell-o Wrestling Special, 153
Nye, Joseph S., Jr., 20

Oduber, Daniel, 96–97
Omusi, Raphael, 146
"One World," 131
optical character scanners (OCRs), 69
Organization for African Unity, 115
Organization for Economic Cooperation and Development (OECD), 160
Organization of Petroleum-Exporting Countries (OPEC), 3, 17
Organization for Tropical Studies (OTS), 99, 105, 116
Osa Peninsula, 84
Our Foreign Affairs (Mowrer), 5, 6
Out of Africa, 145
Overseas Development Council, 57

Pacheco, Freddy, 116–117
Pacific Bell telephone system, 27
Pacific Data, 31
Pacific Rim, 141, 160
Pakistan, 11, 162, 167
Panama, 80, 84, 87
Pante, Filologo, 62
Paraguay, 85
Pelton, Joseph, 68
Peru, 80, 84, 104
Peyton, David Y., 34, 65
Philip the Fair, king of France, 3
Philippine Association of Data Entry Corporations, 44
Philippine Long Distance Telephone Company (PLDT), 51–52
Philippine Overseas Employment Administration (POEA), 70
Philippines, 46, 83, 131, 147, 159; biological resources in, 56, 72, 80; communication networks in, 41–42, 50–53, 55–57; copyright protections and, 64; cultural identity, threats to, 66–67; data entry facilities in, 31, 38, 39,

44–46, 57; economic problems,
49–50, 51, 71, 72; emigration
from, for jobs, 68, 70–72; global
banking in, 42; global
competitiveness of, 44–57;
information flow, 49, 64–65; low
wages in, 38, 44, 47–48, 49, 57,
69–72; per capita GNP, 44, 49;
profit potential in, 46–47;
technological training, 54;
telephone service in, 51–52, 53;
threat of communications
technology to jobs, 55, 69–72;
trade, 42, 49–50, 60, 61, 62, 68,
70–71, 168; unrest in, 47–48,
71–72; U.S. and, 46, 66–68,
70–72, 168–169. *See also* Saztec
Philippines
Playboy, 27, 34
poaching, 141–142, 143, 149
Polo, Marco, 3
Porto Santo, 81
Portugal, 81, 125
Presse, La, 17
Presstext News Service, 33, 34
Price, Mark Stanley, 141
privacy of information, 58, 62–64, 68
protectionism, 18–19, 54–55, 68,
138, 149, 166
Puerto Rico, 48, 109
Purificacion, Rene, 52

Quesada, Carlos, 95, 104, 106

Ramachandran, Rageshree, 131
Ramírez, Gonzalo, 98
Rico, Raymundo, 67
Reader's Digest, 31
Reagan, Ronald, 2, 13, 14, 65, 102, 166
Reed, Thomas L., 32, 33, 35–36, 47,
48, 53, 54, 69, 73
Rick, Charles, 84–85
Rivera, Vicente C., Jr., 51
Roces, Alejandro, 168, 169
Rodale Research Center, 86
Rodríguez, José María, 104, 107
Rodríguez, Silvia, 103
Rogge, Carolina, 71
Rohatyn, Felix, 2
Romulo, Roberto, 49, 50, 56

Rono, Henry, 155
Roosevelt, Theodore, 140
Rovinski, Yanina, story by, 116–117
Rushdie, Salman, 132

St. Kitts, 38
Satanic Verses, The (Rushdie), 132
satellites, 8, 28, 38–39, 41, 50, 53, 56
Saudi Arabia, 9, 11, 125
Saunders, Harold H., 13, 163–164,
165, 168
Sauvy, Alfred, 7
Saztec, 34, 42, 61, 72, 159, 160;
founding of, 29–32; Saztec
International (formerly Saztec
U.S.), 32, 33, 35–38, 39–40, 42,
44, 67, 69, 73; Saztec
Philippines, 27–28, 32, 33, 35,
43–48, 52–53, 54, 59, 62, 70, 71.
See also data entry industry
Schlafly, Phyllis, 153
Schneider, Stephen H., 106
Schneider, William, 19
Schubert, Karel R., 84, 108
Schwartz, Eleanor, 140
Scott, Winfield, 169
Sed, Rafael, 137
service industries: copyright
protections, 63–64, 68;
emigration for jobs in, 68, 70–72;
privacy of information, 58,
62–64, 68; trade in, 28, 42–43,
60–62, 68–69, 137. *See also* data
entry industry; tourism
SGV Group, 42, 54, 64; Institute of
Advanced Computer
Technology, 71
Shultz, George, 162, 163
Shuman, Michael, 14, 163, 164–165
Siegel, Daniel, 72
Simon, Julian L., 107, 109
Simon, Paul, 25, 127
Singapore, 131, 141, 160;
information revolution, 48, 50,
57, 59; low-wage labor in, 30–31;
trade, 11, 141, 149
Smith, Adam, 28
Smithsonian Institution, 129
Smithsonian Tropical Research
Institute, 113

Society of Professional Journalists,
    foreign news project surveys,
    21–22
Society of Worldwide Interbank
    Financial Telecommunications
    (SWIFT), 42
Solomon, Anthony, 18
Solórzano, Raúl G., 103
Somalia, 141
Somoza, Anastasio, 105, 117
Sonnenfeld, Jeffrey, 131–132
South Africa, 167
South America, 81, 83, 161. *See also*
    individual nations
South Korea, 13, 131, 160;
    information revolution, 38, 48,
    50, 64; trade, 11, 18, 149
South Pacific, 121, 139
South Pacific Peoples Foundation,
    145
Southern Governors' Association,
    126, 170
Soviet Union, 2, 6, 7, 152, 160
Spain, 4, 7, 80–81
Sri Lanka, 38, 55–56, 91, 139
Stand and Deliver, 131
Standard Industrial Classification
    (SIC), 60–61
Stein, Todd, 35, 43, 47, 73
Steward, Michael, 10
Stewart, James, 142
stock market, 8, 10; crash of
    October 1987, 8, 33
Stokes, Bruce, 61–62
Strategic Arms Reduction Talks, 14
Stride Rite, 27
Sudan, 106
Sullivan, John H., 133
Sweden, 28, 62–63, 64
Switzerland, 9, 18, 135
Systems Resources Inc. (SRI), 39

Tabjan, Marian, 27, 43–44, 46, 47,
    73–74
Taiwan, 11, 18, 38, 118, 131, 141,
    149, 160
Tanzania, 142
Technobank, 50, 55, 56
telephone capabilities, 36, 38, 41,
    42, 51–52, 53, 55–56, 125

terrorism, 159, 160
Texas Instruments, 41, 42
Thailand, 64, 104, 160–161
Third World: communication
    networks in, 8, 9, 50–53, 55–57;
    communications technology and,
    7–13, 28–29, 50, 52, 53–57,
    60–62, 64–72, 158; competition
    for markets, global, 16, 44–57,
    72, 114, 139, 145, 146–147,
    149–150, 160, 161–162; cultural
    diversity in, 66–67, 125–134,
    145–146, 161–162; cultural
    influence of U.S. in, 66,
    127–134; defense issues and,
    11–13, 148, 150, 162; definition
    of, 7; emigration from, 68,
    70–72, 115; environmental
    concerns, 77–78, 88, 91–92, 93,
    104, 106–110, 115, 119–120,
    139, 140–144, 160, 161; foreign
    debts of, 10, 14–15, 22, 49, 78,
    101–102, 103, 110–111; foreign
    scientists in, 116; genetic
    diversity, 77–78, 79–80,
    115–116, 118; global
    interdependence and, 6–7, 9,
    10–13, 22, 54–55, 64–72, 97,
    100, 101, 127–134, 148–151,
    158, 159, 160, 161–162; Indian
    cultures, 85–86, 87, 114–115,
    119–120; information revolution
    and, 8, 49, 53–57, 64–72;
    investment, foreign, and, 10, 55,
    111, 113, 117–118, 160;
    low-wage labor in, 14, 30, 38, 41,
    44, 47–48, 49, 57, 69–72, 73,
    158; population growth, 78, 79,
    94–96, 97, 110, 140, 144, 153;
    raw materials, dependence on,
    158; services trade, 28, 42–43,
    60–61, 62, 68–69, 137; tourism
    in, 105, 112, 113, 119, 125,
    134–144, 145–146, 149, 152,
    153; trade, 7, 9, 10–11, 12, 14,
    16–17, 22, 54–55, 65, 68–69, 97,
    100, 101, 102, 110, 113–114,
    118, 137, 142, 149, 158, 160,
    162; U.S. foreign policy and, 13,
    14. *See also* Costa Rica; Kenya;

Philippines; tropics; and other
individual countries
Time, 121
Tong, Alfred, 50, 67
Torres, William T., 49, 57
tourism, 126, 151–152; "alternative
tourism," 139–140; competition
for markets, global, 139, 145; in
Costa Rica, 105, 112, 113, 119;
cultural sensitivity and, 138,
139–140; in Kenya, 125,
134–144, 145–146, 149, 153;
trade in, 137, 138, 142–143, 149
trade, foreign, 3, 4, 7, 8, 101, 110,
150, 152, 153, 166; agricultural,
16, 22, 100, 101, 102, 113, 114,
118, 160–161; beef, 97, 110, 171;
communications technology, 28,
49–50, 54–55, 60, 61, 65; crafts,
144–147; entertainment, 8–9;
GATT regulations, 68–69; gold,
100, 101; illegal wildlife
products, 141–142;
manufacturing, 10–11, 15–17, 20,
43, 113; protectionism, 18–19,
54–55, 68, 138, 149, 166;
services, 28, 42–43, 60–62,
68–69, 137, 138, 142–143, 149;
Third World and, 7, 9, 10–11,
12, 14, 16–17, 22, 54–55, 65,
68–69, 97, 100–101, 110,
113–114, 118, 137, 138, 142,
144–147, 149, 158, 160, 162, 168;
United States and, 7, 8–9, 10, 11,
14, 15–17, 18, 20, 21, 22, 54–55,
68–69, 97, 100, 142, 162, 166,
168, 171. *See also* competition for
markets, global
Tropical Science Center, 91, 93, 98,
112
tropics: biological importance of,
77–78, 81–89; crops endemic to,
81, 82–83, 84–88, 108, 118;
deforestation, 81, 106, 107, 109,
110, 115, 121; European
plundering, 81; forests, 79, 108,
119–120; genetic diversity of,
77–78, 79–80, 81–89, 107,
108–109; industrial products,
source of, 88; species loss, 78, 81,

87, 91–92, 96, 107–109, 121. *See
also* Costa Rica; other individual
countries
Tunisia, 152
Turkey, 127
Tuwei, Hillary, 155
Tyler, Michael, 28

Ugalde, Alvaro, 105–106, 109, 122
Umaña, Alvaro, 78, 79, 100, 103,
113–114, 115, 120
United Association for the
Protection of Trade (UAPT). *See*
INFOLINK
United Nations, 6, 7, 18, 163, 167,
172; UN Environmental
Programme, 167
United Nations Conference on
Trade and Development, 62
United States, 113; banking
industry, 10, 22, 42, 69, 101, 111,
163; biological diversity of, 79,
80, 171; biological importance of
Third World to, 81–89; budget
deficit, 17, 170–171;
communication networks in, 8–9;
competition for markets, global,
14, 16–17, 18–19, 56, 57, 152,
169, 171, 172; copyright
protections, 64; cultural
influence in Third World, 66,
127–134; defense issues, 2, 11,
13, 14, 148, 150, 163; drugs,
illicit, 4, 19; economic strength,
162–163; education in, 131,
169–171; environmental
concerns, 18, 21, 88, 106–110,
115, 119–120, 121, 159, 171;
foreign debts and, 2, 3, 14, 15,
17, 22; foreign influences on, 7,
8–9, 127–134, 155, 171; foreign
policy, 13, 14, 172–173; global
interdependence and, 5, 15–23,
64–72, 162–174; government
structure, 171–173; immigration
to, 4, 9–10, 18, 71–72, 83, 88–89,
115, 125, 159, 172; information
flow, debate over, 65;
information technologies,
manufacture of, 28; international

perspective, necessity for,
168–171; investment, foreign,
and, 10, 15, 19, 111, 113,
117–118; isolationist tendencies,
1, 15, 18–19, 163, 166, 171;
Japan and, 6, 11, 57, 152, 153,
161; lobbyists in, for foreign
governments, 147–151;
multilateralism, 166–168;
Philippines and, 46, 66–68,
70–72, 168–169; privacy of
information, 62–64; services
trade, 28, 42, 60–62, 68–69, 137;
trade, 7, 8–9, 10, 11, 14, 15–17,
18, 20, 21, 22, 54–55, 68–69, 97,
100, 114, 142, 149, 150, 152,
153, 160–161, 162, 166, 168, 171
U.S. Agency for International
Development (AID), 91, 112–113
U.S. Bureau of the Census, 60
U.S. Congress, 21, 62, 153, 159, 173
U.S. Department of Agriculture, 82,
86, 88, 122; of Commerce, 61; of
Defense, 2; of Labor, 9; of State,
34, 172; of Treasury, 21
U.S. Library of Congress, 37, 153
U.S. Office of Technology
Assessment (OTA), 61, 62, 69
University of Delaware, 63
University of Kentucky Cooperative
Extension Service, 97
Utalii College, 134–136, 137, 138
Utalii Hotel, 134

Valéry, Paul, 8
Vancouver, B.C., 130
Vanrenen, Jumbo, 129–130
Variety, 131
Vaughn, Jack Hood, 110
Vedova, Mario, 113
Venezuela, 80
Vietnam War, 13, 172
Villalobos, Victor M., 86, 87
Villasuso, Juan Manuel, 102, 103

Virgin, Craig, 155
Virgin Records, 128, 129
Voice of Kenya (VOK), 129

Wall Street Journal, 17
Wang, Victor, 131
Wanyandeeh, Andrew, 147
Warner, Senator John, 1
Washington, George, 6, 15; farewell
address, 1–2, 23, 166
Washington Post–ABC News poll
(1989), 152
Washington University (St. Louis),
83, 118; Center for Plant Science
and Biotechnology, 84
Washingtonian, 127
Wathigo, Jack, 129
West Germany, 2, 9, 10, 127
West Indies, 87
Whichard, Obei G., 61
White House, 34; Conference on
International Cooperation, 172
Wildavsky, Aaron, 107, 109
Williams, Maurice, 171
Wilson, Edward O., 80, 107, 109
Wilson, Woodrow, 166
Wood, Richard, 169
World Bank, 41, 101, 113, 159, 166,
167
World Commission on
Environment and Development
(Brundtland Commission), 87,
92, 106, 109
World Health Organization, 167
World Resources Institute, 93, 107
World Wildlife Fund, 111
World Without Borders (Brown), 20

Yankelovich, Daniel, 163
Year of Living Dangerously, The,
153
Yugoslavia, 7, 131

Zaire, 129, 142, 161

Notes on Author and Contributors

JOHN MAXWELL HAMILTON has reported from Latin America, Asia, and Africa, as well as the United States, for the *Christian Science Monitor*, ABC Radio, and a variety of other news organizations. He served in the U.S. Agency for International Development during the Carter administration, specializing in Asia; on the House Foreign Affairs Committee, specializing in nuclear nonproliferation; and at the World Bank, where he is currently. He has a Ph.D. in American civilization and is author of *Main Street America and the Third World* and *Edgar Snow: A Biography*. He lives with his wife and son in Alexandria, Va.

NANCY MORRISON is a journalist specializing in relations between the First and Third Worlds. She has written for the *San Jose Mercury News* and the *Congressional Quarterly*, as well as for the World Bank, the European Community, the National Geographic Society, and the Bretton Woods Committee. Her reporting assignments have taken her to Turkey, Indonesia, Japan, Kenya, and Europe. She has master's degrees from Yale and Stanford universities. She is married and lives in Washington, D.C.

ERLINDA BOLIDO is editor of DepthNews Radio, a Manila agency serving about 20 Asian countries. She previously worked as a reporter on the *Bulletin Today*, now the *Manila Bulletin*, and in 1980 she was a Fulbright-Hays grantee at Stanford University.

YANINA ROVINSKI is a free-lance writer, editor, and communications consultant specializing in science and natural resources. She is currently on the staff of the International Union for the Conservation of Nature, working in their office in San José, Costa Rica. She has a B.Sc. from the Universidad de Costa Rica and a master's degree from the University of California, Berkeley.

LESLEY ANNE SIMMONS is currently on the World Bank's Public Affairs staff, working with the business community and on development education. She was a librarian in her native England prior to joining the Bank's Energy Department in 1980. She has a bachelor's degree in sociology from London University and holds a master's degree in information science from the Catholic University of America.

WAHOME MUTAHI is associate editor for social cultural affairs for the *Nation* in Nairobi, Kenya. He writes a popular satire column, "Whispers," as well as human interest stories for the *Sunday Nation*. He has served as subeditor and assistant features editor of the *Nation* and as features editor of the *Standard*, also a Nairobi daily.